AGAINST ABSTRACTION

BORDER HISPANISMS

Jon Beasley-Murray, Alberto Moreiras, and Gareth Williams, series editors

AGAINST ABSTRACTION

NOTES FROM AN
EX-LATIN AMERICANIST

ALBERTO MOREIRAS

University of Texas Press ⟱ Austin

Requests for permission to reproduce material from this work should be sent to:
Permissions
University of Texas Press
P.O. Box 7819
Austin, TX 78713–7819
utpress.utexas.edu/rp-form

♾ The paper used in this book meets the minimum requirements of ANSI/NISO Z39.48–
1992 (R1997) (Permanence of Paper).

Library of Congress Cataloging-in-Publication Data

Names: Moreiras, Alberto, author.
Title: Against abstraction : notes from an ex-Latin Americanist / Alberto Moreiras.
Other titles: Marranismo e inscripción, o el abandono de la conciencia desdichada. English
  | Border Hispanisms.
Description: First edition. | Austin : University of Texas Press, 2020. | Series: Border
  Hispanisms | Originally published in Spain as: Marranismo e inscripción, o el
  abandono de la conciencia desdichada. Madrid : Escolar y Mayo Editores, 2016. |
  Includes bibliographical references and index.
Identifiers: LCCN 2019021419
  ISBN 978-1-4773-1982-6 (cloth)
  ISBN 978-1-4773-1983-3 (paperback)
  ISBN 978-1-4773-1984-0 (library ebook)
  ISBN 978-1-4773-1985-7 (non-library ebook)
Subjects: LCSH: Moreiras, Alberto—Interviews. | Sociology—Philosophy. | Political
  science—Philosophy. | Critical theory. | Deconstruction. | Latin America—Politics and
  government.
Classification: LCC HM598 .M68 2020 | DDC 301.01—dc23
LC record available at https://lccn.loc.gov/2019021419

doi:10.7560/319826

Once again, to Teresa. And to Alejandro and Camila, because they lived through these years.

To Cristina and Gareth, who also did.

And to Federico, who prompted me to publish a book like this in a log cabin in the Córdoba Mountains.

One has to get one's own back a little.

GRAHAM GREENE, *The Confidential Agent*

In the design I have outlined here, he had intuitively hit upon the best way of hiding his shortcomings and giving full play to his strengths, the possibility of rescuing (albeit symbolically) that which was fundamental to his life.

JORGE LUIS BORGES, "The Secret Miracle"

What we must never do is willingly hand over our own bodies or the bodies of our friends.

TA-NEHISI COATES, *Between the World and Me*

Contents

A PRELIMINARY NOTE

The following book is a translation of *Marranismo e inscripción, o el abandono de la conciencia desdichada* (Madrid: Escolar y Mayo, 2016). The change of title was thought appropriate for the English version. The texts the reader will find carry some emotional weight for me. Self-identifying dimensions and critical aspects are found throughout: most of the people whose work I use polemically have been close to me at certain points in my life, but they are no longer. The second chapter speaks for itself. The sequence of writings attempts to trace the figure of a particular itinerary that I call, metonymically, a marrano destiny. It also draws a line toward a phrase that was my subtitle in the Spanish version, "the end of unhappy consciousness." The phrase, but not the experience, has been eliminated here. Readers may want to read the Madrid interview first (chapter 1) and decide whether their curiosity is strong enough to warrant the potential disappointment of reading the rest of the texts. But there is at least one other way of approaching this book, which is to read the other interview first, chapter 9, about present and future work. I think chapter 9 proposes a cipher that explains this book, whose secret cannot really be named even if I wanted to. The appendix, I should add, confounds everything intentionally, or rather it restitutes the book to its obscure nature, lest people think they have understood everything all too soon.

I translated the book myself, except for chapter 9, which was translated by Jaime Rodríguez Matos. In the process, I have introduced some changes, usually just nuances and clarifications, some of them suggested by the press's anonymous but very helpful readers.

AGAINST ABSTRACTION

INTRODUCTION

After dinner the last day of our Second Transnational Critical Seminar meeting, which was held at the University of Madrid in July of 2015, José Luis Villacañas handed me the questions for an interview with me that he and a small group of faculty in his department wanted to videotape the next day at nine in the morning for archival purposes. Those questions, in spite of their gentleness and the honor they represented, gave me a feeling of panic, and not just because, like most unaccustomed people, I am camera shy and have a fear of making grievous and irreparable errors, but also because I knew the interviewers would ask, if not about my biography directly, at least about aspects of my career that I myself did not like to dwell on. It made me restless. So that night, at the hotel, I looked over the questions, went to sleep, and had some disturbing dreams. But the interview went relatively well—the questions were well prepared, and the answers flowed quite smoothly. In the parallel sound recording I made, since it is unedited, one can hear my recurring worry: did I go too far? Was that untactful, was it indiscreet, should we do it again?

But José Luis and the other interviewers, namely, Antonio Rivera, Rodrigo Castro, Juan Manuel Forte, and Pedro Lomba, did not allow me to try again on anything—they were incurably optimistic on the issue of nothing to regret. That night, or the following day, since I had a couple of extra days in Madrid before returning to Texas, I posted my voice recording on an internet site frequented by some of my friends. Willy Thayer, who was also in Madrid at the time, thought of entertaining his lack of sleep by listening to the recording. He advised me to publish it, since it mostly dealt with the recent history of our professional field, and some people would enjoy having access to the written text. José Luis and Rodrigo agreed with him.

My anxiety returned when I started transcribing the text, and it led me to complement my answers with some footnotes I thought necessary. Days later, when my friends read the transcription and the notes, some thought the notes undermined the relative spontaneity of the interview; it amounted, they said, to asking myself some extra questions in order to produce answers for them, which was an act of dubious elegance. They preferred that the interview be published without any supplements—although Rodrigo said he would prepare notes offering contextual clarifications. I am not sure my final decision, which was to put this book together, was the correct one. Yes, I had been looking for the opportunity to do this book for some time, and the interview gave me a good one—after all, the latter should be understood in the context of some work of mine produced within the last years that has an explicitly polemical nature and of some other work that speaks about the professional field and my increasingly uncomfortable inscription within it. So I thought it was a matter of course, even a courtesy to potentially interested readers, to publish the interview with those other works of mine—better than my footnotes, after all, since those were summary references to the other work and have now been dropped. The sequence of texts offered here is perhaps more than the history of a professional trajectory, and it has dimensions that can only be seen in their traces by an astute reader (if any still exist and we are not already terminally inattentive).

The Madrid conversation, then, opened the possibility of publishing these materials as a book—it created an architectonics for the book. From my perspective, it is not any book, and this is why I am still uncertain about the possible defensiveness, the possible opportunism, the possible aggressiveness in the decision to go ahead with it; in any case, let me disavow all of those strategies. This is my first personal book since the publication of *Línea de sombra* in 2006. The Spanish version appeared in 2016, so it is ten years between books, and that is a long time, and they were years in which I had been lazy or reluctant or possessed with tedium regarding the academic book form and its fetishes. It wasn't only laziness, though, as 2005 began a period of disillusion that destroyed for me, as one of its effects, any notion of an audience for whom to write—perhaps I should not tell you this. Although I no longer write for my ostensible professional field, or because of it, this book brings that period to an end, without apologies.

Writing on Miguel Delibes, Ramón Buckley says something that belongs to him but that he attributes to the very heart of Delibes's oeuvre: "What is relevant about a life is not what happens but rather what does not happen, what was there at the beginning and continues to be there at the end" (23). This book turns what did not happen into what happened in my professional life. I can now see that putting it together represents an archaic gesture, perhaps not transferable, perhaps unshareable, responding to the impossible desire of abolishing profane time. If there is only one opportunity in life to attempt something like that without becoming preposterous, this is my inadequate, syncopated, elusive, and reticent attempt. There will be no further attempts—no more autography, or no intentional autography.

One of the first questions I was asked in Madrid had to do with my early choice of profession. At some point, I felt the need to become familiar with the archive of my primary language as an imperative. I now kind of regret the feeling, which no longer seems particularly warranted, but it had momentous consequences for me. What does it mean, today, to think within one language, to think from one linguistic archive? Can it mean anything other than, precisely, to think against said language, to think against such an archive? And is this not merely quixotic? That from/against alternative guards a certain key to the so-called crisis of the humanities, which we are only beginning to think about and for which we find ourselves not just without some basic tools but lacking the indispensable conceptual vocabulary. That we are incapable of seeing our way through the crisis of the humanities—as we do not yet understand it—is of course the true crisis. We find ourselves in a peculiar moment of destitution and desistence for which it is no good to invoke, say, Friedrich Hölderlin, and to request from such lofty heights the return of a national mediation, the coming of some god or other, more grand poetry or grand literature. If we could allow ourselves to imagine what the return to poetic thought might mean, to a real poetization of the archive, it would not take long to see that such poetization would be the very problem, not its solution, except that it would have gone from being a patent and passive destitution to being an active and possibly catastrophic one. That is only one example.

When I made the decisions that would determine the course of my life (career choice, move to the United States), I did not want to become an academic expert, a scholar, a researcher, a professor—I do not know about others on similar paths, or whether these things follow a certain generational logic. My idols and models in my formative years were not primarily professors but rather Friedrich Nietzsche, Maurice Blanchot, Georges Bataille, or Pierre Klossowski, or the writers that I had passionately read through adolescence: Marcel Proust or Samuel Beckett or Jorge

Luis Borges or Antonin Artaud or Albert Camus. To get a PhD was a nuisance of a practical order—I would get financial support I had been unable to get in Spain. Later, the realization came that, in the United States, with a PhD in the humanities, one could only do one of two things: start another doctorate or become a professor. The issue did not disgust me, but I never found it attractive. In retrospect, since I had a good time in Georgia, a bad time in Wisconsin, a good one at Duke for about eight years and a bad one for about six, a bad time in Aberdeen, a bad time in Texas and then good in Texas—more or less half and half, good times and bad times— I think what I have enjoyed the most has always had to do with friendship, with conversation and discussion. But such moments of friendship and exchange have unfailingly happened at the margins of conventional academic discourse, always on the outside and in resistance, never in what the profession would consider a typical or normal form. Of course it is always a pleasure to share what one knows or thinks with the younger people, which is the conventionally good image of teaching, but it is much more fun to learn with others, to take risks, to push what is permissible, and to expose oneself—if there is a friend on the other side. The university, I have learned, no longer tolerates such things, perhaps it never did—they could only happen at its borders, at the margins. The promise of the US university in the 1980s, which formed me, no longer seems to be there. For years I thought of myself as someone centrally committed to university discourse, to the university as an institution, and I did everything I could for it. Today, I must admit that is no longer the case. I still try to do my job as best I can, of course, but something has fundamentally changed, and it is not just that I am older. Today, for me, being a university intellectual has lost the prestige it once had. There could be other forms of intellectuality where the enjoyment one sought can still be found. That enjoyment, at the university today, is probably only possible when it happens against the university. I do not know whether the university has failed us, or we have failed the university, or both.

Another interview question whose answer I would have liked to supplement had to do with the issue of the totality of my writing, which Spanish calls *obra*, my "oeuvre." I hope I am not making excuses for the insufficiencies of my work if I say that the notion of "oeuvre," old-fashioned and almost unthinkable today for a university intellectual, is particularly difficult to sponsor for a critical project of deconstructive analysis. I have been accused of being a suspicious destroyer, as if the labor of critical destruction could only be in every case a prolegomenon to a despotic reconstruction, threatening in its very unsubstantial spectrality. It may be part of institutional thought to think that the questioning of petrified pieties and inertial and routine comportments always anticipates a dictatorship, but the worst feature of dictatorships is rather the indifferent continuation of petrified pieties and routine comportments when they have had their teeth sharpened by an institution now hostile to thought and innovation.

There is a production of academic work that necessarily implies institutional peace and quiet, as if one could only do it from an unthreatened positionality, with your back covered, as it were. That has never been the case for me. I have no interest in presenting myself as a good man in a wicked institutional world. I am happy to confess, as Lazarillo de Tormes put it, to "not being holier than my neighbors." But it is no secret that academic struggles are sordid by definition, since they are usually a matter of petty egos fiercely claiming territory on (supposedly) lofty grounds, which comes directly into the terrain Immanuel Kant identified as "radical evil" (*Religion* 15–39). In that context, a special problem probably arises for expatriates like myself. Expatriation is one of the basic facts of my life, as I imagine it is for all of those who decide to leave their country of origin to live and work elsewhere, perhaps not necessarily forever. But twenty or thirty years go by, and then an effective return is no longer possible. Expatriation into academic work, to boot, is a double expatriation, because the university configures a fundamentally clerical world without an outside. For the academic expatriate, this only means, of course, that an outside life is hardly accessible. It is not only that for long career periods there is no time. The truth is, in the United States, for the most part, there is no street life, no life about town, which for an expat academic, no matter how reluctant, means that there is hardly air outside the air-conditioned institution. The North American rituals of Sunday church, children's soccer, and the sports events that are among the few visible social links remain alien to the expatriate (excepting, of course, a radical voluntarism that one does see appearing occasionally, though it is normally excessive, counterproductive, the harbinger or the symptom of a neurotic state). Normally, one is abnormally sunk into the institution, having lost the forms of life associated with the social and material landscapes from childhood or early youth. Outside one's own family, if one is lucky to have one, work is everything. Friends, when they do exist, are generally also academics (in thirty years in the United States I only have a handful of nonacademic friends, even if they are among the most beloved).

As a consequence, in that context that I do not think I am presenting in any exaggerated manner, certainly not from the perspective of my own life, any structural failure in the libidinal compensations the institution may offer—lack of support, betrayal, indifference, sustained hostility—becomes catastrophic and soul-destroying, whether one is saintly or wicked. This needs to be said so that the next potential expatriate learns the facts, and may therefore establish some degree of psychological protection if nothing else.

The general field of Hispanic studies in US universities benefited from the arrival of numerous exiled or expatriate intellectuals after the Spanish Civil War (1936–1939), many of whom took positions in language departments at elite institutions. At the time, Hispanic studies was dominated by interests in historical philology, historical linguistics, Golden Age literature, and to a lesser extent in the novels and poetry of the twentieth century. The period was strongly marked by mild avant-garde conventions and their emphasis on novelty and aesthetic quality. Spanish literature was by and large studied in a compensatory mood, as a tool to think about, and to a certain extent redeem, the tragic substance of a country whose imperial history seemed of a piece with the postwar authoritarian regime and its projections of eternity. Latin American literature was by then underestimated on formal criteria, and attention was paid only to a handful of modernist poets or *criollista* novelists who were said to be good interpreters of the various national souls. But in the 1960s, the "Boom" in Latin American literature, the influx of Cuban exiles, and French structuralism started to push things into some novel terrains. During the 1970s and 1980s, literary prestige moved toward Latin American production, although a small handful of Spanish authors kept theirs. Through José Donoso and Severo Sarduy, Salvador Elizondo and Osvaldo Lamborghini, Néstor Perlongher and Juan Goytisolo, together with the more obvious Boom names, the old national-identitarian critics started to lose their interest for the rest of us in a major way. It was the first split, the first rupture, but there would be others: feminism, which produced a real emphasis on women's writing and cultural production; poststructuralism, which changed critical language much more radically; and, horribly for some, the culturalist conceit that literary studies were structurally elitist and exclusionary and that something else was needed. The 1990s were the decade of the consummation of the long decline of the traditional academic humanities—a forced decline, based on geopolitical realities, from which we have not recovered. And this was the second rupture.

The history of philology had been functional for the European inter-state system during the long nineteenth century and up to the end of the Cold War. The humanities at the university had never been literature's refuge but rather, from the beginning and structurally, a mechanism for the capture of the literary endeavor for the political order. Philology, the history of literature, literary criticism, the understanding of the cultural specificity accomplished more or less by the different "lettered cities" in every case and every country guarded a certain key for sociopolitical hege-monic domination. Comparative literature and, in general, comparative philology allowed us to understand that the quality of the artistic produc-tion of "a people" was a direct glimpse into its political temporality and its possibility of either domination or hegemonic subordination. For the same reason, they also gave powerful formal indications as to their defeat or irrel-evance. The university was, of course, a function of the state apparatus, just another dimension of what was then called the "military-industrial appa-ratus." There was no ivory tower—only functionaries of hegemony. Every piece of narrative is a national allegory, Fredric Jameson used to say toward the end of the 1980s. Not just literary studies, but literature itself, from its formal beginnings as literature in the nineteenth century, came to be seen as a political tool and as a way of preparing the nation for its historical des-tiny. But the end of the Cold War, globalization in its first and second waves (that is, before and after September 11, 2001), the hegemony of the United States, the global imposition of financial capitalism in neoliberal guise, and the ascent of China and the BRIC countries (Brazil, Russia, India, China) emptied from the inside the humanities model of Western society. And this was a third rupture. If today all culture and cultural production is amply subjected to the principle of indifferentiation that general equivalence em-bodies, it means first of all that culture has no aura, and that it has become, in the best of cases, some sociological datum nobody knows what to do with. All of this may be terrible if you want to see it that way, but it cannot be ignored, and it is a major indicator in terms of what may still constitute the task of thinking. Coming to terms with it was our unfathomable gen-erational task—for my generation and for every generation after mine. And it determines, needless to say, very harsh conditions for the development of any real relevance for so-called Hispanist reflection.

And there was a third interview question that left me wishing I could have said a little more: the one about my books, and in particular on *Línea de sombra: El no sujeto de lo político*. I published that book with Palinodia, a small Chilean publishing house that was fairly new then and that some friends of mine were supporting. I had already moved to Scotland. Óscar Cabezas, Alejandra Castillo, Miguel Valderrama, Sergio Villalobos, and Federico Galende took it upon themselves to write about the book and help disseminate it. They will never know how important their gesture was for me. Nelly Richard wanted to publish their commentary in *Revista de Crítica Cultural*, and she asked me for a response. All of those articles are available for review.[1] I am very grateful to those Chilean friends and others, specifically Willy Thayer, Elizabeth Collingwood-Selby, and Pablo Oyarzún, because they have all been essential to my own development since the 1990s. Without their presence, and the interlocution they were able to offer through mutual visits, things would have been harder and more dubious than they have been for my professional life in US Latin Americanism. Since *Línea de sombra* is the book of mine that was published last before *Marranismo e inscripción*, I would like to suggest a possible link between the two.

Alejandra Castillo, in her review of *Línea de sombra*, mentioned a Nietzschean-Derridean "perhaps" whose uncertainty shelters, she said, "an exercise in displaced nomination." To name diverse figures or de-figures for an infinite displacement regarding metaphysical or hegemonic capture would hold the possibility—a possibility always promised, but promised only as possibility—of a future. A redemptive force is always at play in the more or less messianic drift of the uncertain promise of the possible. For Castillo, although she does not quite say it, *Línea de sombra* plays out the "perhaps" of a redemption. It is my fault, once again, and an old fault, since it is inherited from other books of mine where it was said that the possibility of another history could break into a savage event. So it is fair for Castillo to ask. I do not know, and probably have not wanted to know, whether my writing strategy, not just in *Línea de sombra* but also in *The Exhaustion of Difference*, *Tercer espacio*, or *Interpretación y diferencia*, depends fundamentally on a secret narrative—visible as a symptom—of historical redemption without which there would be no place of enunciation. If the very motor of the de-naming or displacing process, if the motor of critical negativity in the text, were to be the precarious possibility of an end of the process, of an accomplishment in de-naming, then the motor of the process would be working against its own goal: the text would be concealing a longing for a name, a desire for coincidence, a desire for the end of desire. It would not be compatible with the project of "overflowing the politico-theological *repraesentatio*." Everything would in fact be modeled on the shame of the lack of representation, and the de-naming drift and the deconstructive negativity would only be screens for a secret polit-ico-theological will. The text would have become incoherent, which may be the case. And not just incoherent: if a writing is theoretical, if there is writing without conditions, or if writing wants to advance toward the unconditional, not in the sense of refusing responsibility for the real but rather in the sense of accepting it fully, if writing wants to be moral on its own determination and not from spurious politico-academic determi-nations, then there is a question about whether such a writing is always beforehand anti-political or reactionary, or courts that risk. It is probably always reactionary to move against the spirit of the times, and it is anti-political to refuse to enter the calculations that may support supposedly progressive academic agendas, so often injected with horse-killing loads of moralism. One must choose rather than compromise, as Kant put it: "One cannot compromise here and devise something intermediate, a pragmatically conditioned right (a cross between right and expediency)" (*Toward Perpetual Peace* 347). I have chosen and, at the end, I offer no apologies. My drift toward infrapolitics was determined by a very definite need to move against the spirit of the times and the facile compensatory "politicization" so many believe can save them. Things are not so easy. Even politics is not so easy.

I will conclude this introduction, still annotating the Madrid conversa-tion, by alluding to the populist thematics that appear in my last responses to the interviewers. I think they cipher, in a certain way, the orientation of my present work, which the reader will see as centered on the hybrid nouns of *infrapolitics* and *posthegemony*. Populism, as I try to speak of it in the pages that follow, is mobilization as a demand for life, as an excep-tion to the labor regime, as an exception to the political state of affairs. Populist mobilization is always exceptional. It is constituted as an essen-tially infrapolitical counterclaim for the suspension of the hijacking of life by politics, in our time against the biopolitical or technical totalization of life, the supposed normality of an existence ruled over by an economy of time that has become intolerable. Populism is in that sense politics for a time of crisis. We can understand populist mobilization as the temporal production of unity; as a decision without a principle; as a political act that interrupts, through demotic irruption, the habitual economy of time and political calculations as usual. But, if a mobilized populism is always and only viable as a critical exception to the state of affairs, then popu-list irruption is always posthegemonic: an exceptional mobilization can only ever produce a phantom hegemony, a mirage of it. As mobilization, and under conditions of mobilization, no hegemony can become stable. Populist mobilization is posthegemonic.

In his book on Peronism, Daniel James noted that there is no mobilization without demobilization (*Resistance*, 32–40). Mobilization is always haunted by a shadow demobilization, and it is the latter that enables the rise of both charismatic verticalization and its obvious counterpart, identitarianization. But it also enables something else. At the moment of demobilization, the phantasmatic character of populist hegemony becomes manifest—a hegemony now become ideology wants to make itself eternal. But this means that populist demobilization marks the time and the opportunity for posthegemonic infrapolitics: the kairos for the materialization of democratic existence. It is the moment when the demobilized, people in general more than "the" people, come to feel that they are and have always been the part that will not become the all, when they give up on the unification of the all that is never consistent with the chain of equivalential demands: that sober time, no longer enthusiastic, the time of renewed solitude that refuses every messianic mediation but is still loaded with political potentiality, is the democratic time. There is also a shadow mobilization behind every demobilization. This is why I am in favor of a marrano—nonidentitarian, dirty, skeptical—populism over every messianic-communitarian one. This is the democratic populism that, withheld within its minimal conditions, can withstand verticalist hegemonization against the theft of the time of life. In it, a certain politics of passion stands against despotic co-optation; a rejection of the biopoliticization of time demands the nonexclusion of the singular; and every totalization of the social field is rejected in favor of a politics of the not-all. European democratization could happen over against its very history. In Latin America, the very possibility seems to be receding now, but it could come back. There is a democratic marranism—this book proposes it—that is only possible as a critical fold in the day after, in the moment of demobilization that happens in the wake of demotic irruption, without which democracy is only the name for the anti-populist administration of the state of affairs. Before breathing with and among the innocent, before living at ease, the price on our heads must be lifted, and that can only be accomplished by taking power away from those who currently have it. This book could not place itself outside that fervent desire.

Finally, I would like to acknowledge the friendship and support of José Luis Villacañas, who co-organized the Madrid interview together with Antonio Rivera and Rodrigo Castro and later was instrumental in getting this book published in Spanish. In the same way that my life in the 1990s would have been more boring without my Chilean friends, from 2000 on, more or less, José Luis's friendship became literally a saving grace. I owe him many of the most intense and gratifying moments in my recent professional life but also something more difficult to express: he kept my faith in intellectual work, in the task of thought, alive at a time when I did not have the resources to do it by myself. He was not the only one, there are others, but he was one of them.

This book is a book of transition—from what I call in the Madrid interview the "desert years" to a period that starts to emerge in 2013. I want to mention here the great importance that our conversations in the Infrapolitical Deconstruction Collective, and particularly with the score and a half of close friends who are tenaciously committed to it and to whom further books will be dedicated, have had for me in recent times.

Some of the chapters that follow were published in versions that have now been slightly modified in various journals, namely, *FronteraD*, *Centennial Review*, *Cuadernos de Literatura*, *Romance Notes*, and *Papel Máquina*. I would like to thank Héctor Fabián, Gerardo Muñoz, Jaime Rodríguez Matos, Gareth Williams, and Teresa Vilarós for their reading and critical commentary on draft versions of this book, which forced me to clarify a number of aspects and helped me feel minimally confident about its publication.

Chapter 1

MARRANISM AND INSCRIPTION

This is the transcription, with editorial revisions, of an interview held at the University of Madrid on June 9, 2015. The interviewers were José Luis Villacañas, Rodrigo Castro, Antonio Rivera, Juan Manuel Forte, and Pedro Lomba.

JOSÉ LUIS VILLACAÑAS: The reason for this video interview has to do with requirements of our program's online teaching and outreach dimensions. For us, it is important because it highlights several initiatives. The first refers to our Master's in Ibero-American Thought, where you are a faculty member and where you have taught. It also refers to our research project "Ideas That Cross the Atlantic," in which you also participate. And the third one is the research group that we have had, in different avatars, for the last twenty years, and where you have been a central presence. This long conversation with you, we believe, is an opportunity for the whole research group and for our master's students. We will publish it online in a complete form, but we will also select snippets and various fragments for our MOOC courses whenever there is an opinion or a reflection that becomes relevant in those contexts. I would like to begin by asking a question whose aspiration is to understand your take on the evolution of Latin Americanism over the last thirty years. You begin your doctoral studies in the United States in the early 1980s, right at the time when Latin Americanist reflection starts to give up on the great essay writers (the *ensayistas*), is moving beyond the literary Boom, and begins to transform itself—we may remember Ángel Rama's *La ciudad letrada* or Bolívar Echevarría's work on the baroque—and become more receptive of what we may still call philosophy, which you had previously studied. How do you see this evolution in the last thirty years?

ALBERTO MOREIRAS: I went to the United States, to the University of Georgia, in 1980, having finished my degree in philosophy at the University of Barcelona, and with the purpose of familiarizing myself, or of continuing my familiarization (I had also finished the first two years in

Hispanic Philology at the University of Barcelona), with the Hispanic cultural archive. Slowly—my doctorate took seven years; today it is done in five—I followed a still very traditional cycle of formation, strongly based on the reading of literary texts but no longer only on them. For instance, for my preliminary examinations, I asked my advisor, my dissertation director, José Luis Gómez Martínez, how I should prepare, and he replied: "Do you remember the *Crónicas emilianenses*?" "Yes." "And the Yellow Pages in the Madrid Phone Book for this year?" "Yes!" "Ok, you have to prepare to produce answers on those two items and everything in between." And, sure enough, the questions I received for my written exams—exhausting exams that lasted a whole week—were not exclusively literary. I remember a question about Erasmianism and the Mystical Body of Christ and another one on Nietzscheanism in Spanish philosophy during Francoism. At the same time, they were questions that centered exclusively on the Hispanic intellectual tradition (they could ask about Nietzscheanism in Spain, but they asked about no comparison with France or Italy).

It was still a time of strong disciplinary emphasis on the specific program of study one followed, but it may have been the last years of it. There were contradictions. In 1985, when I underwent those examinations, the disciplinary structure was falling historically; it was becoming unsustainable. I would be asked about philosophy during the long Spanish dictatorship or about theological doctrines in early modernity, but on the other hand, they insisted on the knowledge of literary texts as my fundamental responsibility. The implied contradiction was the symptom of an awakening to the fact that there would be no real knowledge of the literary texts without familiarity with the letter of the archive, but that meant the total letter of the total archive—the archive of other languages, of other disciplines, but also of the destroyed archives, for instance, through colonization—which of course tended to become an impossible demand for a twentysomething student, really for anyone. When I got my first job, at the University of Wisconsin-Madison, I started to realize that things in the professional world did not quite match my formation process or its intent. A push for what we can call interdisciplinarity was already there, and it has not stopped becoming explicit, even if in mostly trivial forms, over the last thirty years. The traditional paradigm—not quite philology, which was older, but let us call it literary-critical studies—was in crisis, was in fact entering its terminal crisis, even though there are still people today who continue to fail to understand it.

It was demanded of us, it started to be demanded (we do not know who issued the demand: the agent of the demand was anonymous), I myself started to demand of myself and my students that we multiply and open the range of reading and study to include theoretical linguistics, anthropology, sociology, film studies, art, history, and, naturally, philosophy, which was important to me from the beginning and without which I would not have entered any academic garden. But this was not to be done, as it had perhaps been done by the old nineteenth-century philology, in the name of a better knowledge of the sacred text, the national text, literature as the queen of culture. Instead it was done for the sake of a knowledge drive, a form of desire that we could not quite identify and that perhaps today remains unidentified. This is a bit strange. We gave all of it the generic term "theory." Those were the years, the 1980s through the end of the 1990s, of the strong expansion of "theory"—we could call it hegemonic expansion—in the US university. "Theory" started off as "literary theory" and for a few years it was in effect literary theory and started to evolve into what we started to call "critical theory," not in reference to the Frankfurt School but to distinguish it from proper literary theory, which inevitably receded and lost its central position—a logical development, considering the loss of the specific weight of literature itself, not to mention literary studies. During the early 1990s, theoretical paradigms, trans- or postdisciplinary, came and went, and they marked the evolution of North American Latin Americanism and Hispanism. I speak of their US and perhaps Canadian variants because at the time I was not following the discipline in other regions—my impression is that the evolution in those regions was not quite the same.

For instance, there was the irruption of cultural studies, in whose configuration the various kinds of feminism and other forms of thought and of academic activism that we can call identitarian had a central role: queer studies, ethnic studies, race studies. A general interest developed in the US Latino/a world, but it was and has remained rather superficial and more sociological than anything else. There were, of course, diverse openings and exposure to mimesis of movements coming from Latin America or Spain and of tendencies coming from related fields in the North American university. Spanish and Southern Cone postdictatorships, and thought connected to the various political transitions and their cultural particularities, started to become a pretty overwhelming concern, and it was obvious that their referents could not be conceptualized in any way or manner as exclusively or even predominantly literary. Also, the situation that derived from the various Central American civil wars—*testimonio*, for instance—became central to Latin Americanist reflection. Postdictatorship and civil war marked the evolutionary drift toward the hegemony of cultural studies in the field, and it is important to underline here the relevance and influence of Southern Cone intellectuals committed to the same reflection from their perspective, and of Central American but also Southern Cone and even Andean testimonialism.

But Latin American cultural studies started to take on a postcolonial flavor on the basis of loans from reflection on British postimperial and Indian and Caribbean postcolonial studies, as well as Francophone studies. The United Kingdom, as an eminent receptor of many postcolonial populations, through the work of the Birmingham School and of scholars such as Raymond Williams and Stuart Hall, first moved toward an understanding of culture that was perhaps not fully cosmopolitan yet but neither was it exclusively national (or imperial), as it had been in the past. Those novelties in fact dynamite old literary-critical disciplinary configurations. After them, one is hardly able to keep working on, say, form and content in the tales of Gabriel García Márquez or on the memory of gauchos in Peronist literature as if nothing had happened. Or not without paying the price of the growing irrelevance from which cultural studies had precisely tried to escape. These are moments of a certain if short-lasting enthusiasm.

There was an obvious problem in Latin America that Ángel Rama, among others—since you referred to him—deployed and set into circulation in a very efficient way: there is a "lettered city" that structurally excludes a number of historic populations, some of them originary, some mestizos or descendants of slave groups. The Latin American lettered city was exclusively and militantly liberal-criollo (except for a handful of reactionary criollo intellectuals, there are all types) and exclusionary of essentially nonwhite populations and also women. But it was not exclusionary because it would not mention the indigenous or women (sometimes it did), it was not exclusionary from a merely identitarian perspective. It was rather structurally exclusionary: so-called *indigenismo* was not at all incompatible with criollismo, for instance, but the moment the indigenous is discussed from *indigenismo* other possibilities to think about indigeneity are foreclosed. All of this started to become notorious and patent through changes and displacements in forms of work, in ways of framing a relationship with the field of study that left behind literary priorities in order to center themselves on the geographic or geopolitical area as such. One was no longer predominantly a literary critic—even if one was also a literary critic—but rather a "Latin Americanist." And there were similar developments in other areas: one was a "Europeanist," or a South Asian studies scholar, or an Africanist, and the pretension, the claim, was that one no longer wanted to be a mere expert or specialist in one or another specific endeavor, but rather an intellectual engaged with the totality of culture in a given area of the world. Little did we know that "area studies" was going to take a drastic institutional hit not so many years later. But that is a different story.

Cultural studies became radicalized for Latin Americanism through the influence of South Asian subaltern studies scholars, who had done a quasi-systematic postcolonial historiography labor from the 1980s. The Latin American Subaltern Studies Group basically intensified Latin Americanist culturalist parameters. A certain paralysis in the political but also the theoretical terrain had already become visible in the mid-1990s for cultural studies, which seemed mired in a multiculturalism that was easily adopted—in fact, thoroughly instrumentalized, some of us believed—by the neoliberal regime. The Latin American Subaltern Studies Group tried to do something about that. It was a small group, created by John Beverley, Ileana Rodríguez, and some other people, and it had to face clear animosity and political hostility. The resistance of the so-called literary establishment had always been there, and the limited tolerance they had displayed, perhaps only for reasons of distraction, toward cultural studies vanished when subalternism, which claimed an effective politicization of the field of knowledge, showed up. Perhaps through its very name, subalternism could invoke an enemy, hegemony, while cultural studies could slumber without invoking any antagonism. But those of us interested in subalternism could not care less about those resistances that came from no solid intellectual place and were only pathetically political. We wanted to internationalize reflection, to break the ghetto, to stop thinking that Spanish could only fulfill a role as a subaltern language destined merely to reproduce models developed through other languages. And we wanted our conversation to have the same rank other conversations in other languages and intellectual traditions had. It was all against the grain, given the majority composition of our academic field, but it was something that subalternism could have a chance at, because it opened up, potentially, a way of carrying out a counterhegemonic reflection in our own field of study: it enabled, potentially, a new discursivity, politically as well as theoretically, and for many of us, it had nothing to do with transplanting and reproducing South Asian conceits: rather, we wanted the latter's forcing and radicalization. This should not be forgotten.

All of it was difficult, and it still is. It is not just the fierce resistance to theory in our field, thoroughly triumphant today (the new modality: the worst resisters themselves claim to also do theory—I suppose it could be called theory "light"). It is also because Spanish is still a language lacking theoretical legitimation, a subaltern language in the United States for sociological reasons, in spite of the fact that it is the second most-spoken language in the country, and that the United States is, after Mexico, the second-largest Spanish-speaking country in the world. But Spanish has a diglossic position in the United States, always in a subalternized position for reasons that are easily imagined. Theoretical reflection in Spanish has not reached legitimation in the US academic world—and let me make it clear: it is not enough for me or others to write in English, because an English-speaking Latin Americanist is still someone who translates and is perceived as a mere translator. But that means that anybody who insists on theoretical production—which, at this point, with all due respect to the tradition, means anybody who wants to do more than opine on texts from the tradition—gets caught in a sort of crossfire that is difficult to elude (and cannot be eluded without a humiliating mimesis: you must try to become them). That may be one of the reasons why the Latin American Subaltern Studies Group did not last long. Very soon a number of internal confrontations developed that broke the backbone of the group, destroyed any residual faith in it, and made most of us go, institutionally speaking, into a wasteland—the years in the desert—where not much could be accomplished.

JOSÉ LUIS VILLACAÑAS: What years were those?

AM: I think the desert, or wasteland, or wilderness, the scorched earth, starts to grow in 1999, becomes manifest for all in 2001, and lasts through the early 2010s more or less. A good dozen years. That is to say, leaving aside the fact that the establishment continued to do what the establishment always does, but now without a challenge, a state of affairs developed where there was no north, no orientation, no theoretical project that people could interact with—an internally annihilated field had been created, in willful devastation, where, nevertheless, something was developing, almost secretly, or resisted, dormant, in a state of latency. You can easily imagine how tough it was for those who attempted to complain at any public or private level. Of course, during those years, some books were published that have a significant status in the professional field, some people managed to be properly formed, things moved on as things always move on in times of destitution, limping slowly, secretly, but newer generations are perhaps now getting ready to make a move. There are a few signs—not many yet; unfortunately, things are still quite predictably boring. In any case, those new people are not postsubalternist—that word has been used by John Beverley in a sense I do not want to copy or even accept here. It is a matter of a possible intellectual turn, no longer culturalist (culturalism was dominant everywhere in the 1990s, and it was ultimately responsible for the wasteland that followed). But culturalism, in its "decolonial" avatar, the only option that existed, basically cancels itself out shortly after 2010 in spite of some residual middlebrow glory, and it comes to be substituted by a "political turn," which is where we still are, although something else has begun to stir.

To return to your initial question, I would say that those are the basic lineaments of the last thirty years in our field of academic reflection: first, the strong residue of the old liberal-criollo literary philology, lasting well into the 1990s. Culturalism is already alive and kicking then, in fact becoming hegemonic, and it marks the field for about twenty years. But, starting in the mid-2000s, a growing "political turn," politico-theoretical if you want, exists alongside a new geopolitical configuration, post-9/11, that no longer allows us to keep talking about area studies, or Latin Americanism, in any real sense. Latin Americanism is today a quasi-phantom entity that should be buried, given its irrelevance, its fall in intellectual productivity, its inefficiency as a field of thought. Most people have by now given up on thinking about the subcontinent as such, of establishing connections, and, I think, for good reasons. We could say that, during the time of area studies in the United States, which is a time going from the 1940s until roughly the end of the Cold War, the fundamental ideological paradigm was the literary-philological one, sustained on a nationalist state of affairs; from the end of the Cold War until 9/11/2001, culturalism, as the ideological precipitate of neoliberal rule in the atmosphere some called "end of history," dominates; and from 2001 onward there is a growing politicization, to some extent merely reactive, anti-neoliberal but without any substantial positivity, supportive of populist movements in Latin America, and that, like them, shows a good deal of wear and tear. Of course, things are not so clear-cut in reality: all of these critical deaths and births overlap for years. If the best manifestation of Latin Americanism before 2001—the best, since there are others—was a kind of critical regionalism that could already project itself as world thinking or cosmopolitan thinking in and through its regional specificity, today I do not think Latin Americanism can be thought of in those terms (namely, as critical regionalism). It is enough, maybe, to talk about narco-trafficking and wonder how it is to be thought about. Confronted by narco, for instance, Latin Americanism becomes an outmoded academic tag, conventional and residual at best, or administrative (there are still many Latin American studies programs out there). But I do not think it conforms to any real productivity of thought.

JOSÉ LUIS VILLACAÑAS: We would like to know, we are very interested in knowing, how you position your own work in relation to this story of Latin Americanism, how you position a book of yours that is well known in Latin America, *Línea de sombra*, how you position your book project *Piel de lobo*, the rest of what you have been working on, collecting different things, and what you wanted to do with *The Exhaustion of Difference*.

AM: I have never thought about my work in terms of "oeuvre"; really what I have tried to do is to survive, to last, not to bend, to keep standing up (without giving up on my own personal well-being and happiness). It has not been easy—it is easy enough now, but it wasn't in the past. My trajectory has been crisscrossed by conflicts and confrontations I believe I myself have not sought; they have been imposed on me, and that has had an impact not only on my production but also on my interest in having a production—out of boredom rather than fear, I should say. I don't think I am special—it is a matter of positioning. Anyone with similar interests and provenance and in that context will have had to deal with unsolicited confrontations. To that extent, I could say that my books are militant, perhaps the proper term is "belligerent," and can be conceptualized from those notions. But the belligerence has had to do with attempting to keep alive a theoretically inclined intellectual call against the grain, because the will to theory has been a huge problem for many. This can be hidden, there is dissimulation, but Latin Americanism and Hispanism are fiercely, one could also say, violently resistant to theory, and finally just hostile to theory and therefore to people who want to do it. And, as a consequence, since theory has always been my primary interest, I have always wanted— I might have only ever wanted, in the US university—to move forward while trying not to let myself be destroyed. I am not particularly proud of that, mind you: it is what anyone would have done in my place, to seek survival—I would have preferred a thousand times over not to have had to abide in such a vipers' nest, but things are as they are, and our profession is full of senior and not-so-senior people who are unstoppably moved to blood and poison when they smell "theory" from afar; that is and has been my experience—even today. They will invent all sorts of reasons for their hatred, but hatred it is.

Under those circumstances—it would be nice to go into details, into stories, to name names, believe me, old and young, but I must give that up, we would never be done with it—my "work," as I see it, is little more than the expression of a will to survive, to persist. I have always had good friends, I am very proud of them, and I have always been part of a group, not large, that has attempted to follow that orientation and maintain themselves in it with full respect for intellectual freedom and ambition—after all, we ended up in the university for no other reason, though I suppose not understanding well what we were getting into. I think the books I have managed to write, the first, *Interpretación y diferencia*, on deconstruction, which was my doctoral thesis; a second one on the Latin American literary archive, already under the fundamental category of mourning (I think *Tercer espacio* already dwells on the end of a bisecular paradigm: literature as the queen of humanities; when I write about literature and mourning in Latin America, I do not realize, it takes me years to realize, out of distraction or stupidity, out of naïveté, but retrospectively it is clear: mourning was also a mourning for literature, not just mourning and literature, mourning of literature). And *The Exhaustion of Difference* is a book about the end of the culturalist paradigm.

JOSÉ LUIS VILLACAÑAS: It is already a book of the "political turn," clearly.

AM: Well, that was beginning then. At the time I continued to work in deconstructive analysis, in which I was formed, since for me there is no analysis without "destruction" (*Lichtung*), and the same work I had tried to do on literary studies in *Tercer espacio* I tried to do on cultural studies and culturalism in general with *Exhaustion*. So this was an anti-culturalist book within culturalism, which caused great consternation. I remember— at the ball, of all places, of a Latin American Studies Association meeting— the violent denunciation of a fellow who would soon move into the depths, if there are any, of the decolonial territory, although he was not coming from there, who told me that my book was demonic and nihilist and no student should ever read it (yes, I have had to put up with being called a "corruptor of youth" too many times). I also remember my abrupt exit from the editorial board of a certain prominent journal, a so-called gatekeeper journal in the cultural studies field, on the basis of the fact that I was "really an enemy" of cultural studies. The ill-advised, slightly treacherous, hapless editor told me he had no choice but to take my name off the editorial board after reading my book. All of it very pathetic, but . . . impunity was on their side.

JOSÉ LUIS VILLACAÑAS: But your book founded a critical tradition regarding culturalism, and in that sense the book was also very well received. Your very students have followed those lines.

AM: I have always been lucky to have very good students. I have contributed to the formation of very good people, and those people have been producing, I think, work that is among the best the field has produced in the last thirty years. And at this point there are quite a lot of them, perhaps, or yes, no doubt. But I think my friends and students, with some exceptions, are on the same side I am, and we all face a professional field that is, generally speaking, antagonistic. It is always better not to totalize, not to exaggerate. It could be that everybody feels in their jobs that they are not comfortable or secure enough, and that the situation of conflict or struggle is endemic in the intellectual field, and perhaps necessarily so. In that sense, we are contenders in a conflict whose terms bore us, or, more precisely, we are contenders because we find the terms of the conflict quite uninteresting—this is the problem: we refuse the choice they give us, which makes them mad. Many withdraw and prefer to abstain, though at some price. The conflict can be latent or kept at a tenuous level for periods of time, but sometimes it opens up and becomes accentuated—and, of course, in times of crisis and of general paradigm shifts, things get worse.

To continue with your question, *Línea de sombra* departs from the acknowledgment that a political turn has taken place, and that one has to take it into account. We are still there, but with one reservation I will try to explain. That book is published in 2007. I am in Scotland at the time, trying to settle there, unsuccessfully. I had decided to cross the Atlantic once more, to return to Europe, which for me meant in a nontrivial sense to leave Latin Americanism behind for good. For me, for complex and, I imagine, totally private reasons, Latin Americanism was over not just conceptually or geopolitically but also as an option for personal involvement. At that moment, I no longer want to be a Latin Americanist, I want to get out of it (please do not misunderstand: at the end of the day, most of my Latin American friends had nothing to do with Latin Americanism and had no interest in it), but I fail to do it, because my own trajectory will not really let me. I do not realize, when I leave for Scotland, that it is not so easy to escape, and that inertial history does not just follow, it also chases. I could not find a space for myself in Scotland, so I ended up returning to the United States (something I am very grateful about, of course) for another job in the Latin American studies field, which was all I could find, so I had to try to inhabit the ruins of my earlier work and try to relaunch an intellectual project that could still train students at the highest possible level. The task of creating room, opening up and protecting a space where younger people could freely deploy their own intelligence—well, that has always been fundamental to me. So, what kind of a critical and exploratory space could open up in the midst of the political turn? We are now talking about infrapolitics, understood as a general critique of the political turn. We may close the circle, and this new avatar is a return to what had taken place before the linguistic turn, what the linguistic turn interrupted: intellectual history knows it under the fallen name of existentialism, but clearly there is a thinking about existence (as opposed to "life") that is a pending task.

RODRIGO CASTRO: Alberto, I wanted to consult with you, to ask you a question, about something that you have already mentioned in your trajectory through late-twentieth-century Latin Americanism, which is the episode concerning the Latin American subaltern studies project, in which you were very involved. I think that is a very significant moment, perhaps a point of inflection in that recent history of Latin Americanist reflection, in which, of course, a reception of the South Asian subaltern studies project, of the South Asian postcolonial writers, takes place in some way. That project comes to an end, to closure, in the opening of two lines of work: the line that Walter Mignolo will follow, a subalternism of identity, which goes through a certain rejection of South Asian subalternism, since the latter is supposedly contaminated by so-called postmodern thought, and another line that I think opens up, which is the possibility of a subalternism of difference, which is in itself an opening to the traditions of poststructuralist thought, especially to Jacques Derrida. Those are two different drifts—I think they constitute a very important moment—and I would like to know whether you can dwell first in that moment of the breakup of the Latin American subaltern studies project, and then whether you could evaluate that first drift, not the one you took, but the one concerning the subalternism of identity, which now figures as the Modernity and Coloniality

Group, or the "decolonial project." From the perspective of that group, whose presence is still important, its importance is out of the question; in different places of the North American and South American academies, they would probably not agree with your diagnosis about a Latin Americanism at its terminal end. They would, in fact, vindicate the possibility of an authentic Latin American thought that would refer to a kind of history underlying Latin American cultural traditions that would enable thinking alternative to European or Western thinking. Then, two things: can you dwell on that episode, that moment, since it has become kind of notorious with the passage of time, the breakup of the Latin American Subaltern Studies Group, and then can you dwell on that decolonial drift or project?

AM: Your question includes many things, and I must be careful not to say too much or too little. Latin Americanism was always a kind of leftist academic project, at least it conceptualized itself predominantly in that way, partially as a reaction to US imperialism in the region after World War II. At the university, Latin Americanism thought of itself as a machine for resistance, symbolic resistance, no more, since it is a resistance in the US university, against Yankee imperialism. As such, it was strongly influenced by Marxism, even if it was a rather generic Marxism, whiffs of Marxist rhetoric rather, without much specificity (except for some seriously committed fellows, who were rather too specific). But, when I start my professional path, Marxism in the United States (and not just there) is in an open crisis. The crisis only becomes deeper through the 1990s. Subalternism begins in the 1980s somewhere between India and the United Kingdom as a reaction against the crisis of Marxism and Marxist historiography, rather than as anything else. It is, from its inception, a Marxist reaction, philo-Marxist, to the crisis of Marxism, and specifically of so-called world Marxism (that is, not only the crisis of Soviet or Chinese Marxism, or the crisis of Eurocommunism). I will save you details about how the Latin Americanist group was formed and how it grew a little, not much. I belong, along with several friends of mine such as Gareth Williams or John Kraniauskas, to a second or third round of growth, and there was no fourth round because the group collapsed when it was about to happen. Between the second or third round and the collapse, the group establishes a relationship with the South Asians: we have several important conversations with Ranajit Guha in Houston, for instance, and later with Gayatri Spivak and Partha Chatterjee, with Gyan Prakash and

Dipesh Chakrabarty—well, it is the beginning of a serious relationship—the contact is precarious, developing, but it constitutes, such as it is, the moment of international legitimation for Latin Americanist subalternism, the exit from the institutional ghetto. At the same time, it is also the moment of disaster and catastrophe, because that is when internal territorial disputes emerge, with groups of people wanting the legitimation for themselves, which meant refusing it to others, well, you know, that kind of greedy, jealous, petty, and destructive drive that is so typical of the academic world and in which some of our senior members excelled. What happens in the end?

You must forgive me, but I will not give you many details. It is not really for me to do it; somebody else should do it, somebody younger, not linked to the group then could do her or his research and get it done; somebody, if our field were strong enough (but it isn't), should write the history of those years, which not only goes through the meetings of the group or the internal communications of the group but extends to publications, interviews, semisecret and semipublic conversations, institutional and generational jealousy, and unheard-of bullshit that poisoned the atmosphere, undid the intellectual promise itself, and demoralized those who, in the group or close to it, had anxiously but merely expected to devote themselves to research and thought. It was not possible. But you have to ask others and see what they say. My version would necessarily only be partial, and there are things I am still not willing to share.

We organized something at Duke. In 1997–1998, Walter Mignolo is the chair of the department and he tells me: "I want you to help me organize a big conference, I am the chair of the department so I am very busy, so you organize it, you take care of it, with my help." And we began to do it, of course. At that time, we are friends, or that is what I think, and we are colleagues, we have a close relationship, we have a journal together, we go on camping trips, we taste wines, and we have dinner with our families basically every other week. Our intellectual differences are obvious, on the other hand, but I have never really cared much about intellectual differences if there is friendship and good faith and basic cordiality in the middle. For that conference we invite the entire Latin American subalternist group; we invite some very prominent people of the South Asian group; we invite another set of people we figure may have an interest, such as Ernesto Laclau, Aníbal Quijano, Enrique Dussel; and we invite others who are our colleagues at Duke, among them some academic celebrities who have at least an indirect relationship with our thematics, such as Fredric Jameson, and some other people I prefer not to mention or have forgotten, and also, and importantly, our Duke friends and students, some of whom—Danny James, Jon Beasley-Murray, Horacio Legrás—have made their interest in joining the group explicit. The program can be looked at on the internet, I suppose, "Cross-Genealogies and Subaltern Knowledges" was the name of the event, and we had a nice poster. It is a great conference, but so great that, from the very beginning, nay, before it starts, weird things emerge: nerves, neurasthenic meltdowns, stupid confusions, mysterious organizational secrets, and psychotic breakdowns camouflaged in political or spiritual keys (Mignolo, for instance, gets very mad because I tell Chakrabarty to come directly to the conference from the airport; it turns out Mignolo had told him to go to his hotel, which would have made Chakrabarty miss several panels). So, inevitably, for there is no reason to think it was merely coincidence or an accident, at the last meeting an accusation emerges, previously prepared, previously plotted, not spontaneous, not in good faith, but in fact, stated with unforgettable spite, that we, the organizers (not just Mignolo and me, but the Duke group more generally), had done everything with the sole purpose of hijacking the group, of stealing it to satisfy spurious and opportunistic political interests, industries and businesses at Duke, academic glories, and what not. Total bullshit, as far as I was concerned.

I had nothing to do with any of that, the accusations came at me as if from outer space, but, for just that reason, I am doubly perplexed and see that nothing is to be salvaged: they had broken the toy for good. True, other things had happened in the meantime, had continued to happen to help me reach that conclusion. Among them was an intervention by Mignolo that is published out there, so I reveal nothing by telling you about it. I will get to it in a second. In the meantime, Latin Americanist subalternism gets murdered the last day of the Duke conference, in the fall of 1998, and goes down into a foul sea of accusations and suspicions that are certainly without the least foundation as far as I and those close to me were concerned. I will not judge others' intentions. The group dies at the moment of its greatest glory, when it had finally become possible to do something serious, influential, perhaps decisive in our small world, and that is sad, albeit consistent with what I have lived and experienced in the academic world. An opportunity was lost that was perhaps undeserved by us, I do not know. It was an opportunity for collective work with strong institutional support, from a flexible, open, plural, and nondogmatic perspective. We lost the possibility of long-lasting theoretical and political conversations, legitimate agreements and disagreements, at a moment when many of us vitally needed that platform. Professional history from then on would have been a hell of a lot more interesting than it has been. Even now, responding to your question, I can get into no intellectual differences, into the proposals that were being made at the time and the ideas that were being discussed: they drowned all of it, the intellectual discussion, I am afraid, with the petty political interests.

Mignolo opens the conference, as senior organizer and departmental chair. The way I look at it, we are putting our resources at Duke—which are many—and our symbolic capital, whatever it may have been, at the service of the project, without any reservations. But of course at the time I am a recently promoted associate professor, probably a lot more naïve than I should have been. I have already said I prefer not to judge the intentions of others. But Mignolo allows himself a public gesture that, retrospectively, and once naïveté has been forcibly shed, is very harsh, very grave, because he is actually splitting the group, breaking the group in two, performing the division of the group into two sides, which he calls, respectively, the "properly" (or "authentically," to use your word, Rodrigo) postcolonial and the postmodern one. Those are loaded terms. When Mignolo says "postmodern," that was obviously pejorative; anybody who had had some exposure to him knew it. And all of us had had enough exposure to him. "On the postcolonial side," he says, "there are Quijano, Dussel, myself, and some others [they were not mentioned at that moment, but he was talking about Sara Castro-Klarén, Fernando Coronil, perhaps José Rabasa, Ramón Grosfoguel, with Javier Sanjinés still in the interrogation room]." On the side of the postmoderns, everyone else. The division itself was poisonous: even allowing that many of the younger people could be "postmodern," which would of course verge on the definition, it excludes and erases people, like John Beverley or Ileana Rodríguez, but also others from the founding group, who would not tolerate being excluded. They consider themselves classical Marxists and therefore do not accept their definition as "postmodern," but, on the other hand, they are also belligerently not "postcolonial" (itself a loaded and suspicious term in the faux-radical lingo Mignolo used at the time, by the way; it would soon be replaced by "decolonial," which removes the exogenous impurity from the first term). But, given these games, and what went on after them, the tension would become irreparable in the following days. The accusations in the final session, although very poorly directed, are probably a consequence of it. In fact, all of it ends up causing my departure from Duke a few years later, one thing leading to another until things become thoroughly intolerable. It is, of course, hard not to blame anyone, I had eyes to see, but I force myself to think that nothing is ever personal—a collective dynamic unleashes itself where the final agency is undeterminable. But the actors know what they did and what they wanted to do and how they may have been wrong to do it. Or right. Someone else will have to study this. But any destructive intentions people had in those days were demonstrably idiotic, because the results benefited no one and everybody lost out—the decolonials most of all for anybody in the know, as they lost credibility terminally and irretrievably. Not many days went by, however, before we heard that Mignolo, Castro-Klarén, Coronil, and a few others had organized another meeting at the University of Chicago, with Prakash and Chakrabarty, who allowed themselves to be manipulated, incredibly calling it a meeting of the Latin American Subaltern Studies Group, to which most of us—certainly the postmodern ones—were not invited. So it might have been true: there was a hijacking attempt in place, as Beverley and Rodríguez had anticipated. Or was the hijacking a consequence of what Beverley and Rodríguez did? But the whole thing was moot: the group was already dead; it had been assassinated.

As you said, not everything is necessarily disastrous for everyone. The death of the group was a precondition for the decolonial line to develop unhindered. The death of the group marks the beginning of the desert years, and in that desert the plastic flower of decoloniality goes through its latency period until it begins to gain international visibility as "the decolonial option," Coloniality and Modernity, Modernity and Decoloniality, call it what you wish. One hears that it has now self-imploded, which is not surprising in the least. I was never interested, truth be told, but it is beyond question, as you say, that it has had an influence on many people, that it is a visible trend, and that for a few years it obtained the kind of large international recognition, particularly among the younger people, reached by very few politico-theoretical tendencies emanating from the academy. It obviously connected with some salvific or messianic vein, quasi-religious, but in any case very popular. There is an easy common sense in their positions, which are derived from three or four initial axioms repeated unto exhaustion: we have to admit that with generosity. They are or have been popular. Again, I have been hearing that things are no longer going well, but perhaps they will reconstitute and move on from those simple truths until they may reach a higher degree of intellectual rigor and truth—the intellectual field is not helped when it has to confront weak positions, and most of the writing that has come down from the decolonials is weak indeed. But I think you are right that their original gesture of foundation can be traced back to the 1998 Duke conference, and it was the Mignolo gesture: "Not you, but us." Dussel, Quijano, Mignolo are the founding icons. The latency period goes from 1998 to 2004 or 2005, when the popular glory starts. There is a lasting impact of the group, which they also borrow from the fact that they radicalized culturalism, of which they are the last residue, the last "*cri*." They are identitarian and fundamentalist in a world that was and is complacent enough with identitarian fundamentalism; they are radical particularists (as Laclau called them) in a world where radical particularism is comforting, and they pursue and propagate a subalternism of identity, as you say. And many find great enjoyment in it, lacking everything else.

The rest of us, the so-called postmoderns, had to swallow their accusation of being "Eurocentric," hence also racist, male chauvinist, and so many other bad things—in fact, everything bad that in the dubious Latin Americanist left is identified with not being in the politically correct position, which is the authentic, the proper, the identical one. There were people who, in those desert years, suffered professionally, lost academic positions, were denied tenure, were punished for belonging to the group of hypocrites, the fascistic, arrogant theory mofos, well, marranos, old story, double exclusion, we have never been anywhere else. But these problems, which were the function of an institutional defeat in which many who had nothing to do with the decolonials participated, did not affect the decolonials (or the "Marxists"). They held on to the little symbolic power the profession distributes. It only affected the rest of us; do not ask me why because I can't explain it. When John Beverley, many years later, published his book about Latin Americanism after September 11, where he speaks about postsubalternism, he makes no mention of the decolonials, but instead speaks very critically of our group, which he now calls "the deconstructors," in order to say that we are finished, dead, and sunk into the ruin of history. Beating on a dead horse, they all like that. Why does Beverley not talk about Dussel, Quijano, and company? Because, at the moment of publication of his book, they were at the peak of their middlebrow popularity. They were, for the likes of Beverley, untouchable, but we were easy prey, the apparent losers of a kind of parochial battle for critico-political truth. But he is wrong, as usual, because things are changing. Leaving me aside, and given the narrow range of ideologues Beverley approves of, the theoretical and intellectual pull in the field is represented by those he critiques. His identitarian culturalism, leftist or not, serviceable as it has been to neoliberal regimes, is becoming less useful for a geopolitics of the present, except in a reactive manner. Not just Beverley's culturalist populism but also decoloniality are reactive formations with scant political productivity—it does not matter how many hapless graduate students and Facebook users support them. When, in an introduction to a decolonial cult book, the scribbler says that every Latin American who does not look at the world with indigenous or Afro-American eyes is a faceless imperialist, I think the no exit, the impassable ideological wall, becomes clearly delineated—it is not just that they won't be able to pull themselves out of that path: they have no intention and no means of doing it.

Jon Beasley-Murray was astute enough in the mid-1990s, when he was still a student at Duke, to realize that subalternism, particularly in the Latin Americanist variety, was a populism, and that it had developed as a reaction to the crisis of Marxism. He writes an article that would later become a book chapter in his *Posthegemony* in which he says that the great impact Ernesto Laclau has had on cultural studies is directly dependent on that: cultural studies is a form of populism, so subalternism is populism squared. From that perspective, it was our task to establish critical positions within populism, within the populist dimension of the political, quite outside any politics based on principles. The decolonials prefer and support verticalist and identitarian populisms, dogmatic and authoritarian, but this is also the kind of populism Beverley would support. Incidentally, it is also supported, given the lack of alternative options, by the self-appointed communists who circulate in our academic field. Our option was different and moved in a quite different direction from the beginning. I am now trying to call it marrano populism. We persist in the pursuit of a form of thought that is an alternative to the fallen majoritarian academic ways: possibly more Marxian, certainly more critical and destructive, theoretically more radical, anti-identitarian, anti-authoritarian, an-archic. But we are still in a situation of institutional weakness—although that matters to me less and less.

JUAN MANUEL FORTE: The question of difference has come up several times in this conversation, so my question is easy: what is the role in subalternism of Martin Heidegger's and Jacques Derrida's respective thoughts on difference, and what role have they had in the genealogy of that trend?

AM: This is an important question for me, since I was formed in a certain Heideggerianism and a certain Derrideanism, and I keep both of those authors as central references in my own work. But that is not necessarily the case for my friends and associates. Some people I work with were not formed in any Heideggerian-Derridean schematics, although we are close and work together in similar directions. But I was. I was also educated in Marxism, at the University of Barcelona in the 1970s, although I was never any kind of devout follower, since the internal crisis was already producing all kinds of worrisome symptoms. I suppose I already looked at Marxism, and studied it, from a poststructuralist frame of mind. For years in Barcelona I was an assiduous reader of Friedrich Nietzsche and Gilles Deleuze and Félix Guattari, but in my years at Georgia, in my work with Bernard Dauenhauer, I started to develop a strong interest in the work of Derrida. Heidegger had been a constant for me since high school, and Derrida's (and Dauenhauer's) interest in him only increased mine. I suppose deconstruction soon became my theoretical position, although always with a strong Heideggerian drift, I think. Derrida's 1964–1965 seminar on history and being in Heidegger was recently published, and I found it exciting, when I read it, to note that Derrida's reflections and thoughts on that very early work of his—in 1964, Derrida is only starting his career—leaving his genius aside, had been constitutive for me from the beginning and almost in all of its aspects. I suppose it was all in the air.

There is a primary relationship with the history of philosophy, with metaphysics, culminating in G. W. F. Hegel, and Marxism is part of it, since Marxism cannot be fathomed without Hegel. For me, Heidegger's work was, from the beginning, and to a certain extent, given my context in Barcelona and the interests of my professors and friends, a mode of critical relationship to Marxism. And then Derrida's work became a mode of critical relationship to Heideggerianism. I think I am still there, more than ever. Heidegger repeated something Henri Bergson used to say, namely, that people only get to have one single idea in their lives; the problem is that it takes a while to recognize that single idea as such, and we get lost in marginalities. Somehow my single idea, if I may claim to have it yet, is there, connected to that particular relationship with the history of thought that I do not consider a Eurocentric relationship because I do not accept Eurocentrism as my horizon. Eurocentrism explodes once a critical relationship to Hegelianism is assumed, and the latter forces us into a cosmopolitical configuration of intellectual work; we might as well use Deleuze and Félix Guattari's term and talk about "geophilosophy" or "geothought."[1] For me, the work of both Heidegger and Derrida is a key step toward that geothought or philosophy of the future. I am limited myself, lazy also, so results are meager, which I lament, but I think that is what I am trying to make explicit, to let happen, to initiate in some way, together with my friends, from our presuppositions and our complex position as Hispanist or Latin Americanist intellectuals, and against resistances that, because they are external and powerful, become internal also. That this is so difficult to accept may seem unlikely, but the difficulty is real and effective. People cannot understand and prefer not to understand that, yes, we insist on speaking about, say, the ontico-ontological difference or the history of beyng or the trace structure when talking about Latin America—they actually consider it abominable, like a sin, an arrogance, or an intolerable whim. But I do not think that is the case.

There is a state of affairs, a state of the situation, that of course overflows the cultural parameters or the coordinates for Latin Americanist understanding, which is very parochial to start with. That is the situation we try to understand and in which we try to intervene, of course starting from a certain archive, like everybody else does as well. Except that our archive is not the identitarian and tellurian archive so beloved by our "authentic" colleagues. To return to the previous question, there is an uninterrupted liberal-criollo tradition based on identitarian parameters that decolonialism is only a specific avatar of. Just as Roberto González Echevarría may allow himself to say that it is not necessary to read Borges through Walter Benjamin, since we can read Borges through Ortega y Gasset, in exactly the same way Mignolo will fall into the faintly ridiculous (were it not so sad) claim that it is not necessary at all to read Antonio Gramsci, since we have José Carlos Mariátegui. It is the same thing, the same gesture. Identity is the only dominant thought produced by the Latin American intellectual tradition, or even by the Spanish intellectual tradition. There is, of course, an alternative, historically always vanquished, always humiliated, always repressed: nonidentitarian. Heidegger and Derrida, as critics of history and of metaphysical temporality, essentially revitalize that tradition, offering alternative points for various entries and exits from that critical tradition that enable us to think of a future epochality. This is the reason why they are essential thinkers for our present. We can talk about all of this with further details if you want, but to the extent that we are discussing an intellectual field rather than my personal trajectory, we may want to leave it there, even though I would still like to offer a couple of additional reflections.

The first one is that, contrary to common objections, the relationship our particular forms of reflection may have with the Heideggerian-Derridean schematics cannot be derived, either in specific or in general terms, from any state of affairs in the North American university. We have kept quite distant from both US Heideggerianism and US Derrideanism or deconstructionism. I have no interest in critiquing the latter or in maintaining precise critical distances—it is simply a fact. None of us (meaning my friends), with a couple of exceptions, have been educated in the environments or schools that have kept those traditions alive for the English-speaking world; we do not go to their meetings, we do not participate in their discussions, we do not publish in their journals, and, generally speaking, we barely know one another, with obviously some exceptions here and there. Therefore, the tedious pretension that our group or sector or faction—call it what you will—somehow "applies" schemes dominant in the US academy to a historical matter that is alien to it is wrong from the ground up (and down, as a friend says). These are pseudo-genealogical allegations, no matter how predictable. At the same time, I have no interest in claiming for Heideggero-Derrideanism the medal of highest truth of our time or anything of the kind. Everyone works from their readings, their history, their interests, and their style, and it seems to me that welcome always needs to be offered to any discursive formation, wherever it comes from. Of course, it will be a critical and open-eyed welcome, but intellectual freedom and anti-dogmatism should be points of departure—I do not know whether that sounds paradoxical.

The other point I would like to make regarding your question, Juan Manuel, is that the thematics of difference, as ontico-ontological difference, was the central one in my first book, *Interpretación y diferencia*, and is continued in other books, beginning with the title of *The Exhaustion of Difference*, for instance. It has a key role in *Tercer espacio*. I do not want to reify the concept, however, or substantiate it in any way or manner, and I don't think I have done that. This is why, when Rodrigo asks, in his earlier question, about a "subalternism of difference," I understand the use of the expression when it is to be opposed to that other "subalternism of identity," but I would also like to express my distance from that designation, since it might be a bit too ambiguous. I would think that, at this point, nothing in that lexeme calls us: neither subalternism nor difference. The words have been overused and are exhausted now. I am making an effort to remember the work of my friends, that "we" that I sometimes use is also ambiguous and never to be trusted, but I think in this issue I may confidently say that nobody is committed to any "subalternism of difference," and that is possibly another outcome of the bad history of the 1990s—the deck of cards was damaged thoroughly, and by now we have to welcome the thought and go elsewhere.

But it is also possible to say that the attempt to think through or from the ontico-ontological difference—this bothers some people—that is, to take the Heideggerian thematics seriously in all its complexity is one of the threads of what we call infrapolitics. Just a few days ago, a new book by Arturo Leyte was published, namely, *Heidegger: El fracaso del ser*. I read the book with infrapolitical glasses, let me say, and I confirmed in my reading that infrapolitics can be defined as the attempt to think or rethink politics from the region of the ontico-ontological difference and its Heideggerian variations; that both infrapolitical analysis and infrapolitical destruction are mutually, intimately involved or are indistinguishable; that infrapolitics could also be said to be the only properly political interrogation of politics (the rest is a program); that infrapolitics "shows up only as suspension and distance regarding the impropriety where one always already is," as Leyte says about something else on some page of his book, not claiming any other region of propriety, by the way; that infrapolitics, which is in every case a demetaphorization, a practice of demetaphorization, is also ever an errant demetaphorization and must endure the transit, as it is all there is; that infrapolitics is the suspension of the relationship between nihilism and the principle of general equivalence; that infrapolitics, therefore, raises a central objection to any resistance regarding the notion of an "other beginning," so strongly hated by many in its Heideggerian version; and that infrapolitics, since it is also a politics, is necessarily already the "other beginning," or it cannot be understood without an affirmative relationship with the notion, deeply historical, of an "other beginning." I think in a nutshell this sums up the links between the thinking project that has me busier than subalternism in any of its emphases today and the Heideggero-Derridean line on the history of thought.

ANTONIO RIVERA: I wanted to ask you about the importance for your work, whether or not it is a "subalternism of difference," of the archive. You have already commented on the fact that you start your career with an interest in the literary archive. I also wanted to ask about your work on history, about the importance the history of philosophy, the history of political ideas may have for you. With us, the group connected to the Saavedra Fajardo Library [of Hispanic Political Thought], which is a group that occupies itself with the history of political ideas, you have a relationship going back several years. I want you to speak about the importance of historiographical work for you, and whether you establish differences between literary and historical sources. I am also very interested in the relationship you may establish between archival work and theory, as I think that is something that marks a difference with what other Latin Americanist scholars do.

AM: When I finish my degree in philosophy in Barcelona, I am already studying for another degree in literature, that is, in literary studies or the history of literature or philology— hard to say what it was with any precision: Hispanic philology, they called it. I decide to go to the United States to get a PhD, which I understood to be a continuation of my work on literary studies. I had always been a voracious reader of literature, and I still am. For me, the study of literature, that is, the academic study of it, versus the study that may flow from a mere desire to read more, initially had everything to do with my need to get to know the entire historical archive in Spanish, since I had studied philosophy, and Spanish and philosophy are, for whatever reason, two things that have never really come together well enough. So I was unsatisfied. If one wanted to think in Spanish, it seemed hard to do it from philosophy. I did not want to become a permanent paraphraser of the history of German philosophy, or of French or Greek philosophy, like many of my professors, most of them, really, and very respectably so. I do not know what bug bit me; I now see that my argument made little sense. I thought that in order to think in Spanish, one had to absorb everything that had been said in the language—which, in the case of Spanish, meant historiographic and literary sources much more than philosophical sources. I went that way, probably making a mistake, because the truth is, literary scholarship, or archival work, properly said, although I love it and admire it in others, and it gives me great joy when it is well done, was never my thing. And I already knew it then. But then, at the same time, I also knew that there was no thread to be picked up in Spanish or Latin American philosophy, that what there was, not just in so-called philosophy but also in terms of the essay, for instance, was hopelessly dated and implausible. But the tradition is the tradition, and what happens to be the case is the case.

I was between a rock and a hard place: there was a problem, although it did not feel like one in the early years, since there was so much pleasant reading to do. But in point of fact, retrospectively, taking my deeper interests into account, I should not have become either a Hispanist or a Latin Americanist. What interested me was theoretical reflection, philosophical

reflection, but the misery of the Spanish (and Latin American) philosophical archive trapped me, and before I knew it, it was too late to do much
about it. As a young student, it did not matter to me—I did not even think
much about becoming a professor. But you must imagine that when you
do become a professor, then you have to adopt an intellectual field, its history, its problems, its people. And you have to do it seriously, or else you
will never get to train students in it at the right level (and besides, your own
career may also go to hell). The truth is, I was more interested in what Latin
Americanism lacked than in what Latin Americanism was. And I did my
best, but to have to teach courses and seminars every semester on things
that are only indirectly interesting to you at best, to have to be responsible
for the development of every one of your students, which means you must
make sure they can find a job, that they may be suitably launched in the
profession, and to do that on the basis of ceaseless work on thematics that
are of a secondary personal interest, meaning they are of interest, naturally, but only in the same way they can be of interest to anyone, that is,
not intimately, since nothing was decisively at stake at a personal level in
any of that: well, I am not going to say it was tough. It was simply not quite
what I should have been doing. Of course there were compensations: There
was Borges, for instance, and not just Borges but other authors I liked.
There was the good work of my students. But ultimately it was all a bit
schizophrenic, some kind of doomed structure that marked my career perhaps only negatively, I am sorry to say. I have lived—and all of this comes
from the original expatriation, I think—in the trap of the fissure between
my real interests, always in withdrawal, always receding, always in second
place in the order of priorities, with limited time for them except for some
exceptions, like Borges (and that would be true for any other literature in
any other language; the problem was not the literature in Spanish), and
the realities imposed by the truth of the situation, always banal, always
forceful: the need to do what the department needs you to do; the need
for professional progress, tenure, promotion, respectability; the need to be
respected by your peers—all of those things that for me were mortgaged
to a field of engagement I never really liked or felt to be mine: not a glove,
rather a boot tree with some little nails inside, something like that. And I
was the shoe. This is simply the truth, since you are asking. I am not proud
of any of it. Or even complaining. One makes some mistakes, and it is then
difficult to pull out of them. But one should see them.

Of course, as time goes by one adjusts, and at the end of the day, literature and history and culture and politics had always been of great interest

to me, so that to teach those things, to comment on them in class and at meetings, was never a form of torture or self-torture—far from it. I did my reading and my writing, like everyone else, but in my case from a notion of text perhaps learned from Derrida that helped, because it enabled me to suspend the notion of rank, it diminished the distance between the literary text and the text called literary (there is a big difference, if you think about it), between the critical text and the theoretical text. For me, I could argue that it canceled it, it canceled the difference, perhaps phantasmatically, only to the extent I needed it to be canceled, because the cancelation enabled me to read, I don't know, *Don Segundo Sombra* or *La vorágine* otherwise. I persuaded myself that the issue of rank was not in play, which was important when the time came for me to read interminable bores (no matter how short they were) from which nothing interesting enough was ever to come out—the condemnation was to read forever eternal variations on *Fray Gerundio de Campazas*, or it felt like it sometimes. And to that problem, probably only mine, another little problem was added that was also a direct result of that historical archive I had made such a big deal of for my sins: it became an almost libidinal problem that so much of the Latin American literary tradition, as one had to teach it, in its dominant and canonic texts, at certain periods and for certain countries in an exhaustive and exhausting manner, was a liberal-criollo tradition whose only interest seemed to be identity, national identity in particular, which to me seems not necessarily a false problem, since it seems to be real enough for so many people, but certainly a boring and not very enriching problem: more boring and reductive the more obsessive it became. So, what was to be done? Given not just, say, *Terra nostra* or *Los pasos perdidos* but so many other texts with such limiting thinking horizons, their repetitive monotony, their conceits, their prison, how was one to move ahead? How was one to say something that was actually saying something? It seemed difficult.

I am probably exaggerating these internal conflicts in order to make them clear, but I think they have overdetermined my decisions, perhaps out of a certain need to escape tedium. Regarding your question on history, I have tended to concentrate on the present, but not out of disinterest in the past. I have rarely worked on the historical or historiographical archive—but perhaps only because I have not yet found my way into it; it is a long path, and I figured I still need to clarify my relationship to the present to develop proper questions about the past. Please take this as self-critique or simply as a statement of fact, personal itinerary, private conflict, fractures in desire—I am not justifying anything. But, clearly, all of this then has a projection on work in the professional field. Everybody lives with their personal variations of those conflicts, starting from the fact that even if many have a deep literary calling, there are only a few who may feel an intense calling to spend their lives as exegetes and doing paraphrases of other people's literature—and forget history or historiography: this is what the professional field does for the most part, which is a public secret, and not a very venturous one.

Some, of course, grab the bull by the horns and decide early on that they are going to commit passionately to the glimmer of other people's literature, which they will ceaselessly polish. They are the ones who are militant: "No, I will only do 'literature.'" They tend to call what they do "aesthetics" for some reason. At that point, they have turned "literature" into a personal fetish—always connected to somebody else's phallus, as we know. That is fine and dandy, of course, I love fetishes myself. The problem is when they try to impose their fetishistic tastes on everyone else, and particularly when they do it at a time when they fail to find extensive social echoes. We can probably say that the West was largely a literary world until the end of the Cold War, in the sense that literature was an important aspect of social hegemony. Up until then, our languages understood themselves and were socially understood as literary languages, from their capacity, overdetermined as it was by the geopolitical context, to express cultural difference and degrees of glory. I think it is only a minor exaggeration to say that languages were then, more or less secretly, hierarchically organized on literary history and capacities. Western universities sought to support and promote literary production, for that was their function, their political contribution to state discourse. Literary criticism was a powerful instrument for national ideology, for ideological normalization, and, of course, for ideology critique, for all kinds of comparisons. Literature today may not have lost any expressive capacity, but the discourse on literature has, because it no longer responds to any real social or national need. The notion of culture came up, through cultural studies, to replace literature as the main ideological referent, but culture is too vague a notion and it fails to fill the empty throne as queen of humanities. Culture is an entelechy that should probably be understood, historically for us, as a reactive product, a substitute formation given the crisis of the literary apparatus, which is part of the crisis of the national state in times of globalization.

But we can choose otherwise, and from love of literature refuse to fetishize literature, particularly as literature is rarely given, it is a rare thing, and not everything that calls itself literature deserves the dignity of the name. They speak of aesthetics, and aesthetics is supposed to account for any scribblings as well. I have a certain aversion to that word, and I do not quite understand why. Or I do. It is a word that has come to be falsely used; it is the joker for a strategy of avoidance. When it comes to having nothing to say, they invoke aesthetic depths we can only fathom or unfathom. Taking shelter in the aesthetic, constituting "the aesthetic" as an object (the primary object for professional business), is a form of false consciousness—or so I see it, hence my visceral reaction. If they want to talk about art, let them talk about art! But "the aesthetic" is all too often the form in which those who do not dare speak of art talk about what is not quite art or does not seem art, but then it is not any other thing either. It is a thing without thing, an unthinged thing that "aesthetics" addresses, hence my panic: the unthinged thing is horror itself. And yet it is everywhere: at professional meetings, in titles of articles and papers, as banal justification for what the profession does, as immutable witness to a discursive void, to the incapacity to talk about a work in a strong sense. There are very few works, still fewer unworks. And everything that does not dare be work or unwork is aesthetic, it would seem. Performance, *testimonio*, installation, shorts, even novels are no longer works: they are "aesthetic production"—go figure what that means. I do not want to attack anyone's serious labor and efforts. Everybody does what they can, and I suppose everybody tries their best. But there is, beyond people, a professional or institutional responsibility in place. I understand the appeal to "the aesthetic" as a critical symptom, not a substantial region of reflection (for instance, not a region that would enable us to identify productions that are not "aesthetic"), and it is better not to turn it into a false fold of truth: it is only just another proof of a deep historical de-orientation and a real crisis in the humanities. The archive is profoundly more real: everything is in the archive, the real and the unreal, the aesthetic and the nonaesthetic, and as an impossible totality, it marks our task and delimits and circumscribes and frustrates our desire.

PEDRO LOMBA: I wanted to press you a little on the use you make of the archive and I wanted to ask you about an issue that is very present for us here in Madrid, on which we work a lot, and I know you do too in Texas, and that is the recovery, against the identitarian tradition, against conventional thought, inside the archive, that recuperation you do in your latest work, what you underline forcefully and intensely, the concept of marrano thought. I wanted to ask you about that, how you modify and how you use the archive for your elaboration of that concept, what it means, really, and what is the political interest it may have vis-à-vis that subalternism of identity, what do you make of these elaborations of yours?

AM: Right, I think what we can call the marrano register is the register of our relationship to the archive, what I was calling the total language archive in its relationship with the total archive of languages, that is, if you want, with the geophilosophical totality. It is a perspective, an intended will, an intention: to work from that marrano will is a way of eluding the traps of identitarianism, but it is also at the same time a political way of accepting the tradition, the archive. There is a certain belligerence in saying one wants to have a marrano relationship with the archive. It politicizes the relationship in an immediate way, we know that well. José Luis's book ¿Qué imperio? has been very important for me. In it, José Luis traces the history of Hispanic *marranismo* as a counterpart to the identitarian domination of Catholic inquisitorial, *castizo* culture. The book speaks mainly of Spain, but it could easily be extended to Latin America. He traces a rebellious tradition of thought, a tradition of the vanquished, connected to a historical minority, but of course, as tradition of thought, exceeding the minority, and constituting something like an alternative historical pole, an unfinished part of a possible history of freedom. What are the marrano elements in the last five hundred years of Latin American culture, the elements for which the identity paradigm fails to account? That is what interests me, the flights from a history of identity, the escape from hegemony. That is why, for me, the marrano—marrano history, which is on the one hand the particular history of the group of people at some point called "marranos," and on the other the history of a marrano register of thought and existence, which is of course something else, no longer connected to race or religion, no longer directly connected to specific members of the converso minority, as I said, an unfinished part of a potential history of freedom—is an essential element in what we are calling posthegemony, or posthegemonic thought. If there is hegemony, it is never marrano hegemony—marranismo and hegemony are incompatible. Is that enough of an answer?[2]

PEDRO LOMBA: I would like to hear more about the use of the concept of *marranismo* to escape the traps of identitarian thought. I would then like to ask you whether, in the end, *marranismo* is not another way of building up an identity; whether, therefore, it is impossible to escape the trap set for us by a thought that constantly builds identity.

A M: I just remembered a barber in Bryan, Texas. I used to live some years ago in an old building in downtown Bryan. One day I had to leave on a trip and I had to have a haircut and I had forgotten to make an appointment, so I got out of the house looking for the first barbershop I could find that would take me, and I entered a rather rundown establishment, empty of people except for a gentleman reading a book. He asked me very politely whether I could be helped, and on noting my accent, he asked whether I was Hispanic. "Yes." "From where?" "Spain." "Ah, me too!" I was a little perplexed that a Spanish barber had landed in Bryan, Texas, of all places, and besides, the man did not seem to me to have exactly geographical origins in Spain— call it a hunch. So I asked him to explain, and he told me his family had come to the Rio Grande Valley from Salamanca toward the end of the eighteenth century with a land title given by "His Majesty Carlos IV" for twenty leagues of land. And that his family did very well indeed until the Texas Rangers took the land away from them, dooming them to misery, and the family took shelter with a tribe of "Mescalero Apaches," he said. "I hate the Rangers," he said. "I spit when I see them." And he said: "So here I am, Don Chus Espinosa Murguía, a mix of Spaniard and Apache, at your service." It was clear to me that his Spanish identification was only a way of marking his de-identification with Texas hegemonic power or hegemonic culture. He had a history that made him a sort of Texas marrano, something that he somehow intuited, since he immediately asked me something else. He said he presumed that I, as a university professor and therefore somewhat cultivated, would know whether there was a chance he might be connected by family ties to that Jewish philosopher Spinoza of whom he had heard talk. I told him I did not believe so, since Spinoza's family had left Spain long before the eighteenth century, and his family had probably moved to Portugal from Galicia, not from Salamanca. Don Chus was relieved, and he told me he was glad of it, since "I have enough with my Apache blood and it would be too much to have to deal with Jewish blood on top." Don Chus, it seems to me, lives clearly in a marrano register, which of course does not prevent him from making partial identifications (with Spain, for instance, as well as with the Apaches). When he makes them, they are clearly not marrano identifications—what is marrano is precisely the impossible identification; what is impossible in the identification. So, as to your question: you ask about an inescapable or hyperbolic dimension of thought that would not let you escape something through a mere inversion or negation. To that extent, the inversion of an identity is still identity thinking, in the same way that inverting a metaphysical postulate is still an operation internal to metaphysics. My point is that there is another way of looking at this: the marrano dimension is not an identitarian dimension—although it can certainly be made to be, but not necessarily. It is rather the aporia of identity, a de-identification that will never let itself be simply reconstituted as its opposite. Starting from the fact that "marrano" is not something one is but rather something that happens to one—they call you a marrano, and it is an insult, it is the stigma of double exclusion. It is the consequence of a radical (indeed, lethal) exclusion from identity. Whoever is called marrano must swallow it possibly in disagreement with the intentional tonality of the naming. She or he will not be marrano in the sense of the accusation, a pig, a degenerate, but she or he understands that the other's perception performs or corroborates an exclusion from hegemony, an exclusion from the political game, in an abject (and abjected) situation from the game, just an outsider, just an outcast that could be killed without murder or sacrifice, to paraphrase Giorgio Agamben. The marrano never wants to be where they place her, in any way or manner, neither before nor after the accusation, and that silent and unconditional rebellion, that radical no, is perhaps a source of endless conflict: one is not to be captured in the nets of hegemony nor in the nets of counterhegemony. This can be very disconcerting for the others, eventually becoming suspicious, eventually becoming intolerable.

Can we imagine a marrano politics? Posthegemonic? I talked about this the other day, mentioning an "other populism," an anti-verticalist and anti-identitarian populism that would not succumb to pressures for political conformity. We can imagine that the crisis of Marxism in the 1970s was first of all a crisis motivated by the verticalism and the hegemonic push for conformity in actually existing Marxist societies and institutions (the parties, and not just the parties). If Marxism, as a critique of capitalism, as a critique of the capitalist structuration of the world, is the fundamental horizon of thought in late modernity, then to talk about the crisis of Marxism is to talk about the crisis of modernity, or of the political structuration of modernity. It amounts to saying that Marxism cannot overcome modern parameters and remains internal to them. To speak of populism, as is done today, as a way of solving that political crisis is not enough. Populism must also be internally deconstructed. Two essential elements of the deconstruction of populism, of the affirmative and politically productive deconstruction of populism, are the critique of identity and the critique of authority and hegemony. A posthegemonic marrano populism is my political proposal. I know it is only a formal framework, a possibility of thought, not thought itself, only a call to it, which is what marrano thought, which means "thought in the marrano register," or infrapolitics or posthegemony merely name or point to.

ANTONIO RIVERA: Rats, you have already responded to the question I was going to ask.

JOSÉ LUIS VILLACAÑAS: Antonio, you could perhaps ask about some of the theses in *The Exhaustion of Difference* about society as infinite, which is the ultimate critique of a populism of hegemony. If society is finite, then society may be in a position to accomplish some equivalential equilibrium between its parts. But if society is infinite, then it cannot be equivalentially captured.

AM: Right. But, curiously, the thesis that society is infinite is Ernesto Laclau's own thesis.

JOSÉ LUIS VILLACAÑAS: Indeed, it is a thesis of Laclau's that he magically cancels out when he reduces the infinite to equivalence, which is ontologically impossible. He takes his departure in a Deleuzian premise and then proceeds to erase everything that would follow from it into equivalence and the equivalential chain.

ANTONIO RIVERA: Alberto, I am going to ask you about something you have already hit upon several times during this conversation, but I would like you also to offer some genealogical reflections on how it is that you came by this notion of posthegemony. We know you directed Jon Beasley-Murray's thesis on posthegemony and that, years later, a few years after the publication of his book, we organized a summer school course here, in El Escorial, on posthegemony, in which the Madrid group also participated. That resulted in a book edited by our colleague Rodrigo Castro, entitled *Poshegemonía*, and published some time ago by Biblioteca Nueva. You have stated what is otherwise obvious, namely, that Latin Americanism, postcolonial and decolonial thought, subalternism of identity or of difference—that all of that is leftist thought that must therefore accept more or less critically twentieth-century Marxism, including Gramsci's notion of hegemony, and also Ernesto Laclau, who has been explicitly and implicitly present here since we have spoken a fair deal about populism. I would like you to comment on your relationship with Ernesto Laclau, because, after so much conversation about posthegemony and after these books that have come out and will continue to come out, not just you but your entire group, your disciples, are identified as a sector of the academy, if we can call it that, contrary to or at least in a polemical relation to Laclau's master concepts, hegemony and populism, populist reason. You have said you have not given up on the concept of populism. I do not know whether you would want to talk about it in your response, but I anticipate myself, perhaps it is all right to say now that during this last week, in our Second Critico-Political Transnational Seminar, you gave the first address and you surprised us, because we were not expecting—given the fact that we have heard you speak of populism very critically—your proposal regarding a "marrano populism." We thought you were, from posthegemony, in the anti-populist camp. I also want to note that you have just arrived from Greece, and this conversation could be placed in the context of the Greece crisis, not to be megalomaniac, but after all, it is only a week since the Greek referendum on the European Union proposal, and you have just been debating all of that with Yannis Stavrakakis and other disciples of Ernesto Laclau, and you dropped this bomb of marrano populism right there. Can you talk about the genealogy of all these things, how you came by the idea of marrano populism, and how that has been received by Laclau's disciples? That will be of great interest.

AM: Thanks, Antonio, but let me say first that I do not have any disciples. I have some friends, many younger, who work with me if they want and every now and then. The partisans of hegemony can perhaps have disciples, or seek them, but posthegemony does not allow it. Then, indeed, and this is true even though some people do not believe it, I have never tried to impose my theoretical models on anyone, let alone on my students or my younger or much younger friends. How boring that would be. Regarding Jon, when he decides, in the wake of the brutal confrontation at the end of the Duke fall of 1998 conference on subalternism, when the subalternist project dies for us, when he decides to title his dissertation "Posthegemony," what he is doing, first of all, is providing his own answer to Mignolo's position. He is telling him and whoever wants to hear: "Not 'authentic postcolonials' (or 'decolonials') and 'postmoderns,' rather 'identitarian hegemonic' and 'posthegemonic,'" and that is perhaps the beginning of the history of that term. I do not think there was anything before that, although for several years we had been trying to think about subalternity taking exception to Ernesto's hegemony theory, for which the subaltern was simply the fellow who had not yet successfully articulated his popular demands (which we discussed with him as well). I can tell you that our first activity after the breakup of the group, just a few days later, was to create a small working group on posthegemony. What did it mean? Well, against the grain of most or all of the senior people in the group, we had wanted to keep alive an understanding of life and the world outside their hegemonic capture. The subalterns were part of our interest because the subalterns are by definition outside hegemonic capture. We wanted a thinking, a political thinking, that would refuse the imprisonment of the social within political structures that would be incommensurable with the openness of the world, the social world to start with. Posthegemony is, in the first place, in a first approach, a radical negation of voluntary servitude. It rejects, politically, what Spinoza referred to as "sad passions." It sides with Heidegger's conceptualization, in his seminar on Parmenides, according to which politics, understood as a politics of domination, is the art of getting people to collaborate in their own submission. (Should politics always be a politics of domination, one way or another? Perhaps it always is, in which case posthegemony would have to become a directly infrapolitical concept.) We could go to Étienne de La Boétie, but also to François de La Rochefoucauld, Baltasar Gracián, and others. All of that was always there, since the mid-1990s. It is the initial position from which, for instance, John Kraniauskas (although he has always indicated a distance from the term "posthegemony"), Gareth Williams, and I myself expressed our differences with the rest of the positions in the Latin Americanist subalternist group, and would have expressed them with positions in the South Asian group had there been time. Anti-verticalism, understood as a refusal to submit, both objectively and subjectively, not to submit, not to be submitted, meant posthegemony for us. There was always a drive for an-archic freedom associated with the intuition of the noncoincidence between politics, or power, and the world.

That noncoincidence, the gap between power and world—I want to account for it, it is the site of thought for me. Beasley-Murray makes his own developments in those years following theoretical parameters that have little or nothing to do with any kind of Heideggero-Derrideanism. And from there—beyond a period of relative silence during those wasteland years I have spoken of and that I will mention again—it is only logical for reflection to proliferate into versions of posthegemony that are not at all the same—the book Rodrigo edited includes at least four or five quite distinct ones. (By the way, these differences seem entirely to bypass those who dismiss posthegemony gaily, normally in a sentence or two, not bothering to understand the first thing about it, calling it ultraleftist or postpolitical—they only react to the term.) There is probably, at the origin, a common intuition or a common negation, perhaps binding, that has something to do with the gap I mentioned: the mutual overflow of power and world, their radical noncoincidence, which is for me certainly another manifestation of the ontico-ontological difference, and more proximally an absolute indictment of the so-called priority of politics in the order of thought. This would be true also for books and work done by friends either inside or outside our various groups that do not particularly thematize the notion of posthegemony, like Oscar Cabezas's book on postsovereignty, Sergio Villalobos's book on suspended sovereignty, or Peter Baker's doctoral dissertation on emergent indigeneity, or the critique of democratic consensus proposed by Maddalena Cerrato. I could give more examples.

Posthegemony, insofar as it does not rely on any kind of "hegemonic articulation," rejects what has been called "*pensamiento único*," and can only move through open difference—it cannot contain its proliferation. I did not want to steal Jon's term as he prepared his dissertation, so during those years—say, 1999 through 2001—I rehearse "parahegemony," until I realize that it won't work ("parahegemony" could be a kind of hegemony; posthegemony is not), and that it is better to have "posthegemony," cumbersome as it is as a term, as the common reference, at least until something better pops up. But the term would not really take on collective relevance until the 2010s. I return to the United States in 2010, but to a new place, from Scotland, as I mentioned, and I must get involved in some sort of institutional project, or life would get very lonely indeed. A couple of years later, there was a meeting in San Francisco of the Latin American Studies Association, where a number of panels were presented that, retrospectively, were the exact counterpart to some other sinister series of panels we had had to endure between September 8 and 10, 2001—not just any date—at another LASA meeting, in Washington, DC, just three or four miles from the Pentagon, which the very next day would suffer Al Qaeda's attack.

Those 2001 panels had brought to a close what had started perhaps ten years earlier, in the wake of the publication of Néstor García Canclini's

Culturas híbridas: Estrategias para entrar y salir de la modernidad: García Canclini's book heralded the irruption of Latin American cultural studies as a specific disciplinary field. Beyond the previously mentioned subalternist breakup, although perhaps not completely autonomous from it, the 2001 panels performed the opposite of what they were supposed to produce: they managed to bring about the closure of a field of conversation. Things came to a head in the last panel. Many, if not all, of the most significant people were there: Nelly Richard, George Yúdice, Mignolo, Beverley, Julio Ramos, Kraniauskas, Neil Larsen, among others (many in the audience, of course), and everybody seemed to be saying: "I do not do what you do, and what you do does not interest me." It was rather extraordinary. I think García Canclini put it into words, or Beverley, or both, but it was also a matter of a generalized body language. Nobody wanted to have anything to do with the others' discourse, that was made explicit, and conversation was brought to a full stop for good. It was announced—in perhaps the most extraordinary rendition of academic pompous preposterousness I have ever seen (and I have seen a few). Many will remember it, although no doubt many will have self-interestedly forgotten it: that impossibility of conversation made explicit, that fundamental rupture of professional friendship, let us call it, of a will to dialogue, the abjuration of any discursive link among colleagues who everybody thought had been doing "the same thing" minus some theoretical differences. Well, it buried Latin American cultural studies institutionally speaking, and it finally accomplished the full creation of the empty or voided intellectual space from which the wasteland years would evolve. We brought it on ourselves.

Now fast-forward to 2010 San Francisco, where some kind of symbolic resolution took place for at least some of us. There, in the third panel, I think, one person—I prefer not to mention his name to save him from some relative embarrassment, since he recanted almost immediately and very abruptly—said: "Posthegemony is today the diagonal line that crosses (*"diagonal aglutinante"* was the specific term used) a series of positions that are neither decolonial nor postsubalternist." An alternative position was invoked, if you want, only negatively: what posthegemony was not was the unifying element. But it was enough. Posthegemony had been called forth, and not by us, as an affirmative possibility, as a new field project, a new alliance or confederation of friendship, a new field of conversation, in brief. And that was important. And we took it up. In 2010, most of us were just starting to work through social networks, so it was easy to move fast in terms of giving that "line" some positive content, to create a space, to formulate a systematic proposal for open research around that name. Well, there were complications, of course, but two years later we organized a summer school seminar in El Escorial whose goal was to publish a book, the first book that would result from all of those discussions. There are by now many other publications or things about to be published, many items already circulating through blogs and whatnot. But it is not as if things had improved a lot—that is simply not the case. I am not talking about followers, only about conversation and discussion where disagreement would be welcome. There is a refusal, a tremendous resistance out there even to understand what it is that we are trying to propose—people tell us we are incapable of explaining, it is all senseless, and so forth. But at the same time, and in the middle of so much disappointment, things have improved for us, and they are no longer as they were ten years ago. Our (internal) discussion made us realize at some point that the notion of posthegemony was insufficient by itself, particularly as it was perceived to be all too linked to its opposite, hegemony. We needed to push things a bit more. Posthegemony had perhaps done the job of favoring the installation, or a certain installation, of the gap between politics and world, between existence and domination—and, from there, of consolidating the rejection of the theoretical notion of equivalence (and therefore of community, in most senses of community) as the very foundation of democratic life, which of course it isn't. (In 2012, we created a "secret" group on Facebook, Kapital and Equivalence, now no longer in use. We are far from having extracted all the consequences of the critique of the principle of equivalence.)

I would like to be proven wrong, but I would say the general principle of equivalence is the limit and endpoint of Marxism, which makes a critique of Marxism necessarily also a critique of the principle of equivalence. Marx says clearly in the *Grundrisse* that modern democracy is based on equivalence, which is, generally speaking, a precipitate of the capitalist structuration of the world. He does understand, indeed names, the principle of equivalence. But, from the analysis of money as *Gemeinwesen*, the common substance and foundation of the law of value, Marx seems not to have had the thought that democracy must reinvent itself against the paradigm of money (equivalential exchange) as social community or foundation of the social community. Communism is never defined along those contrarian terms. Heidegger may have seen that failure in Marx, but he did not make it clear enough. It may be implicit in his critique of Marxist productionism as the foundation of the law of value. So, when Heidegger says in his work on Nietzsche that the last doctrine of metaphysics is the Nietzschean doctrine of the will to power, he forgets to index another equally effective "last doctrine," certainly also intimately connected with the Nietzschean one through the notion of force, which is the doctrine of general equivalence, in my opinion the "true" last doctrine of Western metaphysics (and much more alive today than the Nietzschean will to power). Its critique opens the possibility of at least thinking of a posthegemonic democracy, a democracy of nonequivalence whose thought can be traced in the work of the Spanish philosopher Felipe Martínez Marzoa, and that has recently been the object of fascinating work by Jean-Luc Nancy (I suspect he is far from finished with it). We have not yet begun to understand what a real critique, that is, an effective deconstruction of the principle of general equivalence as the metaphysical organization of our world, including what falls under the name of democracy in it, could and would mean. Our project understands the need for the deconstruction of the principle of equivalence, and therefore, Antonio, let me land on your question, it understands that it is essential to deconstruct Laclau's hegemony theory, which is, in my opinion, based, in a way that I would have to consider precritical, on the invocation of equivalential chains as the very meaning of politics.

That would be our populist exception to Laclau's populism and our posthegemonic exception to the equivalential hegemony theory in Laclau. But I say this with great affection for Laclau, who has always been a reference for us, and was a friend of mine, from the mid-1990s, when Jon Beasley-Murray invited him to come to Duke for the first time (and we had to face a complaint from the Philosophy Department, which objected to Jon's use of the description "political philosopher" to talk about Ernesto, believe it or not), all the way to some beautiful days in Salerno and Naples the summer of the year before he died. His presence as reference, even mentor, became productively evident at the recent meeting in Greece you mentioned, Antonio, in the context of a great discussion on populism and democracy. People there, most of them experts, were trying to understand populism from the theoretical postulates of Laclau and the Essex School, but not in any dogmatic or inflexible form, rather openly interrogating the Laclauian model for what was left unsaid and unthought by that model. In that context, formulating the notion of a marrano populism was not so difficult, rather it was the consequence of an open discussion.

In the order of thought, there is no posthegemony without hegemony, in the same way that there is no infrapolitics without politics. Laclau is necessarily, therefore, a thinker of reference. We insist on the prefixes, which bother many, but not us, because we think they have their own content. There is a perhaps paradoxical substantiality in them that make the words say exactly what we mean them to say, insofar as we can control them, which is obviously never the case. But it does not worry us much.

JUAN MANUEL FORTE: The notion of infrapolitics just popped up, along with the issue of theoretical concepts that are the result of the modification of an existing word by a prefix or some other particle that determines them and orients them in one specific direction. I wanted to ask you about infrapolitics. In your books, in *Línea de sombra*, for instance, you have worked on the concept of the political in Carl Schmitt, on politics in Hannah Arendt, and in other places as well, and I wanted to ask you about the genesis of that concept, and its destination. What horizons does it open and to what conflicts does it carry us in its relationship with other consolidated notions of the tradition?[3]

AM: The genesis of the concept as I use it is not in James C. Scott. Scott is a North American anthropologist who has written important pages on infrapolitics understood in a certain way—a way that I like and generally agree with, but that is not my way. When I came upon the expression, the substantive "infrapolitics," I had not read Scott, I did not know who he was or that he existed. I am talking about the late 1990s. Infrapolitics comes to my head, who knows exactly why, how, or when, but I believe it was connected to Jorge Luis Borges and to my readings of Borges at the time. I have constantly read and reread Borges, I have written on him, and I have taught courses on him, but I think it was my work on two specific texts, namely, "La lotería en Babilonia" ("The Lottery in Babylon") and "Tema del traidor y del héroe" ("Theme of the Traitor and the Hero"), where Borges is really confronting populism (in "Lotería") and postcolonial politics (in "Tema"), that prompted the word. Borges is establishing a relationship to populism and to postcolonial politics that we could not call directly or visibly political. Nobody would think, I believe, reading those texts for the first time, even for the second or third time, that Borges is engaging in political literature. But, if those are not instances of political literature, what are they? They are not apolitical or anti-political texts, they are not metapolitical texts. They must be infrapolitical, I came to think. And then that thought, like many others, was forgotten. Again, those were the wasteland years, for me years of mourning; I wanted to escape from what I myself had thought, to start anew from another ground, and infrapolitics and posthegemony were forgotten for years, like umbrellas.

It is only recently, little more than one year ago, in the context of collective work at meetings and in social networks, that I came to think I needed to recover and push the notion of infrapolitics, as there is work it can do. I remember a specific conversation here in Madrid with Ángel Octavio Álvarez Solís, in which he tells me that I should revisit the notion of infrapolitics and in fact publish a quick book on it. We talked for a bit, and little by little it occurred to me—it was all conversation, I claim no particular precedence—that if the fissure between world and politics was to be thought, but not anti-politically, if the excess of the social, in Laclau's expression, was to be thought, if we thought that existence cannot be exhaustively constrained by merely political considerations, then the word "infrapolitics" is as good as any other and better than most. I believe infrapolitics means that "thing" that I will not call excess but rather sub-cess, the sub-cess of politics, if you will allow the neologism, that which flows always already under politics and that is, however, a condition of politics, which, accordingly, cannot be politically subsumed (in the same way that the condition of something cannot be made a part of that something). It requires a different, nonpolitical thought: think of "La lotería en Babilonia" as infrapolitical reflection. I do not know if you remember the text, but it is only half a dozen pages; you will immediately realize what I mean if you reread it. I started to think about that thematics, because it enables a different opening of the world. I think of it as a return to existence, to a reflection on existence vis-à-vis politics; it is another form of coming to terms with that political turn I mentioned before—as a critique of the political turn, as a critique of the totalizing pretensions of politics in our world but certainly not in favor of the romantic and classically reactionary notion of culture. Politics cannot in fact totalize the world; there is world outside of politics, and that, understood not as a "thing" beyond contamination but rather within contamination itself, is what seems research worthy—and politically necessary as well. (At a conference where I had been invited to present infrapolitics, one of the organizers reacted quite forcefully at the end of my paper and told me that he failed to understand how I could even dream of something "under" or below politics: "There is *nothing* previous to politics, nothing at all." My answer was, of course, that infrapolitics was merely the attempt to think about that nothing he so vehemently named, and without which the very notion of politics could not even be articulated.)

In Greece, at one of the dinners, I was seated next to Ioanna, a Greek doctoral student who lives in England. She constantly referred to her work, so I asked her, "But do you work all the time?" And she said: "Of course not! I have my life!" We should all be in a position to say that concerning work and politics. Yes, we understand that both consume time and both are necessary, but we should also understand that they do not exhaust, and should not exhaust, the time of life. It is therefore unreasonable not even to have a vocabulary that can address what sub-cedes work and politics in existence itself. Of course, this is related to a Heideggerian thematics, and we can reformulate infrapolitics as the installation of the ontico-ontological difference in politics—and we can certainly subsume work into politics, since work is increasingly not just a direct manifestation of politics, and everything in the division and assignation of labor, down to its last details, is political— but presumably also one of the most significant battlegrounds for a politics of freedom. Infrapolitics is a thinking of freedom; it thinks freedom, which is not for us derivable from politics but must be gained and lived against politics itself. This is all variously connected to posthegemony, but laterally, because posthegemony is primarily political reflection, whereas infrapolitics is primarily something else, an exception to political reflection (whose political import has to do with its character as exception). Both must be articulated and linked, hence our insistence on the conjunction: infrapolitics and posthegemony, posthegemony and infrapolitics. To name the name is not yet to think, it is only to imagine a possibility of thought. We will see whether we are capable of keeping it open—nothing is consolidated yet, precariousness is still radically there. Perhaps infrapolitics includes an intuition about the concrete uncertainty of the future, which includes its own termination.

In the meantime, those two terms form, I think, a specific opening that is not experienced by us as in any way a renovation of the field of study, a contribution to the discipline, part of our academic-institutional responsibility, or any of those things. I think we have discarded those ideologemes, since they increasingly belong in the region of voluntary servitude, of effective hegemony, and therefore are part of a regime of oppression. Insisting on an intellectual task that needs to break away from its institutional inscription gives our opening for thinking a rebellious character, encountered rather than sought—but it is a marrano rebellion, secret but not militant, albeit belligerent indeed.

JOSÉ LUIS VILLACAÑAS: Marrano thinking wants and seeks no identity, indeed, but inevitably it leaves traces in its escape, tracks, signals, clues. Looking at things reflectively, this attempt to keep standing up or holding your own that you mention has finally meant a trajectory, impressive from a certain perspective: many years organizing things—work, groups, projects, publications, conferences. I speak from a very strong impression at the conference we have just had, which follows other conferences, that of Salonika, for instance, and others, where a real accomplishment, important from my point of view, becomes visible. It is an accomplishment that would not have been possible without you, because you are able to gather a consistent representation of the US university, to bring them to a place, and these are people who also come from speaking and meeting at other places in Europe, well, but finally they come here and they speak in Spanish and they build up a forum for thought in Spanish, and they are no longer translating, but they are expanding, commenting on, re-creating, and improving upon other conversations elsewhere in English, in French, in Italian. From this perspective, it seems to me there is more here than just "holding one's own"; there is a group production, a collective production of thought that humbly, I believe, bears no comparison with anything being done in Spanish anywhere. I see no possibility of anything similar in Mexico, in Colombia, in Argentina, not even in Italy. How do you see this process, how do you value what has been accomplished and its possibilities for the future?

AM: I think, José Luis, our generational mission, yours and mine (and others' of course)—we are the same age, but you remained in Spain after some German detours, and I went to the United States, not necessarily forever; in fact, I spent four years in Scotland and then went back to the United States—but our generational mission, as individuals who pay heed to some call for thinking during the Spanish transition, when Francoist exceptionalism receded, when the hegemony of endemic *castizo* culture seemed to be coming to an end—and we need to understand that this is not by any means reserved to central Spain in the Hispanic world: it is everywhere in Latin America, and it is also everywhere in the so-called "Spanish periphery"—our mission, I believe, is simply to normalize thought in Spanish. This is obvious and seems trivial, but it isn't. We know that the normalization of thought in Spanish has faced and still faces immense obstacles of all kinds, embarrassing as it may be to admit it. The attempt to form, in the university of the last thirty years, researchers and thinkers capable of establishing a conversation on the basis of equality, without condescension, with whatever other thinkers and researchers in whatever other languages or intellectual traditions, well, I think that has been the main professional task in my career, perhaps also in yours. Rodrigo, Antonio, Pedro, Juan Manuel: all of you are younger, that is why I am not addressing you specifically in this. Being younger is not trivial here. Our generation is the generation of the transition. We opened a path, or thought we did, with all the difficulties that entailed, the sacrifices in terms of time and work, and, I must say, as fundamentally irritating as it was personally to have to devote one's time to that (for me, it was hellishly irritating not to have someone preceding or marking the way, hellishly irritating to almost always be the oldest guy in the room, from the time I was thirty or so, whenever there was an intellectual meeting from which to learn something other than opinions, to have to fight fights nobody had fought for me, and to have to do it mostly for others—I know this is harsh, and forgive my arrogance, although of course I do not feel it is arrogance, but I could tell you stories: in any case, it has been a damnation that I never sought or wanted), we opened a path, or thought we did, from our very own limitations and shortcomings so that others can walk it with more ease. Yes, one leaves traces and residues and pebbles and hopefully some water along the way, and the task is not over. For years I thought we had failed at that task. During those wasteland years, I thought we had wasted our time, and it is only recently that I have started to think again that, yes, the normalization is gradually happening, slowly, but it is real. There are many out there (of course, "many" means fifty or sixty, perhaps a few more, perhaps hundreds more, I do not know, I hesitate in my opinion), Hispanic academic intellectuals or intellectuals who chose for their sins to devote themselves to Hispanic studies, who are young or still young, whose formation is finally perfectly commensurate to the formation of intellectual elites in Germany, or Britain, or the United States. We must recognize that as an accomplishment, although it is still hard for me to do so—comparatively speaking, it was just about high time and there is nothing much to celebrate. But we must admit that it was not easy, just as the ghetto has a geopolitical character, and to get out of it is not a matter of sheer will—it is constituted and reinforced in the first place and primarily by the very *castizo* culture even when its *castizo* character is denied (say, by some of the Catalan independentists or the decolonials), we don't only have to blame everyone else. How is it possible that only two or three names of Hispanic thinkers have international recognition in the twentieth century, as opposed to fifty Italians, for instance? Why that enigma? Is it an enigma? Well, our mission is to correct it, that is the only possible acceptable future, and others will have to chip in; we will only have started a path, modestly, but also, I think, with no inferiority complexes, with no absurd identitarian exceptionalisms, and with no excuses. I think we saw some of the results at the conference we just had, and we can only keep doing it in ways ever more intense, looser, freer.

JOSÉ LUIS VILLACAÑAS: Let us hope this interview can help establish the will for that task so that we can improve on what we do and reach what is most difficult. Thank you very much.

AM: Thank you for the honor this interview represents, which I heartfully appreciate.

Chapter 2

MY LIFE AT Z

A Theoretical Fiction

To Elena, on her death, *in memoriam*

To render an account neither from defeat nor from victory but from a passage, starting in the passage, at a given moment of the passage, or when the exit from the passage can only be thought in terms of one's own death. To scorn both the notion of defeat and that of victory. The ground is active nihilism, the confrontation with personal values that die and vanish. I do not seek exculpation, I intend neither to critique nor to celebrate, but without telling, no matter how elliptically, what almost destroyed me, I could not return to writing. And it is time to write. So that emotions, in this way, can be cured, and purged for good. One can always survive as a ghost of oneself, so many do it and so few worry about it, but to avoid it is a condition of writing.

So I wrote a letter to the provost of my old university only a few weeks ago, during a night of sleeplessness, when I was at a hotel in Moncloa, in Madrid, waiting for the morning to return to Texas, traveling from Vigo, where I had gone to visit my sister Elena, on her death bed, to say good-bye to her, and she said good-bye to me, and her courage and her integrity were exemplary and devastating. I woke up from some dream around 2:00 a.m., and I could no longer sleep, and I knew I had to write that letter, be-cause the situation was too uncannily similar to what had happened in the same month of 2006, when I was returning to North Carolina from visiting my father at the Intensive Care Unit of the Meixoeiro Hospital in Vigo. We went to Scotland in June 2006, still with a leave of absence from a university that had been home to us for the previous fifteen years, and not so voluntarily. The decision was ours, but it was forced by the open hostility of a certain number of our colleagues and the cowardice of our supposed friends, and because the then dean had preferred to favor the story those very same colleagues were telling about us without giving us any chance to explain what was really happening. The price of those mobbing episodes—there is no other name for them—cannot not be paid, no normal mortal can avoid it. Our life in Scotland—we had thought it was far enough—was wounded by years of depression and by symptoms that, I came to find out, were signs of post-traumatic stress disorder. All of that is over now, more or less, and it only comes back on certain nights. But the background sadness remains. The hurt does not leave.

In any case, Scotland did not work out. We tried to return to the United States in the middle of the financial crisis, in 2009–2010, and we had the good fortune to be hired in Texas, where we have been for five years.[1] Yes, I had an offer from another institution a couple of years ago, but I could not accept it for irrelevant reasons. I almost became dean of humanities somewhere else, but there was an interference from my own Texas department, rumors, more pathetic wickedness, and the chancellor was afraid to move on the appointment. Our history at Z has followed us everywhere. We could not have foreseen it, or we were idiots and we did not. It has been fatal for our careers, as if what they did to us over there had not been enough. Now we have a beautiful place by a lake, and things are okay, peaceful, but we still miss—we will miss it forever—the intellectual intensity of our years at Z. I told you once, I told the provost, that our lives had been cut in half, in two pieces, by what happened, and that has not changed. Often I think of the unjust violence that took place. I do not think I have to remind you, I told him, as he knew us well, that we gave Z our all, everything, and that we contributed to the development of what was for some years not just the best Spanish department in the country, or one of them, but also a unique place, unique because we accomplished things nobody else accomplished, and those things have remained in people's memories. Certainly in mine.

The question I want to ask you, I told him, has at its basis our conversation some years ago at the bar of the hotel by the golf course, when you told me, I reminded him, after you had concluded your own investigation at my request, that it had been bad for the university to let us go and that it should never have happened, that it was a case of bad judgment and lack of support by administrators who should have known better, and you agreed to initiate a process of reappointment if our former colleagues, you said, were not totally opposed. Can you restore us to our old positions? I am not asking you, I told him, because I have any trust or any good expectations regarding our old colleagues. They are still the same people, even if a couple of the more hostile ones and a couple of their clients are no longer there, and even if others are withering and getting too old and are presumably reluctant to fight for anything, and even if there are some new people who do not know us, or know us solely through what they may have heard. I am actually only asking you because university tenure is for life, for good historical reasons of which we could be a more than obvious example, and we only gave it up at our university under emotional duress, under very heavy stress, or, if you want, out of pride, out of dignity, you may want to call it that. But we have tried to remake our professional and personal lives, and we tried hard, and, so many years later, we are not yet all right. Yes, we are still sufficiently productive, we write, we teach, we train students, we organize things, but I think you understand what I am telling you, and it is not necessary to spell it out in ways that would become hardly kind to institutions that have welcomed us with benevolence. We miss Z as an institution, we miss the students, we miss the intellectual life, we miss the town, and our forest, and our friends there, the other friends, and we will be as efficient as anybody else—or more, as usual—if we are given the opportunity to return to the university that defined our professional experience and gave us some of the best years of our lives. And hugs, I told him, and he replied to me that yes, that he would do it, that he had been thinking of us, that he thought it was a good moment, the money was there, his capacity to move was there, but that he could only try it, he warned me. The decision is not only mine, as you know, he told me, I can only initiate a process and make my position clear. Good guy, the provost, he knows what happened, by now he knows, and he will attempt it, but he is not the provost by virtue of taking too many risks, of confronting people, and he will fold, nothing will happen, everything will come to nothing, you will see.

1

I was running through the forest by our house, as I had done hundreds of times in fourteen years, but only that once did I suddenly encounter a red fox standing up on a dead tree trunk, fallen. He was looking at the path, he was looking at me. He did not move. He watched me run by as I looked at him, startled. Now I understand he was warning me, he was telling me not to leave, but he knew, he was saying good-bye, or both things. But I could not understand him then.

Nobody knows how a destiny is hatched, although sometimes things happen—gazes, words—and one obscurely realizes they matter, that they have a weight, this time, that puts a lie to their seeming triviality; one knows it without wanting to admit it, without yielding to any prophetic mystique or paranoia, with a knowledge that is bodily, like a kick in the stomach or a gentle hit in the nape of the neck: it won't kill you, but it will bother you and worry you as if it revealed that the world is after all the magical conspiracy one always wished for it not to be. Nobody weaves the threads that catch her, not even the motherfucker sitting next to us who wants to hurt and destroy because she knows her own impotence and from that impotence throws her poisoned darts and salivates her malignant slime, betting that this time she will accomplish the damage. Or he will. I suppose that happened in my case, and that everything is, in the last instance, a matter of chance, because everything could have been otherwise—a couple of different actors in place was all that was needed—and it wasn't. Or I could have acted differently toward some of those bad people; I did know they were bad, which is the reason I did not. Still stupid. But goodness is only the reverse of evil, and we are at the mercy of both, and it is absurd to wager anything on ethics. Given that there is no moral law, and that everything is a question of winning or losing, the question gets shifted: it is not how you behave but rather what you want to win. Pride and dignity are involved in the answer to the question. For me, the answer was never political. The rejection of that form of politics that consists of submitting always seemed to me a minimal condition of freedom, or of whatever in a life can stand for freedom. I never knew that it was a bad way of living professionally in the environment where I had come to live.

I do not know whether writing will help me, but I have no other recourse—either for action or reaction. If it becomes possible now, for the first time in eight years, or in ten or twelve years if I count not from the consummation of events but from their visible genesis, in spite of frustrating failures previously, painful attempts that never reached a good harbor, it is still a writing in subjective destitution. I want to save the trace, some minimal remainder of what events destroyed, so that perhaps I can let the events go for good without carrying away my entire life with them. I owe it to my sister, and I owe it to my father—my sister told me without telling me at the time of her death, and then I remembered my father had told me the same thing. The people at Z sought to break a style, an orientation, and the damage may seem trivial to most onlookers, whenever they manage to hear something, to learn some snippet, but it is terrible for the one who suffers it. The loss—a loss that one could never have imagined in advance, mysteriously enough—becomes a life condition; one does not live without it, which also means it is a condition of death. Death, consignment to death, mortification—that is what they did. What is lost cannot be named. And it must have happened to so many, and for many there was only silence, but it seems necessary to tell it so that others know; it seems necessary to speak, even though I do not want you to know that it happened to me. I don't. But it did.

One loses what one had sought, it is no longer accessible. What do you do? You cannot continue to seek. There are many forms of expatriation, and one of them, perhaps the freest, is to expatriate yourself for the sake of another fatherland, another home, perhaps only a symbolic one. But there is an expatriation without the minimal possibility of return, a second-degree expatriation, when one finds oneself having to give up that other home, because it has already been lost. Someone has destroyed it for you, as a personal attack on you, and nothing is to be done—they have won, you have lost, and there is nowhere to go. Then, when one can no longer love his fate, when life as it is can no longer be entirely loved, death begins. Another way of putting it: the only intention you have ever had is to elude boredom, so you run and work and do whatever it takes, and all of a sudden you notice that your attempt to escape boredom has thrown you into the most extreme form of boredom.

In March 2004, my father had started his own terminal path toward death. My wife, Teresa, and I arrived in Galicia to visit him. It was March 10. That night we slept at a hotel on García Barbón Street, and when we got up the next morning, the news of the Atocha Station terrorist attacks was everywhere. I saw the first images on television, in the café across the street to which I went to have some breakfast and wait for Teresa. In the afternoon, we had to be in Santiago de Compostela, at the Hostal de los Reyes Católicos, to begin the second meeting of the "Subjectivity and Subjectivation" project—horrible title—that I was organizing as the director of the Center for European Studies at Z. We went to Santiago. I had invited, in addition to the Z group and some of my friends, an important group of international intellectuals, some very prominent and others who would become prominent. Perhaps given my father's situation and the episode in Madrid, my sensation at the beginning of the Hostal meeting was bordering on the ominous. It is difficult to be precise now, as the memory remains in me in a somewhat diffuse manner, like a stain you would not know what to do with and cannot precisely locate. But I think it was a decisive moment for me, given everything that happened later, which I still do not claim to understand and perhaps never will. This is why I force myself to write it. I have enough scars on my soul to know that surviving the impossibility of understanding is more important than understanding itself.

My mood had taken a step back. I had always been a hospitable organizer, and for the Hostal meeting I had gone out of my way, which is saying something. Given my enthusiasm and excessive commitment, and in spite of the atrocious environment that had been gestating in the university for years and had become very visible to me, I suppose I had not yet wanted to realize something was breaking or had broken. I still figured my many friends, as I thought of them as friends, would contain it. In my institutional behavior, I had always wanted things to go well, in fact, to proceed in the best possible way—things, that is, that were mine to initiate or things for which my collaboration was welcome. But I had started to become skeptical, a new feeling for me, as if everything were becoming hollow. Or perhaps it was only lucidity. Skepticism was a feeling I had had to keep away from me from many years, from the beginning of my professional career in the United States. Many times I could hardly believe what I was seeing, but I had to be discreet and take things as seriously as I could possibly take them—I think it was that desire for seriousness that had turned me into an expatriate. An expatriate remains vulnerable, though, to the most unexpected things.

It was the first time I had risked organizing something in Galicia, on Carl Schmitt no less, for whom Santiago had been important in the last years of his life, and I had been looking forward to it. But now many of my guests—you must forgive me if I do not identify them—began to seem to me alien to what I thought we were doing. Their faces literally started changing in front of my eyes. They seemed to resent the beauty of the place, and they made sarcastic remarks on the food that was offered: octopus, baby scallops, cockles, the white Albariño wine in the taverns. Everything seemed too exotic to them, and they acted full of themselves, and I started to lose both my trust and my patience. There was some obscure animosity there, and I even started seeing how it extended to their relationships with one another. My gaze was changing, and the new one was producing alarm and consternation. Remember, some of these people were old friends, and I started to feel our friendship could only deploy itself against the grain, as if something in the air made it difficult. The international guests were condescending, or worse, to the Spanish guests, as if their very presence—or their accents—bothered them. My disquiet culminated or veered toward disgust the night of the demonstration in Obradoiro Square, right in front of our rooms at the hotel, where many thousands of people gathered who were scared by the Madrid deaths and perplexed at the reactions of the Spanish government. My colleagues started to wander among the multitude, but they were simply bothered by all the commotion or even furious about it: it disconcerted them, and they were not interested in it. It was as if they already knew everything in advance, could predict everything. Could have predicted it. I felt myself losing trust in the group, in the project, in what I was doing, in what I had been working very hard for years to do. It was as if something broke in me, as if I myself broke, but what broke was a certain sense of things. I do not mean that I was right in the way I reacted—I am just telling you how I reacted, and what I felt. I think that moment marked the end of something, of what was more important to me at the time, although it is not easy to know it. Perhaps that was the moment of my guilt.

The Atocha dead died as nonsubjects. My father had begun to die (and in his last lucid conversation with me, a few months earlier, during my previous visit, he had told me to leave the place, Z, to go elsewhere). My colleagues had appeared before me, through a lack of generosity on my side (but generosity had been the problem, and when I withdrew the generosity, I saw there was nothing), as spectral gravediggers, of themselves, but also of my life and my time. Some live their critical life shooting at every duck that abandons the flock. They control academic life as a function of their number, which entitles them (they are like the rest of them, so they feel entitled). And they have ample help from the administration, which is usually composed of more of their number. Real university life, once the generosity is subtracted, is hardly breathable, or only when one manages to subtract oneself from the grasp of the gravediggers, or manages to stay home most of the time. The strategy of institutional life is often oriented toward negating intellectual stimulation, toward disciplining personnel in a context that includes perks to be obtained, awards, salary raises, having one's ass licked, stupendously inflated reports, and doing everything in vacuous and banal ways. And fear cuts through everything, it is almost a way of life. I had managed to avoid most of it most of the time, and I had gotten to where I wanted to be without excessive concessions. But during those days in Santiago, everything became hollow. And I realized my inattention, my neglect, and my contempt for those realities were about to cost me dearly. I think I realized it precisely because it was already too late. How could I have been so blind? So innocent?

2

With one single exception, there was no fear from me at any of the times that followed. There is now, years later, and it surprises me to notice it with momentary trembling.[2] Or I may be wrong. I fear I am inviting conversation from those people, when the truth is I want nothing to do with them, not anymore. Those were times for me in which the least important of things was defending a position I had reached, my institutional position, my career, as the position mattered little to me, or I took it for granted. I thought they could not do anything about it, not really. I had tenure. And there was no particular bravery or arrogance in that either. It was something else: both shame and painful anger for their behavior. My life had become a misunderstanding, in spite of my sustained efforts, and it was like walking through honey. I was under attack and I could only reject the attacks that seemed to have nothing to do with me. I could not defend myself because I could not find out what to defend myself from. But the attacks were fierce. Attempting to avoid the misunderstandings became the worst misunderstanding: a hellish structure, courtesy of malignant narcissists. My reaction was wrong: I attempted to understand the misunderstandings (Nietzsche said thought is nothing but a misunderstanding of the body, and my body was, at the time, a misunderstanding squared), which was an impossible thing. Things were designed as a thread of lies. There was nothing to understand except their evil intention.

As to the others, those who were not already enemies, I suppose, one never knows how they see one, and it is possible I had become a pain in the neck. I tried to explain too many things, and I complained. Perhaps my behavior was odious or could genuinely be perceived to be so. Beyond intentions, my life was what it was. But I do not think my behavior was odious: it was an inevitable reaction to conflict, when hostility becomes patent but one is just not willing to yield, submit, and smile. Others may claim that I was discourteous or said inappropriate things. Well, not enough. I was reacting when I should have acted. They *did* things against me, threatening things, false things, and I could only *say* things back. They would call it arrogance or pride, and they used it against me. "That is very Spanish," the goddamned racists would—and did—say. "You were too proud," I had to hear from one of my hypocrite friends some time later. Meanwhile, far from dwelling in pride, I waited for a word of support, some true reaction, some truth from anyone, enemies or friends; I waited in anguish, for days, weeks, months, to hear from someone or at least from those who owed something to me. I had given them my friendship: they had been to our home, had had dinner with us, talked with my children, said hello to my dogs. But the vicious circle was in place, and it was unbreakable, and the spinning was unstoppable. The feeling of shame was difficult to deal with. I had done nothing bad to them, but they were doing harm to me. The dissymmetry, which I regret now, makes me feel like an idiot. Fuck them. I hope they hear me. How many times did I think how soothing it would be to feel guilty, to be guilty? The same hypocrite fool told me later: "You must examine your own guilt"; "nobody here misses you." False and irrefutable. It was even then intentioned mortification, consignment to social death, consignment to death. Why? It is probably no mystery at all, probably nothing special, probably what those people always do.

I will copy here fragments from a letter to the other dean, the dean who arrived later, when I was no longer there but in my head I could not not be, so I was quite troubled, mad, sick. I see it now, but I could not see it then:

Still not on the plane, rather at home, two hours left. I am going to write you a long letter, and these two hours are not enough, they will only be a beginning. I have something to tell you that seems urgent to me, but I do not think the story will count. The story is not worth telling (or, perhaps, nothing else is worth telling). I know the story well, in all its possibilities, or almost all, but what I know makes no sense. There is something else, some other thing, off scene. For three years I have been under its spell, trying to understand what it is, trying to find it, but I have been unable to. I have the story, a story, the facts put together, a narrative, but it is good for nothing. It would be absurd for me to put any hope in this letter, in the process of writing it, and I have even less of a hope in your response (I already asked you, and you told me "cultural difference," and it was so hollow). There have been stories and counterstories, versions of stories that, at the end of the day, in the maze of lies, will not establish the facts, because the only important fact is what the story does not touch upon. Time goes by, but I am still trapped in events that broke my heart, destroyed my soul, took away the possibility of thinking with pleasure on my past, turned me into an other, a stranger, and I cannot get out of the trap. I look at people in the street, or I look at you, and I feel I am inside a fishbowl, or behind a store window, a prisoner of obsessions that will not let me out. Is this a trauma? But nobody died. I am ashamed to feel this way, and I would like to leave it behind. There are many who are worse off, so many others who have worse disasters in their lives, tangible things, irreversible, determining. For me, there are only some poignant images and pathetic residues of feeling:

disgust, pity, revulsion, embarrassment, and all of that. But something still escapes, and that is what hurts. You came by the house and you told me you were going to be the successor to the clueless fellow, the inept idiot whose incompetence made him complicitous in what happened. And now you are going to sit in his chair, and if you had been there three years ago, I would not be writing this letter. I told you at some point I wanted to write a novel, but then I realized it would be a bad novel, too many unpleasant but thoroughly boring characters, illegible since so tediously legible, both enemies and supposed friends, a lot of bird plop, and I would have to imagine what I would rather know for a fact. It won't do. It is still anguishing to be chained to a set of events, as if there were a story there, as if the story could count. I did manage to write a few pages:

—You are a fool if you believe in betrayal. To accept the possibility of being betrayed you must first believe that a world without betrayal exists. Where did you see it? What happens happens, and one can only forget it.

—Yes, we live in a state of war, nobody is beyond throwing anyone to the wolves if there is a percentage in it.

—Percentage? That sounds like a reason.

—I have a sentiment for wolves, I like wolves, and those who respect wolves. But when someone betrays without benefit to him- or herself, betrayal for betrayal's sake, the luxury of a free act, an excess of expenditure? Do wolves do that? You stab someone in the back, then you sell the corpse, or selling is the stab, you do business on your friend, and the better friend he was the more you enjoy it? Those are the ones who should be eaten. By the wolves.

—Yes, they only did business. A death was dealt, a kind of death, and you cannot undo it.

But I was a sucker. Now I see it, somebody like me, I was ready to be hunted down sooner or later. Not because I had no power or my power could be perceived as tenuous enough not to offer resistance, but because the little power I had was bait. And so they moved to destroy me, for nothing or almost nothing: because I bothered some, and they were more like the rest, so they had more friends than I did. But that is no reason. And it is that no-reason that harmed me through its very unsubstantiality. It was all for nothing. And now an obsession remains that I cannot let go, because without it, the world loses consistency, the fabric of the real gets torn, and there is no return.

But why keep copying a letter I never sent? Things are no longer so, time has served to create some distance, but that anguish was my life. Before it invaded me, for many years I did not feel serious tensions with anyone, or nothing that would worry me. I participated in what I was asked to participate in, I took some initiatives, I critiqued some things, I supported some other things, I exposed myself in the way one must at times, I protected myself some other times, and everything seemed clean or clear enough. I worked, and worked, and worked. I acted as a mediator in other people's conflicts. I accumulated offices—I had three simultaneous administrative appointments for a while—I found funds for a new journal, I directed programs, I served in two departments and two area centers. Everybody asked me to take charge of new tasks, and I accepted them because I thought they asked me out of respect and friendship, I could not disappoint them. It did not matter that I was taking time away from my family, away from my writing. I directed literally most of the doctoral theses in the departments, I directed two or three or four working groups every year, and I was the organizer of a considerable part of the intellectual life in my corner of the campus: the lectures, the workshops, the visiting professors who were constant guests in our home, every weekend, many times more often than that. And nobody else did it. Hundreds of letters of recommendation, and all of my students, without exception, and there were many of them, were finding jobs at the right time. Yes, I wrote less than others (except for letters of recommendation), they made me too busy, I missed some soccer games, I was distracted at home at times, too tired, but I had nothing to hide. I do not think I underestimated the negative force of jealousy and envy, the resentment of those who could not compete, I could smell those things, they were obvious, but I scorned them and I refused to accept them as important. My life was just too happy then. And of course that became unpardonable.

To be associated with me, all of a sudden, became toxic. The power of the bullies—former and present department chairs and their clients and acolytes, their network—became general, hegemonic. They sought to do me harm, and for that they needed to make me lonely, to destroy my support. They used every dirty trick. I tried to endure, but they managed to create an impregnable structure of lies, always behind my back, and to react to it was only to make it stronger. This is the hardest to explain, as it was the hardest to swallow: when the words one says are no longer words for the other, only traps and dangers; when one speaks and realizes that nobody listens; when every word, no matter what it is, becomes another nail in your coffin. Every action on your part acquires the virtue of confirming how much of a dangerous and perfidious fellow you are. I would call or send emails; I tried to explain what was happening to people who knew very well what was happening but pretended they did not; I did everything in my power to protect myself from the most absurd things, the most unreal developments, but there was no protection. I only knew half of it, what came my way, but there was always a lot more. A colleague, one of those supposed friends, arrived at my home one night in order to know, "in truth," he said, he wanted to know, he wanted to negotiate, he said, whether it was true, as it was being said, that I had plans, that I was conspiring to take over the journal he was editing—and it was a journal I had barely looked at, a journal that did not interest me, that was on no radar of mine. There was a woman who, as head of some committee, had totally exonerated a certain individual of serious accusations I had had to process, ex officio, as director of Graduate Studies. That same stupid woman accused me, falsely, of instigating that very individual against some assistant professors. Even though at the time I was having to deal with that individual's explicit death threats. A student came, very shaken, very nervous, to my office to tell me they had initiated an investigation, "informal," they say, "secret," they say, "you can speak confidentially," they say, to find out whether I had ever been rumored to have sexual affairs with students—which I had never done, not once, not by far, how do they dare such vileness. But they knew the investigation itself was the attack, which is why they did it. Old tactic for that crowd. And then the provost asked me whether it was true that I had a lot to do with the fact that several professors had accepted offers of appointment from other institutions—and those were professors whose existence and presence I knew of only from a distance, people I had nothing to do with, who did not interest me, there had been no interaction. It was unbelievable, the orchestration, the goddamn character assassination on a massive scale, and the lack of help from anyone. Another woman professor affirmed in an executive session she had requested that I was directly responsible for the fact that seminars taught by men had more students than seminars taught by women, and I had to be sanctioned. I was thoroughly innocent, even unaware that such was the case, but it did not matter, because the only thing that mattered was the unstoppable proliferation of rumors that turned me into some wicked genius of evil—clumsy and inefficient, to be sure, since they were always able to stop my presumed actions.

I was in permanent shock by then, worried. I gave a lecture saying we should try to touch the *ergon*, the work or the action, rather than limit ourselves to lying words. I became obsessed with the real, hoping perhaps to break through the shadow, and I thought that thinking at the university should also affect university behavior. Was that too much to ask? For well-known scholars to be decent human beings? And they said, see how I had been reduced to pathetic self-defense, see how I could talk only about myself, see how I had been rendered lame. They wanted to drive me into despair and force my departure. Another colleague—somebody I had barely crossed words with in fifteen years, for good reason—said at a faculty meeting I was not attending that I was a corruptor of the intelligence of the young, and that something needed to be done to keep so many students from perniciously wanting to work with me. I could not give credence to any of this—I failed to be able to process it. I had never had similar experiences. I am a big guy, more or less articulate, not very tearful, I had always been socially successful, had never had to fight in order to eat, or to have more soccer cards or nicer marbles or cooler friends. I took all of that for granted, never worried about the more obvious structures of prestige, I couldn't care less, but what was now happening to me was grave, and I did not know how to deal with it. I heard all of these things when somebody or other would sneak around to tell me in the guise of a commiseration or condolence. I would react with incredulity. And they would tell me they only wanted to warn me, they thought I should change my behavior, for God's sake: that is, they had already swallowed all the lies. Everybody talked to one another but not to me. Some really boring assistant professor (she is still boring as a full professor) took the daring step of announcing a lecture against my work, oh what bravery, and she garnered some applause and gained stature. My supposed friends and others that I only knew of or knew without knowing—they knew me even less—had become part of the structure of persecution. The air was a swamp, and the final betrayal of so many of the students (not all of them, and they know who they are, and so do I) was the last straw—not the bitterest, but bitter enough. I knew, or thought I knew, I had to leave the institution when my fascination or practice of the real—what I understood as such, and I now see I was also deluded, I was against the ropes, desperate—ended up producing a sort of terminal negativity, an alienation difficult to endure vis-à-vis everybody who knew me. As I could not make myself heard, I could no longer touch anything either: I was a ghost or an ectoplasm, but not a real body any longer, it seemed.

I requested an appointment with the deans, with the main dean, a newcomer to Z, a know-nothing, a windbag, and with his sidekick, a hapless humanities dean whose function as a lackey was notorious, and I was invited to lunch at the faculty club, but at the lunch there was a guest I had not invited. The main dean told me pompously that he would give me "another opportunity" (another one? He had never given me one, and as to the rest I had accepted every opportunity that was offered, too many of them) to prove my "capacity for political leadership" (which I had no interest in, not with that crowd). Yes, you heard it. He would appoint a search committee of seven people (not three, as was habitual, therefore the only acceptable number) to look for two Latin Americanists, and he would make me chair of that committee, and if at the end of the process the general vote went well and I had sought and reached consensus, and if he received a positive recommendation from the chair of the department sitting next to him, confirming that I had not created conflicts because I had not sought to impose my own candidates, anything but that, well then, in that case, I would return to the good graces of the dean and he would give me a "considerable" salary raise. As I tried to tell him that his offer, which I had neither sought nor wanted, since I only wanted to be left alone and for the persecution and the lies to stop, drastically compromised my academic freedom and was nothing but a trap, since obviously I was only going to be able to move forward by yielding to other people's criteria under penalty of punishment, and how could he possibly make me an offer that amounted to a proposal to buy me through the expectation of a salary raise, the unexpected guest interrupted my words and told me, with an abject wink of complicity that she must have thought could be read as charming, with a kind little poke to my elbow, that nobody needed to know the deal I was being offered. I could not swallow my soup. I told her it would be known because I would tell everyone. But, in any case, I must admit, it was then that I felt fear and deep surprise. They had changed my university, or I had woken up to a corrupted state of affairs I had never known existed. That afternoon I told Teresa I thought we would have to go, that they had finally locked the chain, and that their next step could be dangerous and too brutal for us. That everything was now sinister and uncanny. That breathing had become impossible. (This probably was my most serious mistake—I was so sickened I had decided to leave.)

I had been rereading Marcel Proust, and I got to thinking of Swann, *mutatis mutandis*, how his money, his lands, his personal elegance, his aristocratic friendships, had made him unable to see Odette's essential corruption, which made him go terminally under. Of course, for me, Odette was the image of everything that surrounded me, a Verdurinesque institution, hard to believe, demented and dirty, but still mine. I was not Swann, and I had no world outside Z, leaving my family aside—I had no money, no land, hardly more friendships around than those that had become available at the Verdurin's table, and everybody knew what kind of friendships they were. I had given everything to the university, that was my place, I had nowhere else. When it fell through, I could not allegorize: I spoke, but remained dumb. They had tried to turn me into a slave, their subject, and my freedom, now damaged, could eventually be recovered only by leaving, I thought. In a supermarket I ran into the same woman who had said at the faculty meeting that I was a corruptor of youth. She looked at me and told me Harry Harootunian had told her they had made a serious mistake with me, that I was being grievously mistreated, and he had asked her why on earth she had played along with that game. She told me she did not know what to say to him. "Peer pressure, I guess." She said she was sorry about the role she had played "in the campaign." *The campaign?* Unbelievable: so, there was one, an orchestrated campaign of character assassination. She assumed I knew about the campaign, because everyone did, but I did not: I could only see that they were after me, and at the same time I tried to suppress my own paranoia. Now that I am translating this into English, the anguish and the perplexed incredulity return—along with an awareness that things were worse than I am presenting them here, and that all those people either wanted to murder me or went pleasantly along. They are not to be forgiven, not any one of them, and I hope I am not the only one who does not.

Years later, at a restaurant in Buffalo, New York, another former colleague told me of another lamentable scene, although he did not reveal how it had reached his ears: everybody talked, just not to me. Two comrades that I had thought were reliable friends of mine, after so many years, both of them much older and senior to me, were summoned by the dean a few days after I had sent a note saying that Teresa and I would leave, and that the decision was made and nobody should speak for us (you should know we did not really want this, and our note was an attempt to spare ourselves further humiliation: the dean had already said there would be no counteroffer for retention, and I was starting to see that our false friends were indeed false friends and would take no risks of any kind for us). My former comrades expressed their humble opinion, at the dean's office, that we should be retained, that the whole charade seemed deeply unjust to us, and the dean said something like: "Look, those two will be leaving because they already said so, so you two either become part of the solution or you become part of the problem, and others bring in the solution; you choose." And my dear comrades kindly sheathed their fake swords and promised the dean that whatever they jokingly said, they would always follow the instructions of the dean, now and forever more. And they accepted, right there and then, to be members of a secret committee to hire my replacement. But I was still going to be in town for another five or six months, so the dean said: "Moreiras cannot find out about this under any circumstances, is that clear?" And they swore silence, and they became conspirators against me, they know it, the good old comrades. Yes, they only followed orders, who doesn't? But I was already on the other side of the mirror, bare life, somebody who is now only a face and a name, to whom it is indifferent to lie or to tell the truth, because he no longer matters. It is strange to think about these things many years later, when those people themselves no longer matter to me, but it happened this way, and people should know.

At the university I could no longer talk to anyone (except for Teresa, so many conversations, so many analyses). A recurrent dream started in which my "friends"—ah, but they killed that word for me, how can one still believe?—approached me with masks, and those masks were their faces. The lies, the hurt, the conspiracy—perhaps all of it trivial, all of it so normal in our world, but this time I had had to put up with it. I look at the pictures I have from the years before those years—this was an accomplishment, since I could not look at them for a very long time—and I cannot forgive them for the smiles they ruined, the poison they poured into them. And then the question: those indifferent or bought-for colleagues, those false friends, those incompetent administrators, why do we allow them to have a power of life and death over others? Why do they have the right to destroy the faith of others in things, the very consistency of what there is? Poor Antonio Calvo—this is a story that happened the very same year I returned from Scotland, 2010–2011, and it was an infamous reminder of what I had lived through, as if I needed it—was not very lucky. They also did all of it to him, and he chose to cut his own throat.

We chose to leave, and in the end it was a matter of surviving, of becoming a lonely hunter. I returned from Scotland a few years later, to a job on which it was difficult to rely, lacking institutional conditions to do what they were asking me to do, and I was older, and my hair had white spots, I had gained weight, I had dyspepsia, and I had nightmares like I had never had. But I knew it was necessary to move forward and there was only one way of doing that, of leaving the obsession behind. The risk otherwise was isolation, resentment, renunciation. We left because we wanted to, we returned to the United States because we wanted to, nobody fired us, but that was not all, what exceeded it was something other than nothing. But things are different now, and now it is possible to tell it. And let it be known. Let somebody know who could be helped by knowing it.

* * *

March 3, 2014

Dear Alberto,

I write to follow up on our discussions, copying C, whom I know you have also been talking to and who has also been working on your behalf. He has been strategizing carefully about the possibility of your returning while I have been surveying the broader climate and needs and the budgetary possibilities.

I am sorry to say that the outcome is not favorable, something which is unwelcome but I think fully realistic. There are a number of faculty who would be willing, even happy, for you to return, and some others who would certainly not be opposed. But even for the more enthusiastic, their support is bound to be tempered by an understanding of the divisiveness which might be triggered, coupled [with], and likely reinforced by, the strain over the commitment of resources that would be entailed. The tightness of the budget in Arts&Sciences, caused in no insignificant part by the overexpansion of the Arts&Sciences faculty which now must be corrected, if slowly and by attrition, makes each department evaluate any appointment with the greatest scrutiny and with the keenest awareness of trade-offs and possible internal consequences. I hope you can understand that this is not the best climate for seeking strong and widespread support for two appointments of senior scholars who might, no one can know for sure, elicit an internal battle. Hence, some hesitation is bound to arise even among those who would otherwise be your strong supporters. In this situation, both C and I think it would be best not to pursue your appointments, much as we both are supportive, since effective faculty champions, who must be the protagonists, might appear, but are unlikely to prevail.

I am sorry to have to write this, but I believe what will be a great disappointment now would be a greater and possibly more personally punishing one later.

With all friendship,

X

Chapter 3

THE FATALITY OF
(MY) SUBALTERNISM

And a man should never take lightly anything that happens.

SOPHOCLES, *Oedipus at Colonus*

I. Ego Latin Americanism

I had decided to rewatch some old Western classics as part of my preparation for a graduate seminar on *narcotráfico*. My idea was that we could
learn from those films about the pathological subject, in the Kantian
sense, and that the Western genre might therefore be apropos for studying
some aspects of *narcotráfico*. And one of the films I purchased was Fred
Zinnemann's *High Noon* (1952). By the time Will Kane says, "The judge
has left town, Harvey's quitted, I'm having trouble getting deputies," I was
thoroughly alarmed. People are indeed telling Kane to leave town, as "it
is all for nothing," and nobody wants to see him get killed. Was it all for
nothing? When, at the end of the film, Kane throws the tin star on the
ground with a gesture of contempt, everything seemed to have been set
right—or so I had thought as a kid, as it came back to me. My alarm came
from the realization, this time around, that the worldly judge who leaves
Hadleyville before the train arrives ("I have been a judge many times in
many towns and I hope to be a judge again") was probably laughing, with
good reason. Kane acted like a fool, and it is not like he wasn't told. And
what was he going to do now? Yes, he rides off into the sunset with the
woman, Amy. But what about tomorrow, when his gesture wears off and
his contempt comes back to exact a price?

A few years ago, Jon Beasley-Murray jokingly defined John Beverley as
"the Latin Americanist unconscious." It happened after a Latin American
Studies Association panel where Beverley had been arguing in favor of
Brazilian nuclear rearmament for the sake of the constitution of a Latin
American "great space" or hegemonic block against the North American
one. Jon's joke was a high compliment in the context, I thought, but

perhaps a little undeserved. Not that John Beverley does not deserve high compliments; rather, that particular one was not totally deserved. Beverley has never spoken, on professional grounds, from the position of the subject of the unconscious, as his politics will not allow him to do so. Beverley is very much an ego Latin Americanist or, if you want, an American ego Latin Americanist, as the structure of his recent book, *Latinamericanism after 9/11*, once again confirms. As one would surmise, there are plenty of ego Latin Americanists around, and that is perhaps the secret of Beasley-Murray's remarks: "John Beverley hits the nail on the head for all ego Latin Americanists, he represents their collective preconscious better than anybody else." I think I could go along with that. It is indeed a compliment, but for us closet Lacanians, it is one only within limits.

I can come out of the closet and make a premature and impossible proposal, which in this context is a counterproposal: in his seminar of 1954–1955, Jacques Lacan undertook a critique of American ego psychology as a travesty of Freud's heritage. His intention to "return to Freud" by painstakingly reading Freud's evolution from his early work to the metapsychological texts, in particular *Beyond the Pleasure Principle*, led him to the discovery of the subject of the unconscious, a *nemo* that is not the ego, and that holds the possibility of what the Lacan of those years understood as psychoanalysis proper. *Mutatis mutandis*, I would like to suggest the possibility of a Latin Americanism beyond the pleasure principle, which is also a Latin Americanism beyond culturalism and ego psychology, beyond the humanism of the subject, beyond the pieties of speculative identity and mimetic difference, beyond narcissism and imaginary projections. Such a form of Latin Americanist reflection can perhaps only be announced as a sort of mythical possibility. But all projections of thought are mythical. If Lacan could talk about his own endeavor under the guise of a "return to Freud," we could launch ours in the invocation of a return to the very ground of Latin Americanism, which is, structurally and destinally, the very possibility of an anti-imperial, hence also anti-principial and anarchic critique of the total apparatus of Latin American development. I am not sure it would be a Latin Americanism anymore.

Who is "we," however? No one, *nemo*. The position is unoccupied. There is no "we" here except in a phantasmatic and counterproductive way that should be avoided. I once put my Latin Americanist eyes out (yes, like Oedipus did at Thebes, to my shame, as I do not compare myself to Oedipus), and what I then saw, to the extent that it can be conveyed, was the nothingness of our collective desire: "the essential drama of destiny, the total absence of charity, of fraternity, of anything whatsoever relating to what one calls human feeling" (Lacan 230).[1] Oedipus asks: "Am I made man in the hour when I cease to be?" For Lacan, however, "that is where beyond the pleasure principle begins" (230), and he goes on, enigmatically, to talk about the "negation of the prophecy [*parole*], which takes place within the precinct, upon whose borders the whole drama takes place, the precinct in the place where it is forbidden to speak, the central point where silence is obligatory, for there live avenging goddesses, who do not forgive and who catch hold of the human being at every opportunity. You get Oedipus to come out of there each time you want to get a few words from him, for if he says them in that place, something awful will happen" (230–231). In the infrapolitical grove of the Eumenides, the Dread Ones, Oedipus has become a holy man. His sacredness comes from having become one with his destiny, in full destitution, which is another way of saying that he has become one with his life's desire. The mortal Oedipus remains the embodiment of an a-principial thought of restitution. He could also be the apotheosis of the Latin Americanist postcolonial unconscious. The Latin American Oedipus must indeed pull his very eyes out in order to begin to see.

I can picture former Marshal Kane within the precinct, far from the town, vanquished from the town, in mourning for the town and its fatality, blind and yet seeing. It is the same place Tom Doniphon occupies, in his own burnt home, for the many years after Stoddard and Hallie leave Shinbone, with only the company of his cactus blossoms and his old buddy Pompey, in John Ford's *The Man Who Shot Liberty Valance* (1962). Were they Latin Americanists, they would be Latin Americanists beyond the pleasure principle. And aren't we all? We secretly are, or I am, or I strive to be. But not John Beverley. That is the function his ego Latin Americanism serves: apotropaic, he always indulges in a little bit of the evil so as to then step back and feel fortified by the winds of history, like Polyneices. He talks about everybody else's "paradigm of disillusion" (96) to conceal from view his own disillusion, probably harder to bear, but secret.[2] He must set up the fiction that everybody is impotent but him, the leader of the Seven Against Thebes, so that his recipe for politically active Latin Americanism is immediately legitimized on the grounds of an expediency that comes, naturally, at the price of refusing it to everyone else. But it is a rather constraining universe that he creates, and some of us would feel choked within it.

Will *Latinamericanism*, the book, ever reach its destination? To whom is it addressed? While reading it, I could not help thinking that there is something of Edgar Allan Poe's "The Purloined Letter" in it. The book, like the letter in the story, is designed so that everybody must take a position in relation to it; or rather, it has always already defined everybody's position. So, let us imagine that the book is addressed to the queen, as it might well be. Well, the rogue minister will take advantage of that, and the king will remain an impervious idiot and be used as such. But things change. One could say that "when the characters get a hold of this [book], something gets a hold of them and carries them along and this something clearly has dominion over their individual idiosyncrasies" (Lacan 196). We are all characters, as Beverley has written a book about us, but obviously in ways that speculation will find uncomfortable. You receive an image of yourself back, and who is to say that it is distorted? You thought you were a deconstructionist and you become a neocon, you thought you were a communist and you are nothing but a neoliberal, you thought you were neither and you find yourself pigeonholed and scripted, you thought you were alive and you are dead, and there is nothing you can do about it. And most of us find ourselves in a bad way, anticipated by our destiny of failure, toys of fate, wanting to stay but being refused, which is what Oedipus finally cannot forgive. Not all of us, which makes an interesting point to which I will return, but most of us.

We can call it cartography. Maps also locate characters, including zombies, within them. Beverley's book is a map of holes with only one mountain, which is what makes me think that it is finally addressed to the queen. Let us cut to the chase: the mountain is called "postsubalternism" (Beverley 8). It is a capacious one: it can easily incorporate all identity politics people, and, as we know, within Latin Americanism, they are legion. So people are always already defined and interpellated in their identity, and the ones who cannot escape this, or who can least escape, are precisely the ones whose claim to identity refuses to make itself explicit. The book will do it for them. Did you think you could escape? Think twice. The first thought has already captured you. And into the hole you go. At the end of the day, you climb the mountain, through the preset paths, or you remain in the hole. This is what I call ego Latin Americanism. For all the good it will do you.

II. Follow the leader!

Latinamericanism after 9/11 offered a chance, perhaps, for us all to pull away from what someone once called the Latin Americanist doldrums of the previous ten years or so, and have a conversation yet again. It was in that sense a service to the academic community, if one can call it community. Beverley offers a rather totalizing mapping of the field—of a certain field, perhaps not the totality of theoretical Latin Americanism, as no doubt many did not feel included, no doubt many were in fact beyond Beverley's radar. There is no thinking of the not-all here. Feminism was a conspicuous absence in anything but a generic sense, for instance, and so was queer studies, which turns this controversy into too much of a battle "between men," also in the generic sense. We may have trouble with the map, the map may be absurd, the map may not quite give us the possibility of narcissistic identification we need, or indeed it may give it to us in spades, which is equally bad or worse. But it was a map, and we could all talk about it—for celebration or denigration, for supplementation or subtraction.

I was personally grateful for Beverley's ample attention to my old work, and I could not care less that he distanced himself from it or even that he took it as perhaps the primary example of theoretical obsolescence in the field. Given the present stakes, what I care about is the labor of thought, and the possibility of thinking for the future of our field of endeavor. (I say "our field of endeavor," but I actually do not believe that there is such a thing, as I think I have already said. The rhetoric is here more powerful than my personal belief, and I find myself helplessly returning to the first-person plural.)

It is not easy to find the right place from which to respond, because Beverley places me, impossibly, as the nonconformer of a nonschool of Latin Americanist subalternist deconstruction that was allegedly influential beyond its means for a few years right around 9/11/2001 (43). My "associates" in the alleged enterprise thus share my destiny, which is possibly too unkind to them without being particularly kind to me, and which, furthermore, puts me in serious difficulties at the time of claiming a nonbetrayal: if I were not to speak for myself, I would refuse the opportunity to speak for them. But if I were to speak for myself, I would be falling into the trap of accepting the very premise of my alleged failure to mold my associates into a proper school if only in order to rebut it. I am not interested in anything of the kind, although I will say that the people Beverley mentions at the beginning of his chapter 3 are the metonymy of an ample sector of perhaps two generations of reflection on Latin American intellectual and political history that decided to make a serious investment in theoretical work, whatever limitations we may have had or still have. Whether Beverley wanted it or not, those are the people finally under collective attack in his book, mortified or consigned to a kind of death, and the attack comes from what is at bottom an anti-theoretical and anti-conceptual position that I will not hesitate to call conservative in anything but its self-assigned name. I do not think of Beverley as a reactionary thinker, but his book plays a reactionary card by aligning itself with a fiercely reactionary abandonment of theoretical thought in favor of merely political positioning in the professional field. It is perhaps time to initiate a countermove, to resist consignment to death. About those who care to do it nobody can say we have not been patient, even all too patient.

I remain a subalternist in Latin American studies, to the increasingly limited extent that I still think of my work as within Latin American studies, and I do not want to have anything to do with that particular "post" in "postsubalternism" that Beverley invented. Subalternism is still very much a pending account, and nothing has been solved, and the questions remain, and I find Beverley's rather reductive definitions and attempts at further obscuring the very discussions he actually contributed to silencing inadequate and unsatisfying. Subalternism could actually have amounted to something, but the conversation around it was killed, it was forcefully interrupted, in the name of twisted professional interests (disguised as political), and it will not do to come back and say "let's do postsubalternism now." The idea of "postsubalternism," with all due respect, seems to me little more than a whitened sepulcher. I am not a postsubalternist, but I would have a few things to say about subalternism if anyone ever asks the right questions.[3]

Why should this be important to anyone? It is probably important to no one, *nemo*, the nonsubject of the professional field. But there is a certain fatality in writing, or a fatality that opens up once one decides to write and must say things, to be sure, against the fear and self-censorship that have come to be quasi-naturalized in our field of study. It is not only that people will not talk, or will not talk beyond or outside their own limited circles of friendship. It is also that people tell each other to be quiet, not to speak, not to rock any boats or make any noise. There is an abandonment of professional responsibility in this respect that I have witnessed often and that I find appalling. There is widespread fear in our professional milieu—fear of reprisals, fear of not getting hired, or of not getting tenured, or of not getting published, fear of exposure, fear of standing up for freedom of speech and the rights of open intellectual exchange lest one suffer, it is said, the consequences. It is hard to take it seriously, but it is meant seriously. Where does it come from? How have we allowed a certain number of theoretical discourses—or perhaps it is simply a certain kind of theoretical discourse, a certain style of doing work—to become so dangerous to our professional health that a sympathy for it can only be acknowledged secretly? How did it come to pass? We know that it is routine today in some quarters—everybody always hears too many stories, everyone always knows a lot more than others think—to advise students not to mention a few given names in their job application letters, and we know that petty power games based on ideological alliances, sometimes simply in the name of exclusion, have become almost the norm in many job searches and other professional contests and competitions. Is this the way we want things to continue to be? There is no fatality to the present status quo, which is why it is only up to us, and to no one else, to change it. Beverley, by critiquing people—me, among others—openly, also breaks the silence and the fear and gives us a chance to respond, also openly and freely. He engages in a mortification that could bring us all back to life.

"Fatal" is an adjective, by the way, that Beverley applies to me. He says:

> As for the comment about a "rhetoric . . . as respectable [*tan respetable*] as any other," that is, of course, the scorn of the philosopher for the demagogue, of Plato for the Sophists. But is it in fact true to say that the rhetoric of the Master Race and the Final Solution is "as respectable" as the "rhetoric . . . of Pachamama and *ayllu*"? Moreiras confuses here, in a way that I think is fatal for his position, the *form* of ideology—what Althusser called "ideology in general"—with the *content* of particular ideologies. (59)

The stuff about the "Final Solution" and the "Master Race" is Beverley's own imaginative creation, as those issues are not even remotely mentioned in my book. My sentences in question are, in Beverley's translation:

> It is better to decolonize than to colonize. But the success (desired) of [Evo] Morales will be a function of the ability of his government to encourage the production and redistribution of wealth and to create social justice; not of the rhetoric, which is in any case as respectable as any other, of Pachamama and *ayllu*. It is not the infinite decolonization of the cultural sphere that most matters or should matter to the Bolivian people, but social justice and the republican capacity of the citizenry to obtain a genuinely democratic political and economic system. (Moreiras, quoted in Beverley 57–58)

But there is nothing "fatal" in those words of mine, and they are nothing but trivial common sense. And Beverley's willful association of what I actually said with the Master Race and the Final Solution is nothing but unadulterated hogwash. As any Spaniard knows, when one uses the idiom "*tan respetable como cualquier otra,*" one is not indulging in nihilistic relativism. For instance, I could say, and I probably have said, that if only Celta de Vigo could purchase such and such a player or coach then they could be as good a team "as any other," and it would be crystal clear to my audience that by "any other" I mean the better ones, Barcelona FC or Real Madrid, not the Bouzas Rápido or the Celanova Racing (with all due respect). So when I say that the rhetoric of Pachamama and ayllu is as good as the best ideologies out there, but it still won't particularly do for the main purpose at hand, which is democratic justice, I am not comparing the Pachamama to the Final Solution or the ayllu to the Master Race. I hope this is not too didactic, but sometimes one has to explain things patiently that are too obvious to anyone. Beverley, we know, is not a Spaniard, so perhaps he did not get the obviousness. Or a Galician, for that matter, as he wants me to be.[4]

Beverley adds an endnote to his fatal paragraph, where he says: "Moreiras would respond that the form of ideology *is* its content" (135n18), and he is probably right, and I would furthermore claim that such is indeed Louis Althusser's own position. But never mind. What is at stake here is a fundamental notion that says, on Beverley's part, that since everything is ideology anyway, and there is no getting out of it, then some ideologies are better than others, and we should swallow them whole or, rather, we should allow the people to swallow them whole, and even ask them to swallow them whole, have them swallow them whole, as it is good for them to feel redeemed on the basis of imaginary identifications and projections that give them what they consider an identity and what the academic field in Latin American studies has never tired of calling an identity. But there is an alternative position on this, an opposite position, which I share, and which says that while some ideologies are definitely better than others, and their contextual political valence must be taken into account every time, in every case, so that feminism is good in a patriarchal world and antiracism is good in a racist world and indigenism is good in a criollo world, it is condescending and anti-democratic of us, the ones who are supposed to know better and already know better because we have read, say, Louis Althusser, to accept or promote the fetishization and reification of any ideologies, knowing full well that the reign of fetishized ideology has pernicious effects in the political sphere and militates against any conceivable democratic desire. Besides, we should not be spreading rampant lies, because it is a shameful thing to do.

When feminism, antiracism, indigenism, and any other configuration of rebellious desire go beyond their initial status as political positions, as they sometimes do, and become ideologies, they take over a person's imaginary world. While this is not necessarily bad, it is not necessarily good either. We may think it is better to be a Catholic in a Protestant world, or a Protestant in a Catholic world, or a marrano within Christianity, and I have a lot of sympathy for all of it. But I prefer to leave my options open and not to confuse my critical interests with the adoption of an imaginary identity for myself.[5] And if that is what I prefer for myself, well then, I certainly don't want anything else for others. If Beverley wants to call his position "postsubalternist," and he wants to make of it his principled reason for support of Latin American *marea rosada* (pink tide) governments, I will hold on to my subalternism and very much refuse principled support in that respect to some of those particular populist leaders, and to some of the academic populists who follow the leaders, just as much as I may withhold it from the neoliberals or the conservatives. If I am Plato to the Sophists, then it seems to me Beverley might be a Sophist who has always already assumed that his students are foolish children who must be guided with tall tales and whatever scary stories one can invent so that they sleep comfortably at night and keep quiet while the parents do their work—good or bad, that is a different but always open issue, whatever the political rhetoric. Politics is, after all, the realm of praxis. There is nothing worse about the Pachamama than there is about the Holy Trinity, I suppose, or about the Islamic notion of the godhead, and the myth of the ayllu can only be compared, perhaps advantageously, I do not know, to the myth of the democratic city. But my subalternism does not stop there—fatal or almost fatal as that may be, and has been, within the pious parameters of the North American university and its ever-so-leftist guardians. Or, indeed, within the pious parameters of those who seek to do business, political business, on the backs of the people, whether in Latin America or elsewhere (like many of the politicians Beverley has supported have done, starting, say, with the Colombian guerrillas when they were already thoroughly implicated in *narcotráfico* and the outright oppression of the Colombian countryside. It does not matter that they were not the only ones doing it).[6]

For me, subalternism, one of those dirty words that students in particular are urged never to use, and which was always linked in my personal biography to an interest in deconstruction, another dirty word, is the possibility of a radical critique of ideology and praxis wherever it comes from.

I try not to commune. The possibility of noncommuning critique, how-ever, is finally what Beverley objects to, somewhat clandestinely, to tell the truth, as, on the surface, he will not stop critiquing everyone. But the cards go up when, at the end of his chapter 5, "The Neoconservative Turn," he asks his most profoundly felt question: "To what extent then are we also, individually and collectively, invested in what I am calling the neocon-servative turn? This is a variant of the question that is at the heart of the Christian Gospels: whom do you serve?" (94). That is, do you serve God or Caesar, do you serve the people or their masters, do you serve anyone at all or only yourself? Well, once you have identified your master, put up *and* shut up, Beverley means. And what if the answer given to Beverley were to be, not from the Christian Gospel, but from the Old Testament: "I will not serve, I will serve no one" (yes, no one, the *nemo* or the nonsubject of the unconscious yet again)? We know from previous versions of the essay that resulted in Beverley's chapter 5 that the original question behind the lamer form that appears here is whether we are prepared to drop our intel-lectual façade, bourgeois critics that we are, entrenched in our academic privileges and our pretense of freedom of speech and thought, and in fact "follow the leader!," whether (Hugo) Chávez or (Evo) Morales or the neo-Peronists.[7] The time of truth had come, for Beverley, and Beverley needed little to kindle his enthusiasm as a follower (Lacan had already warned the 68'ers that they should be careful not to end up being mere seekers of a new Master)—but, if "follow the leader!" is the precondition for postsub-alternism, I think it holds a limited future. As it should, no matter who the leader is. And *that*, among other things, comes from the democratic republicanism that Beverley finds so objectionable and fatal in my own position: Arendtian, he calls it, between perplexity and scorn. I will stick to it for the time being, though.

III. A Democratic Critique of Imperial Reason

There is one glaring absence in the cast of characters in Beverley's *Latinamericanism after 9/11*. Aníbal Quijano is mentioned once, and Walter Mignolo is mentioned a couple of times, but no one else in their group is mentioned, and there is no direct engagement with their "decolonial" posi-tion. We get an earful about the hapless neoliberal cultural studies types, about sinister neoconservative litterateurs, about desperado neo-Arielistas, and about obsolete deconstructors, now either dead or in full transition toward neoconservatism, but the tendency that seems alive and well and progressing in the field is not mentioned, let alone critiqued. Why? It is possible that Beverley thinks of himself as a good fellow traveler of the tendency, with it if not of it, as he probably would not be accepted into it. His essential position is, however, different, although I would still place it within what I am calling ego Latin Americanism. So why is decolonial thought never brought to task in Beverley's book? I can't help thinking this may have something to do with ego Latin Americanist troubles—a neurotic symptom, perhaps, this omission of a trend whose specular identification might have brought more baggage with it than Beverley would have bargained for. The decolonial tendency (like feminism or queer studies but for essentially different reasons) goes without saying, which has, of course, the unexpected bonus of making it, since it is placed outside the frame, immune to Beverley's "political critique." The decolonials do, after all, follow the populist leaders, for whom they seem to have great respect; although, to tell the truth, in this particular case, the "respect" is more a matter of expecting the leaders to follow them.[8]

So, here is what the analyst would have to say: the field of Latin American postcolonial studies had been amply taken up, at the time of publication of Beverley's book, by the decolonial tendency, to the extent that one used to read in every other paper on the topic "Latin American postcolonial, that is, decolonial studies . . ." But there is no particular reason why this should have been so.[9] Understanding the structure and the history of Latin American postcoloniality is essential to the intellectual task of our time, and the decolonials have no exclusive purchase on it. Without it, we would not be able to proceed adequately toward what I want to call a democratic critique of imperial reason—another name for the task of specifying a subalternist reflection on Latin American issues beyond the pleasure principle and imaginary identifications. The analysts of empire have shown us to what an extraordinary extent, starting with Antonio de Montesinos or Bartolomé de Las Casas, imperial reason has always been criticized from imperial positions, albeit alternative ones: Dutch imperial reason critiques Spanish imperial reason, English imperial reason critiques the Dutch, and so forth. Imperial reason always develops on the basis of its own critique, and the history of imperial reason is all the more effective when it can present itself as a critical history of imperial reason. Empire, in other words, always imperializes its own critique, and it ends up absorbing it.

If that is indeed the case, one of Beverley's fundamental questions, that is, how can Latin America rid itself of the shadow of the North, of North American hegemony, must be answered by pointing toward the possibility of the formation of a general democratic intellect in Latin America that is, for me, premised on the very possibility of a fundamental democratic critique of empire on Latin American and Iberian grounds. We, as academic intellectuals, may not be able to help form a general democratic intellect in Latin America, but we can surely engage in a democratic critique of empire: and this is preparatory work, and it must continue to be if there is to be a chance of breaking the self-perpetuating cycle of imperial reason—of which, incidentally, "Latin Americanism" as such is a product.[10] It has not happened—not yet. It is, to my mind, the potential (or mythical) solution to every one of Beverley's problems, and it is the intellectual path that, while leaving neoliberals and neoconservatives and deconstructors and identitarians and decolonialists behind, would trace the way for a generational endeavor for which the field—the purported general field of Latin Americanism, which is far from being institutionally confined to the North American academy, and instead encompasses any and all reflection on the history, present, and future of the hemisphere as such—is ripe, although it does not yet know it and perhaps may never know it. Instead, when it can be bothered to, it accepts false solutions, which are not or no longer necessarily the old and tired clichés of multiculturalist identity. And one of those solutions that does not solve anything is, in my opinion, the decolonialist tendency. Oh, sure, they are useful enough sometimes, the decolonialists, but they do not present themselves as researchers whose partial contributions to scholarship are meant to be shared by others, or by anyone. Their theory, they say, must be accepted as a whole. They only understand sharing as communing, so that their question is always perhaps a different but equally choking version of Beverley's question: "Whom do you serve?" So why does Beverley pass up the very possibility of criticizing that option through whose critique he could perhaps find an answer to his own fundamental queries?

No effective decolonization of the Latin American field, that is, no genuine democratic critique of imperial reason, will be made on the basis of the various alleged discoveries, revelations, and procedures offered by the decolonialists. The decolonial option, to speak clearly, is not a democratic critique of imperial reason, nor is it meant to be. The downside, then, is that it becomes an imperial critique of imperial reason; or, inverting the terms but saying the same thing, a colonial critique of colonial reason. This could seem an exaggeration or even a paradox. After all, the decolonial option firmly believes in its decolonializing potency and even posits infinite decolonization as its one and only goal. Decolonials say, for instance, "decolonial conceptualization means to denounce the colonial matrix of power" (Mignolo, "Preamble" 17). But denouncing means nothing or almost nothing. Denouncing (empire, colonial power, the coloniality of power, if I may use the term without being accused of plagiarism, as has happened to others) is far from establishing the possibility of a democratic critique of imperial reason.[11] It is only its parody, and insofar as it is a parody, it remains enclosed in the universe it parodies.

The decolonial option acts as if its denunciations automatically became, every time, events of truth, the irruption of truth into our world, capable of splitting the world in two, capable of opening another history, a history capable of dividing the world, precisely, into denouncers and denounced. Whoever is not with me is against me, they say, following Beverley's Christian Gospel. Over and over again, practitioners of decolonial denunciation denounce and preach, in a double rhetorical movement that is their signature. What is denounced is the imperial "control" of the economy, of authority, of sexuality, of knowledge and subjectivity, even the imperial control of being. And what is preached is that the denunciation of imperial control is a sufficient condition to change the world, a sufficient condition for democratic or popular mobilization, because it is, from its very enunciation, the sufficient condition for the unveiling of an other economy, an other authority, an other sexuality, an other knowledge, an other subjectivity, and an other understanding of being, which are never defined or specified, only invoked. Thus we read: "implicit in the analytical concept of the colonial matrix of power (or coloniality of power) is the programmatic concept of decoloniality" (Mignolo, "Preamble" 18). The analysis is already its own total synthesis. The concept already performs itself. Denunciation is always at the same time revelation and preaching. It would be enough to show a sandal to teach someone how to walk, or the priest becomes a saint because he denounces the sinners. This is no doubt a peculiar colonial critique of colonial reason, full of a *potentia* that always already incorporates its own *actus*. But it is not yet, and it cannot be on its own terms, a democratic critique of imperial reason.

The dazzling discovery, the major *arcanum*, the great truth that the decolonial option claims to have discovered is the following: "There is no modernity without coloniality; coloniality is constitutive of modernity and not derivative" (Mignolo, "Preamble" 22). This is the analytic dimension or the great accomplishment of the analytic dimension in the vision of the coloniality of power. About it we are told that it encloses, rather magically, also a programmatic or performative dimension. In order to enter it, the mere understanding that there is truth in it, that modernity and coloniality are interchangeable, that when somebody says "modernity" she is also saying "coloniality" and when somebody says "coloniality" that person is also saying "modernity"—those understandings are not enough. They are not enough to the extent that some of us can agree up to a certain point, although perhaps not for the same reasons, both that modernity is a specific dimension of Western imperial reason and that coloniality is a specific, even constitutive dimension of modernity.

But the point is that to penetrate the hidden truth, as is the case for any magical truth, one has to agree with it *in a certain way*, with a certain faith, otherwise we will miss what is truly important. If the analytic dimension of the coloniality of power always already anticipates its own program, that is because something within the analytic dimension opens a portent: "The very concept of coloniality of power is already a decolonial move that, subsequently, opens up the gates for imagining possible futures rather than just resting on the celebratory moment of critical explanation of what the social world is really like" (Mignolo, "Preamble" 22). The denunciation is not therefore a mere critique. It is, above all, already a predication, and what it preaches is the futural dimension of another world, of another image of the world under the sign of infinite decolonization. Opening up another world in the abjuration of the present is the only acceptable "game in town for people who would prefer to decolonize themselves and contribute to the decolonization of the world" (Mignolo, "Preamble" 29). The destruction of the world opens up another world. Infinite decolonization is the infinite opening of another world. And it goes without saying that such an infinite opening entails, by itself, the encounter with another form of control of economy, authority, sexuality, knowledge, subjectivity, and being. There is no guarantee that such an alternative form of control not just promised but performatively or programmatically uttered by the decolonial option should be better than the first, except that the preaching itself places it formally as always already better. Or even: the radical improvement is in fact guaranteed by the very word of the preacher, the witness, the prophet, by his or her aura or personal prestige. The argument that the destruction of the authority of the coloniality of power as it is and has been, by virtue of the verbal shibboleth, automatically hands over the construction of alternative worlds does not need any guarantee other than the promise itself. But such a rhetorical procedure is far from contributing to the creation of a democratic general intellect. It is only auratic, charismatic thinking, meant to persuade the gullible, meant to secure the position of those already on board. It requires charismatic reception.[12] And, to my way of thinking, the call for charismatic reception is colonial critique of colonial reason in spades. Colonial reason, after all, has always proceeded on the basis of charisma—colonial reason has always already incorporated a charismatic critique, has always already colonized charisma itself. The decolonial option is a charismatic critique of imperial charisma.

A democratic critique of Latin American postcoloniality, which Beverley's identitarian position would not be prepared to accept either, always rejects in advance the idea that it may embody a programmatic dimension. There is always a programmatic dimension to identity thinking: "I will become what I am." Except that identity thinking is always already premised on being no one, not yet. The gap between the original absence and the fixity of desirable success is constitutive of a program for action, albeit never a democratic one. It amounts to the self-consecration of an ego-sovereign, which is, at bottom, what Beverley shares as a goal with the decolonials.

One of the radical limitations of US academic thinking over the last twenty years, after deconstruction, has been its inability to understand a simple thought: that the labor of the negative embodied by critique cannot be, and therefore refuses to be, always already synthetic. A democratic critique of imperial reason does not have recourse to the authoritarian and magical argument that a democratic analytics includes its own world revelation, and that such world revelation opens the charisma of the world as if for the first time, hence inaugurating another history and splitting the world in two: the infidels (deconstructionists?—the "deconstructionists," in Beverley's sense, have never had anything to do with deconstruction: the word, as he uses it, is shorthand for something else) and the believers.

I prefer to look for a zero degree of postcolonial thought: in fact, for postcolonial thought in a radically anti-chiliastic dimension. Zero degree postcoloniality, that is, democratic critique as postcolonial thought, a democratic critique of postcolonial thought, does not necessarily give up on the establishment of a program: I would say, on the contrary, that it prepares for a program. But it must, by definition, actively renounce the possibility of offering itself up as an example of organization and command because it must give up every possibility of charismatic self-consecration. Beverley's book is crisscrossed by a great anxiety over his own authority to speak as a US Latin Americanist, not from but about Latin America. It is a worry about the lack, his own lack, of charismatic self-consecration. Lacking it is a good thing, and this may be his main difference with the decolonials (not that the latter, for the undeluded observer, do not lack it as well, but they assume they don't, or do everything possible to act and speak as if they don't), except that Beverley's desire is rather to find a way into it, which is, for me, a bad thing and possibly the symptom of an unavowed or disavowed specular identification with the success of decolonial thought, which goes a long way toward explaining its mysterious absence, a glaring form of presence, from the general political critique *Latinamericanism* administers.

But there is no particular authority of the US Latin Americanist to the same extent that there is no particular authority coming from the autochthonous, primal, pure subject of Latin American history, who, for the decolonials, and perhaps also for Beverley, would not be a Latin American in the first place (he or she would be a Quechua subject, or Aymara, or Maya-Quiché, and so forth). The discussion is moot. Going back to Lacanianism, all of us should just traverse our fantasy and forfeit privilege on intellectual grounds. We do what we can from our position. If there is any possibility of linking up knowledge and democracy, that is, a demand for radical equality, a demand for freedom for all, knowledge must learn how to give up its own presumption of charismatic prestige. Is that not, incidentally, a possibility closer to those of us who must study the particular historical modality of imperial reason, the Hispanic one, that has always already abandoned knowledge for power?

As the premise of modern imperial reason, or, to paraphrase Karl Marx, as the "original sin" of modern imperial reason, its locus of primitive symbolic accumulation, Hispanic imperial reason is the one that has given up in advance its own critical possibility, the one that does not have to proceed to self-exaltation as political theology, the one that remains and has remained crudely attached to its own immunity, its privilege. As such, it guards, perhaps better than others, the possibility of its inversion into a democratic critique. If one may call for zero degree postcolonial thought, it is because Hispanic imperial reason is the zero degree of modern imperial reason—the only modality of imperial reason that does not reach constitution through its own self-critique. But this opens the way, at the end of modernity, at the end of democracy, for the beginning of a possible democratic critique of imperial reason, which prefaces the possibility—which

cannot be announced, only prepared for—of the constitution of a democratic general intellect in Latin America.[13] Would this not also preface the
end of (necessarily imperial) Latin Americanism? Were the *marea rosada*
governments on the way to it? One can only hope they were, and that they
may return to it.

IV. "Guillotinar al príncipe y sustituirle por el principio"

At the time of his republican commitment, around 1923, José Ortega y
Gasset indulged in prorevolutionary comments with a thought that has
no doubt become outdated in its terms, but from which we can still learn
a thing or two. He said, talking about the 1790 revolutionaries: "The ideal
future constructed by the pure intellect must supplant the past and the
present. This is the temper that leads to revolutions" (576). But, in 1923,
he found such an attitude petulant, and he wanted to temper it by means
of a reflection on what he termed "life reason," or *razón vital*. *Razón vital*
at the same time expands and limits the horizons of absolute reason into
history, and seeks in history grounds for revolutionary change. But then
Ortega says: "It is inconsistent to behead the prince and replace him with
a principle. Under the latter, no less than with the former, life becomes
subjected to an absolute regime. And this is precisely what should not
happen: neither rationalist absolutism—which saves reason and nullifies
life—nor relativism, which saves life as it evaporates reason. The sensi-
bility of the epoch that starts now is characterized by a refusal to submit
to such a dilemma. We cannot satisfactorily establish ourselves on any of
those terms" (577; my translation). I think John Beverley knows about the
false dilemma, but I am not certain that he has learned not to substitute
the principle for the prince. The decolonials most certainly have not.

Here is Beverley's presentation of "postsubalternism":

> This book is not only "after 9/11," then, it is also in some way postsubalternist.
> This is indicated particularly by the attention given here to the question of
> the state. The paradigm implicit in subaltern studies (and in postmodernist
> social theory in general) was that of the separation of the state and the subal-
> tern. . . . We are now confronted paradoxically in some ways by the success of
> a series of political initiatives in Latin America that, speaking very broadly,
> corresponded to the concerns of subaltern studies . . . a new way of thinking
> the relationship between the state and society has become necessary. (8–9)

And chapter 7, the last one in the book, opens with the perhaps not so surprising claim that "the question of Latinamericanism is, ultimately, a question of the identity of the Latin American state" (110): here is the principle again, the principial-identitarian thinking that has always been the bane of Latin American and Hispanic thought, of which decolonial thought is also a paradigmatic example, from its structure down to its very style, as if we could not do otherwise. This seems to be the only ground from which Beverley can announce his "postsubalternism" in the open denunciation of a subalternism he has now come to associate with "deconstruction," and through it with an entire movement of theoretical thought in Latin American studies that, from a specific point in time, somewhere in the late 1980s for some, sometime in the early 1990s for others, refused principial-identitarian thought in the attempt to seek a critical edge that the Latin Americanist tradition could not and would not offer. Postsubalternism is a regressive proposition that returns to a collusion with the postcolonial state in the name of identitarian thought. It is, after all, nothing but the main thought of the Latin Americanist tradition over the last two hundred years and counting.

The way Beverley sees it, the "elective affinity" between subaltern studies and deconstruction was based on the thought that the subaltern, by definition outside the hegemonic circle within any particular society, was therefore also outside the state and outside any progressive narrative concerning "the formation, evolution, and perfection of the state" (111). What is a bit paradoxical here is that, on the one hand, it was John Kraniauskas who offered the definition of subaltern studies as "a critique of the total apparatus of development," and Kraniauskas would rather be dipped in something foul than have the tag of deconstruction attached to his name.[14] And on the other hand, the notion that the subaltern is the constitutive outside of any hegemonic articulation—hence, the subaltern cannot claim belonging, and must therefore not claim any positive identity whatsoever: the subaltern is the nonsubject of the political—was drastically rejected by most people in the Latin American Subaltern Studies Group, including the totality of the founding members and those members who would later claim a decolonial alignment. It was, however, embraced, shared, co-thought, although not uncritically, by many of those whose continued involvement in the discussion, had it not been interrupted precisely so that they could not speak, might have made it amount to something: Gareth Williams in particular, but also Jon Beasley-Murray, Kate Jenckes, Horacio Legrás, Brett Levinson, Patrick Dove, Danny James, and others, including many who were at the time beginning graduate students and people whose life and work did not happen within the institutional space of US universities. Beverley's move is now—but it was not then, when he was fiercely fighting it, dismissing it, accusing it—to cede the ground to obsolete, "deconstructive" subalternism as definer of the field in order to continue to reject it: "The distinction [subalternity/hegemony] confuses the *form* of hegemony . . . with its *content* (both socialist-feminism and fascism are forms of hegemonic articulation, but obviously with quite different consequences)" (112). We are used to that argument by now, but the point is: it is not a subalternist argument, since, for the subaltern, insofar as it remains subaltern, the form of hegemonic articulation is indeed its content.

It is the argument of a state actor, as the state actor always must argue for the logic of the lesser political evil (that is, less or more gracious domination is better than more cruel domination; a domination by the majority is better than a domination by the minority; and so forth). I will not dispute that: it is the first, or political, articulation of subalternism, albeit not the only one. But Beverley will not go beyond it, and arguing solely for the state in the name of postsubalternism is what he is prepared to do. Chavismo is, for instance, justified based on the logic of a lesser evil: "Yes, yes: we know it is rather terrible, mostly authoritarian-populist, mostly corrupt at all levels, not really socialist, a bit violent, but, hey, it ain't the Right, and there are interactions between the state and subaltern-popular sectors that would not have occurred before the Caracazo."[15] If that logic is the foundation of postsubalternism, let me be spared—I would rather stay where I am. At the same time, I do not reject the political argument that a lesser evil is always better than a greater one—I have never done it, whether politically or professionally, and that was the whole point of my call for a first register of subalternism in the last chapter of *The Exhaustion of Difference*. This first register is the register of political possibility. Beverley talks about it, registering the register, but only in order to say: "He [Moreiras] does not appear to either want or be able to sustain that claim" (52). No? Who says? This is not a minor point, as Beverley thinks deconstruction, and by extension my position, and by extension that of my so-called "associates," "may lead outside of politics altogether" (51). Well, it certainly leads outside his form of politics.

It is true, I think, that deconstruction, but not exclusively, involves an infrapolitical gesture, but for me, such a gesture, which is the very opening of thought beyond the pleasure principle, is the very possibility of properly political engagement: that is, of an always provisional and contingent decision, contextual in every case, and political through and through, not based on the mechanical application of a program. And yet deconstruction, if I had any right to speak for it, which I do not, has never meant taking over the totality of political space. The reduction (of everything) to politics, at the expense of conceptual labor, is perhaps the real exit from the political into the realm of imaginary projection, which may very well, and usually does, wreak havoc. I will argue for the rights of the infrapolitical in Latin Americanist political reflection, and will state, for the sake of argument, that the infrapolitical is the sine qua non condition of thought beyond ego Latin Americanism, beyond the position taking and mere opinionating, beyond the sloganeering and silencing of the concept that the ego Latin Americanist options—say, postsubalternism, decoloniality, and, yes, also neo-Arielism—seem all too often limited to offering. But I will also argue that an infrapolitical thought beyond the pleasure principle, deconstructionist or not, is never and can never be beyond politics.[16] In fact, that has been the problem, and the reason for so much patent hostility, quite beyond Beverley. It is as if only some people were entitled to speak about politics—the rest of us can only be forgiven or forgotten if we do not.

It is most likely useless to continue with any of this instead of moving on, after enough things have perhaps been said or after we have gotten totally bored with saying them. Imaginary projection, that is, the charismatic-narcissistic impulse, is what is finally at stake, which is the reason I opt, in principle, if one is institutionally bound to Latin American studies, for a Latin Americanism beyond the pleasure principle, without recourse to facile desires (sometimes disguised as prophecies) and their expression. Since I reject, as much as Beverley does, both the neoconservative and the ultraleftist positions regarding my own political investment, such as it is, in Latin America's future, what remains immediately important is perhaps the possibility of a new conversation, beyond narcissisms, on the historical basis of our work. The nature of academic intellectuality is also a political issue. Our field is deficient and has shown itself to be irresponsible over the last few years—not so few anymore—notwithstanding the good books that have been published in the meantime. A lot of students, in particular, have paid a terrible price. I may accept my own blame. My gesture of contempt, when I thought I had to leave the field and in fact left it for some years, was an arrogant gesture that has come back to haunt me in rather unpleasant ways. Although I would not put myself in the shoes of my erstwhile hero, Gary Cooper in *High Noon*, as I was saying at the beginning of this chapter, old Marshal Kane can only be thought of as eating his heart out beyond the hills. He was a fool, if not for attempting to play the hero then for thinking that it would be all right for him to leave town in contemptuous dignity, and it is his foolishness that ultimately brings him to the position of mortal Oedipus. It is a good thing when we manage to get him out of his misery and bring him back to talk to us, so that various catastrophes can once again be averted. Once we have him out, once we bring old Oedipus outside the grove of the Eumenides so that he can speak, perhaps a new path will open up toward a liberation of Latin Americanist desire beyond the pleasure principle and egoic projections. There is an awful lot to talk about even when, or precisely because, talk has become difficult. I make no presumptions, but this is the time for a countermove against the willful reduction of thought in our institutional field of endeavor.[17] Will it ever happen?

Chapter 4

MAY I KILL A NARCO?

They say a fair is great if it has gone well for you, and it could not be otherwise in fairs as vast as the Thirtieth Congress of the Latin American Studies Association (LASA), which took place in San Francisco on May 13–16, 2012. Nobody can get an overall perspective. The association had around 5,000 members, of whom about 4,500 attended, and the program listed 999 panels and activities. At the first LASA Congress, in New York in 1968, there were only 7 panels. A wide majority of members come from the US academic field, from all relevant disciplines in the social sciences and the humanities, but many European and Latin American intellectuals are also members or are invited to attend as special guests. The conference, which has become annual after many years of being held every eighteen months, is traditionally a place where the pulse is gauged for the state of discussion in the specific disciplinary fields. It is something like the mecca of Latin Americanism, understood as the sum total of discourses on Latin America—to that extent, it has something of the Borgesian Chinese encyclopedia: the collection of words is always anachronistic and heteroclite. Generations and schools get together, forms of work get separated, contradictory proposals are reconciled, emergent thoughts are glimpsed, and ideas that are no longer alive, even if only half-dead, are sometimes buried but most often allowed to continue a dismal existence.

The visitor explores among many options. She can opt for a film (the film festival offered twenty-nine films that year) or walk around in the area where publishers show their wares, buy a book, speak with some available editor. She can go to panels, receptions, roundtables, cash bars, or presidential sections. And she can also install herself at the cafeteria or the lounge and wait there for the passers-by who need saluting. It is more fun to do all of that, of course, so there is a lot to talk about. The older ones meet the younger ones, and the younger ones confirm the various degrees of deterioration and decrepitude of their elders. Friends get together and conspire with greater or lesser innocence, although there are always some who sit with their backs against the wall to avoid certain visitations. There is a politics of greeting, of gazing, of silencing, and there is a politics of approach, of distance, of intimacy. One always ends up a wreck, and done for. LASA is always interesting or catastrophic or both, and one goes back home inspired or thinking of changing professions—and severely broke. I paid $250 a night at the conference hotel, and dinner at the otherwise excellent Chez Panisse in Berkeley was $169, and we were very careful with the wine.

There were reasons why this LASA in particular could produce in advance some tingling in your gut. It was held on US soil for the first time in six years, since in previous years foreign locations had been selected by the organization as a form of protest for issues having to do with federal policies regarding Cuban visitors. But, beyond that, the last few conferences had produced much disappointment and bewilderment. Leaving aside the individual quality of some of the papers, of course, Toronto was disastrous, and they told me Rio de Janeiro was just as bad or worse. In Montreal, there were some good panels, and that was about it, always within the options I would choose, since LASA is always many LASAs, and mine is just as microcosmic as anyone else's. For many of the LASA-goers, consequently, the story I will tell you will be unrecognizable, but not for everyone. The fact was, from my perspective, things had been pretty bad for a long time, since Washington, DC, in 2001. And "my perspective" more or less means: the interests of a professional field associated with departments of Hispanic languages, literatures, and cultures, open, yes, to other fields of knowledge, and contaminated by critical theory and a will toward political thought.

The day before the terrorist attacks against the Twin Towers in New York and the Pentagon in Washington, in September 2001, I was driving my car back to Durham, North Carolina, from Washington, DC, from the LASA hotel, and I had Eric Hershberg and Óscar Cabezas as passengers. Óscar remarked that the professional field—the one I have just mentioned—could not easily survive the scandal of the series of panels on the state of Latin American cultural studies. And he was right. It did not. We will never know whether it was, as Óscar prophesized, because of the row at the panels or because the attacks changed the state of affairs and brought about a discursive crisis that destroyed the promise of incipient theoretical reflection before the latter had become sufficiently established and institutionalized (institutionalization is not always bad). Everything had begun about ten years earlier. At the beginning of the 1990s, LASA was the site for the coming together of certain conditions that were going to become very productive. For instance, a theoretically informed, cosmopolitan Latin Americanist generation was emerging that wanted nothing to do with the old exceptionalist pieties according to which Hispanic modernity would always have been alternative, baroque and then neobaroque, nothing to do with the rest, and following a historicity that was not comparable to any other historicity. Poststructuralism in general was the dominant or at least more prestigious discourse in the humanities, and it was about to have a strong influence on adjacent fields, say, in social sciences, or in architecture, even in biology, which gave the humanities a certain surplus in symbolic prestige for the first time in several decades. The fall of the Berlin Wall, the dismantling of the Soviet Union, and the end of Central American civil wars raised important and urgent questions for the Left that advanced the need to come up with new answers. And new thinking horizons and new political experiments were becoming visible in the Southern Cone democratic transition processes, and in the initial launching of what later came to be known as "politics of memory." The latter insisted that an emphasis on historical memory was a condition of democratic process, which was relevant for the consummation of the "cultural turn" that was taking over the previous "linguistic turn," according to which language, not life or history or culture or experience, was the final horizon of thought. We were a bit tired of that. They were good years for the academic world: there was a lot to think about, as there always is, but this time it seemed as if new problems came with their own instructions for thought, and there was a concrete task to carry out, and we could do it. The university was expanding, the humanities were expanding, and years of economic growth were coming up that promised a general improvement in personal conditions of life. For those who, like me, were initiating our careers then, they were optimistic years.

In those years, *testimonio* was frequently and intensely discussed. *Testimonio* criticism—having to do with the victims of Southern Cone or Central American dictatorships and military or paramilitary regimes— emerged as one of the sites where it was possible to hatch a new relationship to Latin American studies, since the old relation, for us, until then, had been excessively mediated by literary representation. But it had become a truism of the times that literature would no longer rule over the fundamental representation of the subcontinent in the cultural field. An expansion of the idea of text toward an understanding of the social as text was developing that amply overwhelmed literary representation criteria. This did not happen only because the literati were doing things poorly, although they were, but rather because there were structural limits to the function of literature in multicultural societies where large percentages of the population were illiterate, and where there was rampant social racism and cultural subordination.

Those were the years, in our academic world, of Julio Ramos, a Puerto Rican and then a professor at Princeton, who wrote a book that is now a classic on the function of the literary in national constitution processes in Latin America; of Nelly Richard, a Franco-Chilean, a critic and theoretician of the Chilean Escena de Avanzada and a key figure in Latin American feminism; of John Beverley, a specialist in the literature of the Spanish Golden Age whose political passions had taken him to a strong solidary commitment with Central American revolutionary processes; of Néstor García Canclini, an Argentinian sociologist living in Mexico, whose book *Culturas híbridas* opened up the field of cultural studies in Latin America; of Beatriz Sarlo, an Argentinian public intellectual, the editor of *Punto de Vista*; and of the Salvadoran and New Yorker George Yúdice, whose incisive *testimonio* criticism was a fundamental counterpart to other ways of understanding *testimonio*. They were the foundational years of something that seemed a new distribution of the visible, a new field of the sensible—what we can retrospectively call Latin American cultural studies. Of course, the habitual tensions inevitably arose again: whether cultural studies was a substitute for politics or an instrument for politicization; whether it was merely mimetic of other traditions, notably the Anglo-Saxon ones; whether it was able to absorb a properly theoretical and metacritical reflection or was rather refractory to it in favor of a noseless culturalism reducible to a set of recipes for interpretation; whether it was inspired by the identitarian multiculturalism that had become hegemonic in the US university or was rather critical of those developments; and, above all, whether it was paradigmatically capable of sheltering an authentic reconfiguration of the field of knowledge in the humanities.

Diversification within the field was healthy, as it included the strictly culturalist, like García Canclini or Yúdice; those who put more of an emphasis on critico-theoretical reflection than on reflection on any concrete cultural object (for example, Nelly Richard); the Marxists, like John Kraniauskas or Neil Larsen; trends that were more strictly feminist or more directly engaged in thinking about ethnic issues; and those—it couldn't not happen—who continued the identitarian and liberationist tradition (that is, the anti-colonial tradition that had originated in the context of Peronist populism, and that would give rise to the philosophy and theology of liberation) that had been prominent in the 1960s and 1970s, probably represented as well as by anything else by the great film of Fernando Ezequiel Solanas, *La hora de los hornos* (1968).

Around 1994, Ileana Rodríguez, John Beverley, and a small number of other colleagues decided to create a Latin American Subaltern Studies Group that could produce in the Latin Americanist field the project that South Asian subalternists had been developing in postcolonial historiography for the English-speaking world.[1] Taking its point of departure in the thought that, in the postcolonial world, the idea of nation had never abandoned its upper-class mark and had therefore never accomplished hegemony, subalternism was an attempt to think about the critico-political conditions of a Latin American world where a national hegemonic articulation, that is, the thought of the nation as the primary horizon of political action, had stopped being dominant and could no longer produce the mirage of a general ideological persuasion. If the (Latin American) nation could no longer be the horizon of constitution for politics in Latin America, after the various historical catastrophes in the Southern Cone and Central America in particular, but also in Colombia and Peru, how, then, to think about the future, and how to do it from a will toward social justice, from a will to eliminate—theoretically and factically—subalternity in subcontinental societies? This was the moment of social movements and indigenous claims against any ideology of transculturation and national integration.

Latin American subalternism was born controversially, but it was born, and it became a significant referent within two or three years. It wasn't, or it didn't seem to be, important whether one was in agreement with the Founding Manifesto—a fairly lame text—or with the various texts that started to be published within that line of thought. Certainly ideological agreement was not so relevant for the younger people, who tended to see the group's proposals as an invitation to debate and discussion, which one could enter from a certain commitment to think politically but without any need for ideological straitjackets. I believe that, as often happens, a mere count of those who became formal members of the group (no more than a dozen and a half people) would be somewhat deceiving, because the intellectual success of the group did not depend so much on its closed constitution as it did on its capacity to influence, to call to dialogue, to propose—and this perhaps not even specifically, but formally: in other words, its success depended on its very projection as a thinking machine, which produced great consternation in some quarters, certainly, but also curiosity and desire to engage in other quarters, perhaps reticence, rancor, or sympathy, but little indifference. It became an interesting academic experiment, even an experiment in academic "grand politics" (in spite of its repeated anti-academicist protests), but daring experiments tend not to last, and it was perhaps written in the destiny of the group that it was not going to last. It was formally dissolved after a conference at Duke University in the fall of 1998. Retrospectively, I suspect the dissolution of the group ended up causing the fall of the much larger coalition around cultural studies, as would become manifest in the discussions around a series of special panels on the state of things at the 2001 LASA meeting in Washington, DC.

Those panels were the practical confirmation that the moment of coalition was over. After that, there would perhaps be little interest groups, *taifas* we called them, if they were able to sustain themselves, but there would no longer be an ample movement, reaching the whole professional field, with the ambition of a general transtheoretical and transdisciplinary conversation. The academic machine had failed, or only ours, the humanities machine, or its pretension (an old obsession of US-based Latin Americanists) that it was after all possible to exit the ivory tower and talk to more than a reduced circle of colleagues, and any expectations of influence on the public sphere would have to be newly reduced. The hour of subalternism might not have entirely passed, some of us thought, but the knell of dispersion had tolled. And what happened in the years that followed is the history of a withdrawal: many of the theoretical tendencies whose professional flourishing was a function of critical dialogue with other tendencies proved unable to survive in isolation—almost all of them, really. The field—now quickly turning into a void—made certain tendencies invisible, destroyed other tendencies, consigned some to the archive, and became factically divided, from the perspective of their relative visibility, into the two pathetic notions Walter Mignolo had identified in his intervention at the Duke conference: the so-called postmoderns (it sounds very passé now, but it was equally passé then), who were those said to be willing to continue their entanglement with non–Latin American critical thought and to sustain nonidentitarian theoretical reflection (we could say: posthegemonic or critical subalternism, in a special dialogue with both Marxism and Althusserian post-Marxism and deconstruction), and those who started to call themselves "decolonialists," whose fundamental interest was to keep the flame of postcolonial identitarian liberationism alive, but not in the horizon of the postcolonial nation, rather through indigenous or originary relationalities in Latin America. The latter were able to pull ahead, and their impact has been significant in recent years. But the former failed: their position, our position, could not consolidate itself institutionally.

Hence the tingling. What was going to happen at this LASA? Was it going to be more of the same? Would it be yet another signal to start looking at job ads in, say, the still-flourishing fast-food industry? Become an Uber driver in Calcutta? Or was there a possibility that we could find some spirit, some remainder of it, that would enable us to go on, and that would make it plausible to make new promises to potential students? Benjamin Arditi, who was then the president of the LASA Section on Culture, Power, and Politics, which had been historically important in the development of Latin American cultural studies, had organized a series of panels with a rather infernal common title, but where an open discussion among different politico-theoretical tendencies was sought: "Polemizing Subaltern Culture: The Decolonial, the Posthegemonic, the Postliberal." Something could happen there. The old actors would be present, not everybody, but some of them, and some younger people. And discussion in and around Latin America was increasing and burning fairly intensely: on the one hand, there were the various "pink tide" governments, in countries where democratic and anti-liberal irruptions were taking place about which intellectuals must develop nuanced positions beyond the simple knee-jerk principled support—it was not necessarily easy to do it; on the other hand, there were relatively new phenomena reaching extremely urgent heights: the narco-political system in Mexico threatening the very Mexican nation as such; huge levels of corruption based on illegal capitalist practices flooding most Central American countries; the situation in Colombia, where the guerrillas continued to generate abysmal problems; the consolidation of Brazil as an emergent power and the leader of a Latin American "great space."

What was important was not really what happened at LASA, but rather what people thought had happened. In other words, when the possible constitution or reconstitution of a critical project for the overall field is at stake, one that can gather several theoretical tendencies and move as an institutional war machine, as Latin American cultural studies had almost done in the 1990s, what matters is not that such a machine be properly built with all the bolts and screws tightened up. Rather, what matters is that people think of it, schematically, from their own will to produce it; there will be time later for precisions and corrections, for adjustments and oilings. So the words of the panelists would require attention, but the audience's reactions would be much more fundamentally important, and not just in the Q&A periods, but in the corridors, at the bar, during dinner, even in bed. It was important to see whether a new political will for field construction would be produced or the same situation of inane dispersion that had plagued LASA for the previous ten years or so would continue to obtain.

In the first panel, Bruno Bosteels offered a summary of the state of the situation from four instances that he conceptualized as: political (the one emanating from the crisis and the critique of the legacy of all revolutionary movements from Castroism to Central American guerrillas to Zapatism; deontological (perhaps a product of deconstruction in the 1980s and early 1990s and linked to the radical critique of the academic apparatus of knowledge production); ontological (linked to the association of metaphysics and politics in leftist Nietzschean-Heideggerianism, which would include deconstruction and Levinasianism); and ethical (linked to decolonial particularism, in the absence of the nation as a reference for liberation, and committed not to the totality of the social but to particular subaltern segments of it). According to Bosteels, subalternism would have been able, for some brief years, to act as the common denominator of those four critical positions, even if in an internally divided and potentially conflictive manner. In the 1990s, a politico-critical constellation had emerged that was based on the passage from a politics of militancy to a politics of solidarity, which also produced forms of research that were both critical and self-critical vis-à-vis power/knowledge mechanisms anchored in the research itself; this critical politics of solidarity, or solidary political critique, was committed to a testimonial practice of respect for otherness, both for the differentiated and the nondifferentiated other, and took its departure from local rather than "global designs." This was Bosteels's rather masterful summary of critical conditions in the Latin Americanism of the 1990s. In contrast, for him the current situation in 2011 was a "dialogue of the deaf" in which discourses had become mutually incomprehensible, even inaudible.

Bosteels then made a call—we were hoping he would, but we did not know that he would—to some collective awakening, to the reconstitution of a dialogue not "of the deaf," and, to some surprise, he did it on the basis of, or through his appeal to, the term "posthegemony" (as I have said before, a term first heard at the 1998 Duke conference, then the focus of Jon Beasley-Murray's dissertation and eventual book, *Posthegemony: Political Theory and Latin America*). Bosteels was generous, since his own book, *The Actuality of Communism*, has a clear propositional dimension, in venturing that "posthegemony" could become for the immediate future, if not the mostly common reference that, say, subalternism meant in the 1990s, then at least a new site of engagement from which to discuss collectively, with all the necessary disagreements and disputations, and on the basis of a new will, a possible novel articulation of politics and the critique of knowledge production.

It did not seem as if the idea had great purchase on two of the other participants at that panel, namely, John Beverley and Arturo Escobar. Beverley reiterated his proposal for "postsubalternism" already offered in his book *Latinamericanism after 9/11*, which was that, given the ongoing construction of new state forms in Venezuela, Ecuador, Bolivia, and Argentina, it had become necessary to support the anti-neoliberal "statism" of the pink tide as a simple acknowledgment that politics, at decisive moments, should take priority over any theoretical or critical practice. In other words, he proposed that we should all just celebrate the pink tide and forget or postpone the criticisms. For Beverley, hegemony does not necessarily imply the subordination of the population sectors that are not part of the government coalition, and it is therefore perfectly plausible to posit a reasonably democratic state or neo-state hegemonic articulation on the basis of a commitment to the popular classes that can leave behind the oppressive authoritarianism that plagued the actually existing socialisms of the Soviet bloc. For him, any posthegemonic postulation— that is, any position that departs from the notion that any given power articulation, whether it be an articulation of the dominant, as in neoliberalism, or an articulation of the dominated, as in Venezuelan Chavismo or Argentinian Kirchnerism, deserves critical vigilance rather than either simple resistance or unconditional support—is always already ultraleftism in the classical sense defined by Lenin, and it is therefore a negation of the political as such, a "political" that, in the Latin America of those years, either follows the pink tide or is necessarily neoconservative and reactionary. Beverley, whose position rests on critique of intellectual privilege, made it clear that it is necessary to be a politician before being an intellectual. In Latin America today, "there is what there is," he said, with its glories and limitations, and there will probably not be a "second phase" (by which he meant some kind of revolutionary radicalization) of the pink tide; and what there is, is infinitely better than what there was, which was neoliberalism, hence the pink tide deserves not critical, that is, lukewarm support but simply unconditional support. "Intellectual," Beverley seemed to say or was saying, "it is time to be counted, it is time to count, and you must cease being a bore with all your class privileges. Intellectual, become a follower!"

Escobar, who was representing the decolonials, insisted that an articulation between politics and the critique of knowledge was indeed necessary and urgent, given that the present situation of global crisis makes modern thought incapable of pondering life in its real conditions. For Escobar, the subalterns today are not necessarily the proletarians displaced and ruined by deindustrialization or the various groups of mestizo laborers who work for subsistence in Latin American societies' black infraeconomies, but rather primarily the indigenous communities whose cosmovisions and ontologies were radically denied and silenced by the Western colonial project. To restitute life to politics implies restituting a communal logic, a "relational" logic, he said, on the basis of life processes that have nothing to do with abstract knowledge and that reject Western dualism in favor of an ontology of relationality that includes the animal, the mineral, and the vegetable (say, the mountains, who are agents insofar as they are divine in Quechua tradition), and that rejects the division between mortals and immortals. Against every state logic and against every logic of globalization, the so-called universal relationality (meaning there are no dualist discontinuities between body and soul, or human and natural; rather everything is a relation) is the very logic of community, and the political project of the present and the future, certainly in Latin America, can only be the reactivation of communal relationality, for everyone in their own community, and from there in everyone's community. The ambition of this project is to substitute relationality for Western rationality—a relationality that was always already present in the old pre-Western originary cultures and that is presumably very much still there, even if only latent.

The three mentioned positions amounted to a mapping of the territory: we can call them as they call themselves, *communalist decolonialism*, against globalization and against the state, but more fundamentally against Western and Westernizing rationality; *statist postsubalternism*, looking for an expansive commitment to the anti-neoliberal government coalitions in Latin America; and *posthegemony*, which attempts to think about politics from critical procedures alien to the postulation of and commitment to particular subjects of history. It remained to be seen whether those three tendencies would be complemented by some other decisive or relevant one, or whether the parameters for discussion had already been set. And I suppose it was at that very moment, between the first and the second panel, when a certain decision started to become collectively possible. Communalist decolonialism's and statist postsubalternism's strengths have to do with already preconstituted and mobilized political subjects that they support (and perhaps also pretend to inspire and properly lead). By contrast, posthegemony is reduced to critically contingent positions in every case, without previous blanket commitments, without a priori alliances, only looking for whatever seems more democratic and best guarantees equality. Communalist decolonialism has the drawback of ignoring countless millions of Latin American citizens who would not identify their lives, or indeed their desires, as dependent on any kind of relational-communitarian reconstitution. And the fundamental problem of statist subalternism is its knee-jerk character: once there is a self-appointed "popular" or leftist government in place, we should only follow, we should only say yes: it is good to obey the leader, the movement, and it is good to shut up already with your critiques. Both tendencies revealed their limits in rather blinding ways, and that further reduced their appeal and their strengths: they could never become the center of a transtheoretical proposal for the reconstruction of a field of studies. They could, certainly, recruit adepts and influence opinion, both inside and perhaps outside the academic field, but they seemed destined, once people understood them properly, to insubstantial minority support. Posthegemony did not even look for or need majority support: its own conditions of critical enunciation voided any kind of establishment of hegemonic potency for itself. The real question was then whether posthegemony could start to be seen, by the field, not by those already persuaded, as the possibility of a new horizon for thought: inclusive, articulate, critical, political, flexible, and open, with enough convoking power.

But then, of course, LASA was not only those three panels that Arditi had organized, and people moved on. There was time to keep up the curiosity and get into other panels. I myself was involved in another panel series entitled "Iberian Postcolonialities: A Metahistory of Material Practices of Power." Isidoro Cheresky was rigorously critical of *caudillista* tendencies in pink tide governments, which he named "verticalist presidentialism," endemic to Latin American historical populism, and Javier Gallardo spoke persuasively about the history of Latin American republicanism and democratic practices in government. In that context, it started to become clear to me that posthegemony could be the contemporary name, historically and theoretically situated, for a critique of domination whose point of departure is the critique of the ideological foundations of domination itself. Hence, it seeks to think outside any pacts of sovereignty, whatever they are or whoever their signatories, and it articulates itself, always and in every case, specifically and regionally or locally, as a critique of every hegemonic formation as apparatus of power, including, of course, any counter-hegemonic formation, actual or potential. Posthegemony can therefore be understood as a form of critical regionalism, or rather, its successor. It fulfills the conditions of addressing the critique of knowledge and ideology, and it is endowed with a capacity for practical intervention in the political terrain. It can and should be understood not just as a theoretical trend but as an institutional machine that can also displace what from a democratic perspective are old and unproductive problems, like the problems of statism or the problem of community. Every community excludes, from its very constitution, those who do not belong to it, in the same way that every state form is built on a pact of sovereignty by virtue of which certain classes, set against other classes, acquire a power that is exactly the amount of power they take from the rest, and that they will then naturalize. As an institutional machine, posthegemony is neither against the state nor against community: it is only, and primarily, the place of a possible encounter able to generate new thought along the lines of the republican motto "Everybody counts or no one counts"—something the other two tendencies, doomed to the infinite loop of their own conditions of enunciation, could never offer.

One of those nights, over dinner at Mochica, a Peruvian restaurant, the question came up as to whether it was possible to kill the other only in the case of legitimate self-defense or, if, in fact, in a posthegemonic regime any death is possible, insofar as there is no longer legitimacy outside what is factically imposed by the law—there is legality, but not legitimacy, because principles have been abolished, and now *nadie es más que nadie*, and everybody counts or nobody counts. In other words, the question on posthegemony includes and does not erase the question about the ethical legitimacy of the struggle, but also its limits (and at the limit it moves toward a refusal to turn ethics into the foundation of politics). Immanuel Kant does not discuss the question of self-defense, but, as José Luis Villacañas let us know electronically, Salomon Maimon, a Kantian, does. For Maimon, the preservation of one's own life is a natural right and a necessary priority. When Arturo Escobar says during the Q&A session after the panel that the democratic-republican position is a matter of faith, not therefore of logic, he ignores that it is not necessary to believe in the Kantian moral law in order to sustain that domination breaks ethical obligations not based on self-defense. If I must live in freedom, free from domination, I understand my possibility is based on the same possibility for the other, for any other. If I do not want to be killed arbitrarily, I must not kill arbitrarily. But I also understand that my need to oppose domination is imperative. This is logic, not cultural faith, whatever Escobar says. It is valid posthegemonically and postsovereignly—it depends on no principle, but it is not itself a principle. It opens the political space as a permanent space for the negotiation of conflict, instead of displacing or erasing conflict in the name of the law, of social unity, of the preservation of community, of the security of the citizens, or of a commitment to the goals of some revolution. Because it is posthegemonic logic, it recognizes no legitimacy of command, certainly not one's own, hence death is only valid as self-defense and has practical advantages vis-à-vis communitarian closure (always willing and ready to deny the conflict, which is major violence, in the name of the priority survival of the community) and vis-à-vis populist statism (which privileges not seeing, not hearing, not saying every time seeing, hearing, and saying could raise an objection to the interests of the government coalition).

In the third of the Arditi panels, Beasley-Murray announced that posthegemony was in fact the strictly logical step to take after subalternist theory. Insofar as subalternism was always trapped in the polarity hegemony/subalternity, inherited from Antonio Gramsci, posthegemony takes one step forward in announcing that "there is no hegemony, and there never was one." Beasley-Murray thinks that hegemony is only one more ideological pretension that has little to do with the "real movement of things," and whose disavowed secret is always a will to domination. In the dialogue that followed, Bosteels and Sergio Villalobos objected that a fundamental ambiguity seems to creep into the theorization of posthegemony to the extent that posthegemony seems to refer simultaneously both to its own theoretical stance ("there is no hegemony because hegemony is an impossibility, no more than a theoretical fiction") and to the reality of the social ("there is no hegemony, nobody has it in, say, Mexico today, nobody holds it in Honduras or Paraguay, and so forth. It is a fiction, it is never a part of the social fabric"). But it is an ambiguity that should not be seen as a problem that must be solved; it is a productive ambiguity, because it places theory historically: it would have been, no doubt, more difficult to insist on posthegemony at the time of the national-popular state form, when the nation was still the goal for political constitution. For classical Peronism, for instance, the notion of posthegemony would have been perhaps incomprehensible or merely obstructionist. But we are no longer in national-popular times, or the idea of a return to them is a rightwing retrograde conceit.

Erin Graff Zivin, Josie Saldaña, Gareth Williams, and others spoke up in favor of posthegemony and underlined what they called its line-of-flight virtue that makes it useful for multiple sites of critical engagement: it is a notion that includes in itself a self-critical dimension, since it cannot become reified without contradiction, and it is for that reason useful to think about state problematics (at the level of state politics, for instance), but also inter- or para-state ones (communitarian, local, or regional microphysics, and macrophysics of globalization and financial rule), whether pink tide or neoliberal, populist or anti-populist. And it generates a productivity that is far from reducible to the thought of the political: it is also a fundamental tool to think about culture and about every modality of presentation of the visible. It can intervene as critique of knowledge because it is ideology critique in the first place, and it can propose political and intellectual articulations of all kinds. I thought, in the wake of the discussion and the excitement it generated, that the task was done. Not for everyone, and not in the same way. It is a big box, but it is a box—the tool kit for a new and potentially collective project, for a new program of inter- and extradisciplinary thought that does not have to be only academic. LASA seemed to have fulfilled its long-deferred promise. It was now just a matter of waiting . . .

Chapter 5

THE TURN OF DECONSTRUCTION

I concluded that between the real desert and the idea we have of it there is never a correspondence. "One is only the metaphor of the other," I commented to Professor Pecha. "But it is not easy to discern which of them is the metaphor."

PABLO D'ORS, *El amigo del desierto*

I

Years ago, at the end of a book whose partial intent was to justify a subalternist approach in Latin American cultural studies, I wrote a few pages on Jacques Derrida's *Specters of Marx*. In the third chapter of that book, Derrida is calling for a "New International" on the basis of Marxism, of one of the "spirits," or "specters," or "ghosts" of Marxism. Derrida refers to a "double interpretation" (81) whose need was for him irreducible at the time of accepting the complex Marxist and Marxian legacy. For Derrida, as to Marxism, "There is no precedent whatsoever for such an event. In the whole history of humanity, in the whole history of the world and of the earth, in all that to which one can give the name of history in general, such an event (let us repeat, the event of a discourse in the philosophico-scientific form claiming to break with myth, religion, and the nationalist 'mystique') has been bound, for the first time and inseparably, to world-wide forms of social organization" (91). This is the "messianic promise" of Marxism, which "will have imprinted an inaugural and unique mark in history" (91). Derrida places his own work vis-à-vis such messianic promise: "deconstruction would have been impossible and unthinkable in a pre-Marxist space"; "deconstruction has never had any sense or interest, in my view at least, except as a radicalization, which is also to say in the tradition of a certain Marxism, in a certain spirit of Marxism" (92). Regarding, then, this "radicalization" of Marxism, Derrida's "first interpretation" is close to what Etienne Balibar, in an essay written around the same time (Balibar refers to Derrida's *Specters* briefly [64]), called "fictitious or total universality" (61). For Balibar, "fictitious or total universality is effective as [a] means of integration . . . because it leads dominated groups to struggle against discrimination or inequality in the very name of the superior values of the community: the legal and ethical values of the state itself (notably, justice). . . . To confront the hegemonic structure by denouncing the gap or contradiction between its official values and the actual practice . . . is the most effective way to enforce its universality" (61–62). And Derrida says of this first or fictitious register of interpretation: "Let us accept provisionally the hypothesis that all that is going badly in the world today is but a measure of the gap between an empirical reality and a regulating ideal" (86). Derrida's regulating ideal is what Balibar directly calls the official values of the hegemonic structure. Both thinkers, in the spirit of Marxism, recommend critico-political intervention to close the empirical gap that keeps the democratic ideal so far from everyday experience.[1]

But for Derrida, that first register of critico-political interpretation is not enough, and he seeks a second interpretive articulation that is also, in fact, consistent with the Balibarian notion of "ideal universality," that is, a "latent insurrection" that guards an infinite and absolute claim "against the limits of any institution" (64). In Derridean terms, "beyond the 'facts,' beyond the supposed 'empirical evidence,' beyond all that is inadequate to the ideal, it would be a question of putting into question again, in certain of its essential predicates, the very concept of the same ideal" through a radical critique of its articulations (86–87). Derrida claims that it is not possible, politically, to restrain oneself to either the first or the second interpretation: both are necessary, since a unilateral insistence on one of them would only result in either fatalist idealism or abstract and dogmatic eschatology. The first interpretation, by itself, would dwell on the fact that nobody could pull oneself out of one's own context, that we are always determined by our world, that we cannot get rid of our own ideological prejudices, and that therefore all that is possible is to make sure, or to demand, that our prejudices be kept consistent with reality. This would be Derrida's fatalist idealism. But through the second interpretation, we would fall into a permanent hole of critique without remainder, a kind of absolute negation that Derrida calls abstract and dogmatic eschatology (see Derrida, *Specters* 87).

At the time of writing my own *Exhaustion of Difference* (2001), I associated this Derridean and Balibarian injunction to live or dwell in the ambiguity of the double register to what I called "subalternist affirmation" (289; see also 281–288). That seemed to me what needed to be done, critically or academically, in the name of a politically productive deconstruction, or of a deconstructive political strategy, whether or not it could be said to constitute a certain radicalization of Marxism. But today I no longer find myself in that secure position. The world seems to have changed, or perhaps just for me. As a thought experiment, metonymic, let me reduce the global or generalized political framework invoked by Derrida or Balibar to institutional terms, to the university, for instance, and its small history. Perhaps today we have come to know that the university no longer works in the gap between its pure idea and an empirical reality that is not commensurate with it. Rather, the university seems to have fallen prey to some administratively fostered sclerotic conventionality, or a tendential reactionary-ism that follows some kind of entropic law of decay, and the idea of the university is no longer inspiring. We are not convinced that it is enough to work for a return to the old foundational idea of a free university, because nobody bothers to remember it anymore. The notion of the university has been modified to such an extent within the last twenty years that every kind of "idealist" practice of it in the old sense must assume its internal ruin: there is no longer a regulating ideal of the university, and to say this is neither fatalist nor second-degree idealism but rather the only way to avoid concrete schizophrenia. The first Derridean-Balibarian register is by now critically insufficient and must be abandoned.

Can we then move toward the second one, according to which we must bring into question the very concept of that ideal? The practice of this second register of interpretation could be said to be the deconstructive practice of critical destruction of the idea of the university in view of its potential radicalization. But what are we to radicalize? And how are we to do it? If the political possibility promised by the first register of interpretation falls, this second register falls too—there is no longer a hegemonic construct with an official ideality that we can subject to demolishing critique in a politically productive way. Or, if there is one, it is shamefully disavowed. Indeed, given the fact that the labor of radicalization no longer has an institutional referent, and cannot find a horizon within otherwise secured and recognizable parameters, any exercise of dismantling might very well end up accelerating the transformation of the university into the commercial-instrumental enterprise that it already is. How are we to operate institutionally against the institution, how are we to work beyond work so that, day by day, we can get a glimpse of another world, a perspective that could perhaps subjectively sustain our actions? But the university is just an example. Think about the Venezuelan, or Argentinian, or Spanish/Catalan political processes and how they are themselves metonymic examples of why it is no longer feasible or reassuring to appeal to any hegemonic or ideal structuration of institutional democracy or to any regulative notion of the social that does not immediately explode in our faces. The legitimacy of parliamentary democracy as we have known it is in deep crisis in Latin America, and Giorgio Agamben has recently offered, in *Il mistero del male,* a powerful denunciation of the void of legitimacy of power also in Europe: "If the crisis that our society is crossing is so deep and grave, it is because it does not only set into question the legality of institutions, but also their legitimacy; not just, as it is too often repeated, the rules and modalities of the exercise of power, but also the very principles that found it and legitimate it" (6). The failure of the Derridean-Balibarian first instance of political intervention opens an abyss that threatens to swallow the very possibility of the second register.

Something new is being sought whose orientation and destiny are unclear and not particularly inspiring from the perspective of the old democratic ideal that more or less secular, more or less stable Western democracies can still be said to harbor somewhere. In Latin America, from Zapatista Chiapas to the Mapuches and from peasant areas in Brazil to barrio movements in Buenos Aires, Rio de Janeiro, Mexico, or Bogotá, not to mention Venezuela or Bolivia, there is a proliferation of movements whose political projection is primarily consensual-communitarian, called "consensual authoritarianism" by people like Félix Patzi or Raúl Zibechi (309). Any idea of radical democracy would be hard-pressed to endorse it without having to undergo deep conceptual modifications in the best of cases.[2] This is not failing to manifest itself at the level of academic ideology throughout the hemisphere (that is, including the Latin Americanist establishment in the United States), which is also increasingly neo-communitarian (more than neo-communist), and in many cases explicitly nondemocratic. But is this what could possibly have been meant as fidelity to a certain spirit of Marxism? Derrida said, "If there is a spirit of Marxism which I will never be ready to renounce, it is not only the critical idea or the questioning stance (a consistent deconstruction must insist on them even as it also learns that this is not the last or first word). It is even more a certain emancipatory and messianic affirmation, a certain experience of the promise that one can try to liberate from any dogmatics and even from any metaphysico-religious determination, from any messianism" (89). It cannot be a mere matter of deciding that a change in hegemonic articulation favoring the popular classes should suspend political critique and provoke unconditional endorsement. I suspect consensual, communitarian authoritarianism would not qualify within the Derridean terms just mentioned, to the very extent—and precisely to the extent—that those movements partially find their inspiration in ancestral ideas or traditions or inventions of tradition that are endorsed from messianic perspectives pregnant with explicit metaphysico-religious determination and with revisionist cultural ideologemes laden with decolonial dogma. An insistence on avoiding mythic projections once again leaves deconstruction, as a partisan of democracy understood as radical democracy, on either the wrong or the right side of history, according to opinion, but in any case rather outside either ruling hegemony or aspiring counterhegemonic ideologies struggling for political self-construction. Deconstruction never thought of itself as a participant in the drastically impoverished notion of what is to count as political thought that those with a primary allegiance to political instrumentalization uphold or celebrate. It continues to be critical of the political insofar as it is politically critical. The shifting of political ground that is partially a result of the last fifteen years or so of Latin American political history has not yet solved the issue—whatever progress may have been made in some cases, new questions constantly pop up. At the same time, the Derridean double interpretation finds its limit at the border of political invention. What is to be done, then?

II

To talk about a second deconstructive turn presupposes a first turn, understood as a clearly recognizable discursive process that can be dated to some moment in the presumably near past. But about this first turn one could find a number of alternative positions. For some, there would have been no end to deconstruction's first turn, whereas others would prefer to say that there never was a clearly identifiable deconstructive turn, much less at the level of the entire field of Latin American cultural studies. Others would say, however, that deconstruction has not even begun yet, it is still to come and we will see whether it ever arrives. Yet others would want to say there is no need at all for deconstruction, either now or ever. And finally, some others would opine that only a real and serious deconstructive turn could have us wake up from a dogmatic slumber full of decolonial pronouncements and identitarian mush. And perhaps there is some truth in each of those five propositions, although, in its partiality, it would necessarily be a trivial truth.

Deconstruction, if we think of it weakly (I will try to provide a stronger definition later) as an influential form of intellectual practice associated with the name of Jacques Derrida, known for its tendency to reject facile claims for intellectual closure at every level, and that affected first of all what were then primarily literary studies in the US university, hit Spanish and Latin American literature departments belatedly, not until the late 1980s. As the fortunes of deconstruction in that sense waned toward the end of the 1990s, we could talk about more or less a decade of significant presence in the everyday discussions of the field. After deconstruction at the end of the 1990s, the very word submerged for us (Derrida himself was not really using it, and he dies shortly thereafter). What has happened since then? And what happened during that decade? If there is a future for deconstruction in the field, to what extent is that future premised on past accomplishments? And to what extent is that future, if there is one, necessarily the product of a potentially new invention? Only approximate responses can be given.

I was still a student in Barcelona when my friend Julián Abad showed me a copy of Derrida's *La dissémination*. It must have been 1978. When I started my doctoral studies at the University of Georgia in the early 1980s, only philosophy professor Bernard Dauenhauer, one of my mentors, had a working knowledge of a phenomenon that was in fact, he told me, sweeping through the admittedly rarefied "continental philosophy" establishment out there, which increasingly included people from French and English and Comparative Literature. There was talk of a Yale School, and a book had just been published, with articles from the members of that club, that was to be found in what were then the moribund or just plain dead philosophy shelves in university bookstores throughout the country. Derrida's work was being increasingly translated, and it was to be the new trend, or it already was, in "literary theory." People had heard of literary theory at the time, and we all had to read Wayne Booth and the Russian formalists and Joseph Frank and Wolfgang Iser and Hans Robert Jauss in addition to a little Roland Barthes, who was more confusing, a little Hans-Georg Gadamer and Michel Foucault, and an assorted series of French names that made similar claims—they were "similar" because they were all theoretical: it was a matter of a new language first of all, and at the time it was the "new" part as such that mattered; if you were serious enough, you would subscribe to *Diacritics*—what an exciting and incomprehensible nightmare to have to read through it—and to *New Literary History* (more stolid, good, useful, but a bit boring, when all was said and

. done). This was not quite philosophy, hence it could be ours, but it was not quite, not quite, literary theory, and that was a problem, because what were we to do if we could not use that stuff for our exclusively literary critical endeavors, which is all the department wanted and supported? And feminism? Some professors in English mentioned Julia Kristeva, and Luce Irigaray, and Sarah Kofman, and Hélène Cixous, and it did not seem to be the same as the sociological North American stuff. It was also new. But it took time.

I got into all of it. I had finished my philosophy studies in Barcelona as an incipient Nietzschean and Deleuzian, but in Georgia I really got into Derrida and before him, into Heidegger (thanks to Dauenhauer, my mentor in theoretical issues). And I wrote my dissertation—what was supposed to be the introductory chapter, a way of prefacing my proper literary criticism, became the whole dissertation, and José Lezama Lima and Severo Sarduy and James Joyce were short-shrifted into the final chapter. But I had finished a book on deconstruction (later published as *Interpretación y diferencia*), and my dissertation committee, as my advisor José Luis Gómez Martínez regretfully told me, said they would not deal with it, they would not read it, they could not understand it. I almost quit and applied to law schools; it was perhaps too bad that a compromise was reached through their generosity, although I did not change a word. And by the time I started my first job at the University of Wisconsin in 1987, well, there were a few people there who knew what I was wanting to talk about. And for me that was the beginning of a beautiful friendship.

I am talking about Brett Levinson and Marco Dorfsman and Lori Hopkins, and a few more students, most of them from Comparative Literature. We created the Theory Colloquium, which was soon accused of all kinds of things, including arms smuggling, and between skirmishes and defensive operations, we managed to attend almost every one of the Midwest Modern Language Association annual meetings, great fun at the time, where we were able to find some accomplices and a new host of enemies. The first split in the theory crowd, alas, had started to develop, and those of us into deconstruction were deemed to be never Marxist or "political" enough, never feminist enough, never enough into the various identitarian causes that were already proliferating as a sort of poor man's (and woman's) theory thing. The suspicion—certainly for those of us who were not protected through being perceived as "white," or by the elite reputation of our universities and our major professors, as the Yale and Hopkins people were—of not being correct enough in our politics, of being, say, a little skeptical not as to feminism but certainly about some of the concrete feminists surrounding us, and it must be understood that to come under such a suspicion amounted to falling under the *mysterium tremendum* of social death in the US academy, was always, and still is, a Damocles sword hanging over our heads, and whatever we do or say never matters, because these things are solved by those who count, bless their souls, at the level of rumor and malicious whisper. Or even: it is a question of odor, not honor, like it was for the perhaps perfectly devout new Christian who could not avoid falling into the hands of the Green Cross because everybody knows his skin lacked the luster of the pork fat he does not eat, which made him a marrano, and screw him. In the words of some assistant state attorney in the TV series *Billions*: "If someone says Charlie fucked a goat, even if the goat says no, Charlie will go to his grave as Charlie the Goatfucker." Well, for the longest time the deconstructionists, or at least some of us, and certainly in Latin American studies, have been considered more or less eternal goatfuckers by the academic mob out there. Let them say no if they want to now.

It was not easy to keep one's head on one's shoulders, as condemnation was pretty fierce, but there came a point, subtly, stealthily, perhaps in the very early 1990s, when the theory people (all of a sudden it was not "literary theory" anymore, just theory, though some people added "critical," but was that not the Frankfurt School?) had reached such a critical mass that the enemy hordes started relenting and retreating to their winter quarters. We could look forward, perhaps, to some years of being left, if not alone, then perhaps less than persecuted at least in our own departments. Then I went to Duke, not on my theory credentials, since they were still not presentable for any Latin Americanist, and one rather needed to conceal them, but rather following my wife, Teresa Vilarós. And then, once there, I suppose they had to hire me. And at Duke there was no interest in deconstruction—one had to be a little careful, which I have never been, not very, but the university was rich enough, and generous enough, and liberal enough that one did not have to fight for resources. They ended up allowing me to do whatever I wanted to do in the Romance Studies Department (the Literature Program was a lot more territorial, and certainly hostile to deconstruction at the end of the day). And we had a great time, partially through luck—it turned out that Gareth Williams, a fellow Latin Americanist deconstructionist, got himself a job at North Carolina State University, and Brett Levinson had a partner from Wisconsin, Ellen Risholm, hired by the Duke German Department, so he kept coming down a lot, and we had many meetings and dinners and parties and conversations, and I had made friends in Chile—Nelly Richard and Willy Thayer and Pablo Oyarzún and Federico Galende, all of whom had a serious interest in deconstruction—and I was able to invite all of them to come, sometimes several times and for a full semester, and some of our colleagues in the History Department, like Danny James, were very sympathetic and interested in what we were doing.

The activity at Duke was very absorbing, and I had little kids and the obligation to obtain tenure, so I stopped paying real attention to what was going on in other places. I know what others were doing in some other universities around the same years, but not what they were doing everywhere, and I would certainly refrain from making any kind of claim that, if there is to be talk, even minimal, of a deconstruction turn in Latin American studies, it started at Duke, and it started in the mid-1990s precisely with that group, to which we must add the different generations of students: here I must mention Idelber Avelar, Adriana Johnson, Horacio Legrás, Jon Beasley-Murray, Ryan Long, Alessandro Fornazzari, Marta Hernández, Isis Sadek, Óscar Cabezas, and Kate Jenckes in particular (and also Elizabeth Collingwood-Selby, who was a doctoral student with us for one year, until she decided to go back to Chile) as those whom I felt intellectually close to, and whose work it can be said has been impacted by deconstruction. Also part of the Duke constellation of those years were John Kraniauskas (not a deconstructor, never a deconstructor to his own mind, but a deconstructor nevertheless, given the nature of his Marxist work) and Sergio Villalobos (who came to Duke to give a talk during the second semester of his first doctoral year at Pittsburgh, when Federico Galende was a visiting professor). Not too many of us, after all, never too many, but we had friends and colleagues, and they would come to our gatherings, and students from other departments, particularly from History, or Anthropology, and Literature, and we talked with them, and we invited many people over, and something was going on that was, if not world-changing, certainly world-building for us. But those were also the years of the Latin American Subaltern Studies Group, which turned out to be a mistake, as already explained.

We should have seen it coming, from the first meeting of the group to which we were invited, held in Puerto Rico at the Hostería del Mar in 1996.[3] I do not intend to blame anyone in particular for what happened, not even by implication, but those of us who had just been invited—Gareth Williams, Kraniauskas, and myself, among others—were already old enough to understand that it was going to be very difficult to keep together a group that was, to start with, crisscrossed by all kinds of emotional tensions and political passions, if we joined it—for no good reason other than our own respect for the founding members and our interest in being part of an intergenerational collective—and brought to it what would end up being seen as an irreconcilable intellectual and ideological difference of opinions. I will not speak for Gareth or John, but I do not mind admitting that I was clueless enough to believe that an earnest attitude of friendship and commitment should and would be sufficient to guarantee a comfortable space of critical plurality and exchange of perspectives for everyone.

It was not to be, and some of us, those who were more junior then, probably ended up suffering more than our share until the group broke up shortly after the "Cross-Genealogies and Subaltern Knowledges" conference at Duke in the fall of 1998. Let me simply evoke the moment to say what I think is the case, which is that after that conference, in a clearly reductive manner, the notion that there was a group in the professional field that thought of themselves as people engaged in (overly radical forms of) subalternist deconstruction, or deconstructive subalternism, was given *patente de corso* (consent to pursue). That the group included—phantasmatically, for the fact is the group never existed as such—people for whom deconstruction was not a real formative influence (Danny James, Jon Beasley-Murray, John Kraniauskas), and, in the uninformed eyes of many, also people who had perhaps been astute enough not to want to join the subalternist enterprise, like Idelber Avelar, seemed irrelevant. We had been tagged as more or less young (I was around forty at the time), ambitious Turks, and interviews and position papers started appearing in which we were accused of being opportunists; careerists; Eurocentric postmodernists; anarchists; even, in a notorious episode, Calvinists; and certainly bent not so secretly on hijacking the Latin American Subaltern Studies Group for our own nefarious and nihilistic purposes. (This theme of nihilism, by the way, is an interesting shibboleth for our antagonists, who have never stopped using it and will no doubt continue to use it: a useful word, to their minds, but always for banal purposes and undistinguishable in spirit from the same word when used by Catholic *integristes* or Islamic fundamentalists; it only means they think we believe in nothing and we are diabolical, and someday it will be good to study to what extent so many of the so-called controversies in the North American humanities have as their point of origin the parochial stupidity of so many professors who are like small-town rentiers. The problem is, of course, what they kill before it can be born.) And that killed everything, but at the same time it was, paradoxically, the sanction given by the professional field for something like a deconstruction turn in Latin American cultural studies. So, if there was a deconstruction turn, it was already born with that kind of heavy lead in its wings.

In the meantime, however, dissertations and monographs from people in our circles—those not terminally terrified yet—were being written and would start appearing soon. And, of course, many articles were already being published. I will not talk about the latter for lack of space, but if, for the sake of historiographic punctiliousness, we date the first books that could possibly be considered at the outer limit of this turn to my own *Interpretación y diferencia* (1991) and to Brett Levinson's *Secondary Moderns* (1996), I think it is fair to say that those two books are isolated when they appear and therefore not yet really part of any deconstruction turn in Latin American studies as such. But Levinson's *Ends of Literature* (2002), Idelber Avelar's *Untimely Present* (1999), Gareth Williams's *Other Side of the Popular* (2002), Danny James's *Doña María's Story: Life History, Memory, and Political Identity* (2001), and my own *Tercer espacio* (1999) and *Exhaustion of Difference* (2001) are. Other books would follow, and I cannot be exhaustive, but I would like to mention twenty of them or so, some of them long in the making, which were inevitably published after the very word "deconstruction" seemed to have become a thing of the past in standard critical usage. And yet many of those books are among the best the field has offered during the period. They are Levinson's *Market and Thought* (2004); Nelly Richard's *Masculine/Feminine* (2004) and *The Insubordination of Signs* (2004); David Johnson and Scott Michaelsen's *Anthropology's Wake* (2008), and Johnson's *Kant's Dog* (2013); Patrick Dove's *The Catastrophe of Modernity* (2004); Horacio Legrás's *Literature and Subjection* (2008); Kate Jenckes's *Reading Borges after Benjamin* (2007); Elizabeth Collingwood-Selby's *El filo fotográfico de la historia* (2009); Jon Beasley-Murray's *Posthegemony* (2010); Adriana Johnson's *Sentencing Canudos* (2010); Ryan Long's *Fictions of Totality* (2008); Williams's *The Mexican Exception* (2011); Alessandro Fornazzari's *Speculative Fictions* (2013); Federico Galende's *Filtraciones* (2007–2011), *La oreja de los nombres* (2005), and *Walter Benjamin y la destrucción* (2009); Willy Thayer's *El fragmento repetido* (2006) and *Tecnologías de la crítica* (2010); Óscar Cabezas's *Postsoberanía* (2013); Sergio Villalobos's *Soberanías en suspenso* (2013); Bram Acosta's *Thresholds of Illiteracy* (2014); Erin Graff Zivin's *Figurative Inquisitions* (2014); and my own *Línea de sombra* (2007).

The list is important not just for its own sake. Any reader familiar with a sampling of the books will immediately recognize that "deconstruction" is used here as a tag for a very mixed bag, and that the proper and genuine deconstruction establishment (it exists) would not open the gate for many of them—they would be found insufficiently deconstructive. And yet such is the way of things, and if there is to be talk of a deconstruction turn in Latin American cultural and literary studies, taking deconstruction only in the weak sense specified above, then these are the books, it seems to me, through which one could start to unravel the constellation. They are all, for the most part, Latin Americanist books that aspire to stay away from any kind of dogmatic claim at the level of identitarian or geopolitical formation, that are reluctant to engage in any substantialization of the concept of culture, that do not pursue the literary in any exegetic-paraphrastic way, and that have no interest in national or even continental traditions of constitution. They all privilege reading the historical text from a sort of theoretical force that itself remains at the level of desire, or drive, and is never articulated as a grid for systematic deciphering. They are all politically critical, committed to a certain notion of democracy that is not the liberal one, but skeptical of any kind of prescriptive conceptualization regarding how to move forward socially. They are the books that some of us have been able to produce, often against odds of various kinds, while taking all the risks one takes when one attempts to step out of disciplinary boxes. Although there may be no overwhelming reason to pretend such a list beats any other comparable list produced by our professional field, whether in previous generations or in the wake of some other cluster of intellectual influences, it is simply the list we have (although far from complete). And I think it may be allowed to feel a certain amount of pride in itself. But is that, now, enough?

III

What was John Beverley thinking when he said, in his *Latinamericanism after 9/11*, that it would be dangerous to equate Latin Americanism with deconstruction, or to think that deconstruction can constitute "a new form of Latinamericanism" (52)? He is right of course: it is a dangerous and, moreover, an absurd thing to do. He is doing me the honor of glossing two quasi-concepts I offered in *Exhaustion*, namely, "dirty atopianism" and "savage hybridity." He says:

> Dirty atopianism, Moreiras explains, "is the name for a nonprogramma-
> ble program of thinking that refuses to find satisfaction in expropriating at
> the same time that it refuses to fall into appropriative drives" (23). "Savage

hybridity" flows from this. As opposed to "cultural hybridity," where, as in Laclau's well-known formulation of "hegemonic articulation," a given cultural feature or artifact can be posited as an "empty signifier" for the "national" or collective as such, "savage hybridity is simply the recognition that every claim to totalization of identity, where the one is made to stand for the many, including the claim of hegemonic articulation itself, ultimately lacks foundation . . . As the 'other side' of the hegemonic relationship, savage hybridity preserves, or holds in reserve, the site of the subaltern, just as it preserves the site of a subalternist politics. It is not so much a locus of enunciation as it is an atopic site, not a place for ontopologies but a place for the destabilization of all ontopologies, for a critique of totality—*and* a place for the possibility of an *other* history." (52)

This is the moment when Beverley says I come very close to "proposing deconstruction itself as a new form of Latinamericanism" (52). But it seems to me that it is not deconstruction that has been invoked by me in any of the segments of the long quote. What I was invoking then was rather an attempt to move past the politics of hegemony. With that caveat, I declare myself guilty of proposing or having proposed in the past a posthegemonic Latin Americanist reflection, in the weak sense of a reflection on Latin American issues that does not take hegemony as the alpha and omega of political articulation, whether on the side of the liberal criollo elite or on the side of any conceivable noncriollo, indigenous, popular, or subaltern counterhegemonic push. The question as to whether there needs to be an identification between posthegemony and deconstruction should be answered in the negative, even factically, since Beasley-Murray's proposal and extended presentation of posthegemony in Latin America not only does not claim deconstruction but in fact militates against it. And of course there could be any number of variations on the notion of posthegemony in addition to Beasley-Murray's or mine. Deconstruction makes no particular claim to possess posthegemony, and yet it likes it, or it should, for reasons I will try to mention in a minute.

Beverley is moving toward establishing his conclusion, according to which both any deconstructive "critique of the 'ontotheological' character of politics and the apocalyptic ultraleftism of . . . 'posthegemony' . . . involve in fact a renunciation of actual politics, which means that despite their claim to be 'transformative,' they remain complicit with the existing order of things" (58). Provided, of course, one should say, following the tenor of Beverley's book, that the existing order of things be neoliberal, not postsubalternist. But the problem is, what if what is ontotheological in non-neoliberal politics is not all other politics but the particular brand of postsubalternist hegemonic politics Beverley endorses, and with him so many other enthusiastic sponsors of either instrumental subservience to whoever serves or seems to serve the popular cause or the neo-communitarian consensual authoritarianism?

Any continuation of a deconstruction turn in Latin American studies in general should probably, at this stage, attempt to move toward a clearer articulation of the stakes. We need to recognize that it is no longer enough simply to write, or continue to write, in the loose invocation of a particular set of texts that have been stimulating in the past, just as it is not enough to define ourselves according to that which we are not (we are, say, not decolonialists, we are not postsubalternists, we are not culturalists, we are not historicists or identitarians, and so forth). The books of the last twenty years may have had a collective effect of bringing the field of reflection into a certain maturity. An element of that maturity is necessarily to understand, first of all, that there is no reason to continue to uphold an always uncertain, improbable, and imaginary state of affairs according to which those of us blessed with the sacred mission of teaching about Latin America in the United States, or elsewhere, should always do so in the name of Latin America itself, or worse, in the name of some Latin Americanism that could only function, and has only functioned for the most part, as a prison for thought—a prison easily surveilled and panopticized by the guardians of political orthodoxy, in which our field, on the right and on the left, has always been plentiful. Getting rid of Latin Americanism in order to liberate the Latin American archive for itself is perhaps the first task of a second-generation deconstructive turn. Latin Americanism has only ever been a metaphor, perhaps useful at the time of the Cold War, or useful to the culturalists or those who believe in some form of "clash" of civilizations, or that the world divides itself into civilizations. Latin Americanism, like the related term "Orientalism," obscures more than it exposes, and it is also too convenient an alibi. But there is another potential task, one that is rather more difficult to undertake.

In 1964–1965, Derrida devoted his seminar at the École Normale Supérieure to the question of being and history in Heidegger's thought. At the end of the sixth seminar session, Derrida says: "Somnambulism is perhaps the very essence of metaphysics" (Derrida, *Heidegger* 228). Metaphysical thought is premised on a certain somnambulism incapable of keeping an open eye on the ceaseless process of metaphorical reification that is metaphysical desire as such. If deconstruction can be politically translated as a de-metaphorization of history on the impossible back of a language without metaphor, then deconstruction is the ongoing process of analyzing and destroying metaphorical investments as formations of power. I want to conclude by suggesting that this work on the radical reduction of metaphor responds to an existential a priori existential condition that, incidentally, simultaneously organizes the drive for posthegemonic politics. It is the task of deconstruction, if one wanted to take it up.

One somnambulistic approach to thinking simply moves on in oblivion of the fact that history is not to be captured by political projections, and even fails to note that its very somnambulism is itself a particular kind of political projection. There is nothing anti-political about this. Derrida is clear enough, in *Specters*, when he maintains that politics, as political philosophy, "structures implicitly all philosophy or all thought on the subject of philosophy" (92). If ontotheology—read: metaphysics—is the hegemonic thought of the West, it thereby follows that the attempt at a non-ontotheological thought must be posthegemonic, and very politically so. Deconstruction's detractors tend to think of it as a merely destructive and negative attempt to ruin every piece of stable meaning, so, for them, it is even worse when deconstruction says it wants to move politically; at that point, clearly, a number of individuals give themselves over to a bad orgy of negativity without the people, without the multitude, without a country, without a program, without a horizon, opportunistically bent on poisoning all the beautiful constructive propositions other members of the profession would have been trying to push forward, either in terms of proper Latin American identity or else on the basis of a rather sui generis version of the Marxist philosophy of history.

But we know enough to know that somnambulism may have caught up with Marxism itself and with so many other kinds of well-intentioned political work, and not once but many times. If somnambulism is the essence of metaphysics, *perhaps*, says Derrida, and metaphysics is the hegemonic thought of the West, and therefore of all territories marked by Western empires, like Latin America, then hegemonic thought and the thought of hegemony is somnambulist or it induces somnambulism. To want to wake up, to expose oneself to the trauma of awakening, to abandon oneiric metaphorization, to de-metaphorize the dream of reason, not for the sake of an impossible full or literal language, and still less for the sake of a truth constitutive of a new subject, but rather in the name of a future and of the preparation for a future that we do not yet know but that might imply the de-activation of every presently living metaphor (and is that not what is already happening?)—such might be the project of a new historicity, perhaps revolutionary but not instrumentalizing, never aiming for a new capture of history by allegedly progressive ideology. To return to Derrida's 1964–1965 seminar, if the thought of the truth of being (deconstruction, notwithstanding its perpetual feud with Heidegger, is fundamentally a thought of the ontological difference, of the truth of being as opposed to beings, of the trace-structure of being in beings, or it is nothing, and this would be my strong definition of deconstruction), if the thought of the truth of being is to come but to come as what has always already been buried, in other words, if the structure of the to-come is also the structure of the always-already, then perhaps the political dimension of deconstruction—the notorious democracy-to-come—is also at the same time an a priori existential that first presents itself at a level other than the political. Releasing thought on uncaptured life is also a style of life. A second-generation deconstruction should perhaps move without reservation toward it, politically if one wants, but for the sake of the element in politics that founds its very pertinence, and against every instrumentalization and capture.

Another type of somnambulist appears in the Derridean text. In an essay entitled "Penser ce que vient," published in 2007 but partially read as a lecture a little before the publication of *Specters*, in 1992, Derrida also talks about somnambulism, except that, this time, the somnambulist does not embody the essence of metaphysics. Rather, this time, the sleeper takes upon herself the "absolute risk," beyond knowledge and philosophy, "beyond all models and all prescriptive norms in whose exhaustion we live" (46), of attempting a thought of the to-come/always-already "that resembles the dream of the poetic, with the reservation of thinking the dream otherwise" (46). Derrida wonders about the aplomb of the somnambulist to think the future and links it, strangely, to a word of Lenin on the disjunction or non-adequation between dream and life, on which, he says, the very possibility of justice depends (61–62).

Thirty years will have passed between the tentative affirmation of somnambulism as the essence of metaphysics and the vindication of a certain poetic somnambulism, able to keep the disjunction of the future open. It would be excessive for us to require terminological consistency here, after such a long period of time. Derrida's first somnambulist appears in a particular context. He has just questioned those who, in the wake of Nietzsche, Freud, or Marx, are looking to "solicit" the privilege of consciousness and try to present it as a mere misunderstanding. Things are not so easy. Only an arduous confrontation with Being-as-Presence as the fundamental determination of metaphysical Being, which means only a confrontation with Hegel as the thinker in whose work metaphysics closes in upon itself, hence lets its end be seen, can preempt "gestures of aggression to metaphysics or transcendental idealism [from] remaining prisoners of that at which they aim" (228). In the absence of such a confrontation, the efficacy of the debunkers of consciousness "will have a somnambulistic style." That somnambulism might well be the essence of metaphysics therefore, first of all, means: a confrontation with metaphysical thought that does not elude the fundamental consideration of the forgetting of being as the temporal horizon of being is necessary—in other words, a confrontation with a horizon of thought that brings the alternative thought of the ontico-ontological difference into play also at the political level.

There are two somnambulists: the metaphysical one, who cannot awake from metaphor, who lives in metaphor, and the poetic one, who assumes the risk of what she could not do while awake. There is no conciliation, but their opposition is not total. The first somnambulist has, after all, a de-metaphorizing intuition and refuses to listen to stories about consciousness, self-consciousness, and the subjective domain, from which the second somnambulist has also adjured. It is not enough. If somnambulists live the metaphoric dream, in nonvigilance on the metaphoric character of language, "we could call thought and thought of being (the thought of being constituting the horizon and the call for an impossible non-metaphoric language) what calls for [a] gesture of de-metaphorization" (278). In the final conclusions of his 1964–1965 seminar, Derrida insists: "The thought of being announces the horizon of non-metaphor starting from which one can think metaphoricity . . . it is announced as the impossible on whose back the possible is thinkable as such" (323).

There is a problem with somnambulism, just like there is a problem with de-metaphorization. They need to be worked out. Derrida never again spoke as clearly as he did in the 1964–1965 seminar about de-metaphorization as the awakening of thought, and about de-metaphorization as deconstruction, and about deconstruction as a means to access being as difference (or, soon, *différance*). But he started there. A possible second-order deconstruction in Latin American studies or wherever else could do likewise. In the epigraph to this essay, extracted from Pablo d'Ors's novel, it is said that, given a literal and a figural term, given a gap that both links and separates empirical reality and regulating ideal, it is not necessarily easy to discern which of the two instances is the metaphoric one. The political application of de-metaphorization preempts the security of any hegemonic demand or negotiation on the basis of too premature a naturalization of the figural plane into the literal plane. We do not know what a life without metaphor might be. We do know or may intuit what metaphors betray.

Chapter 6

WE HAVE GOOD REASONS FOR THIS (AND THEY KEEP COMING)

Revolutionary Drive and Democratic Desire

To Bruno and Fred, in memory of old friendship

> The sort of abstract domination constituted by labor in capitalism is the domination of time.
>
> MOISHE POSTONE, "Rethinking Marx (in a Post-Marxist World)"

I

Yes, if we are to believe some of our favorite master thinkers, a specter runs again through the halls of the academic-theoretical enterprise, and it is the specter of a communism or a neo-communism. Jodi Dean says: "It seems more and more that the left has worked or is working through its melancholia" (176). What remains to be seen, to use Dean's own words, is whether the specter is back in ways that do not conform to a merely voluntaristic revival consistent with communicative capitalism: "This decline in a capacity to transmit meaning, to symbolize beyond a limited discourse or immediate, local context, characterizes communication's reconfiguration into a primarily economic form. It produces for circulation, not use" (127). The question, I want to point out, is already a Marxist question, if Marxism is indeed a theory that must account for "the possibility of its own standpoint" (Postone 4). Is communist desire today, as conveyed by academic-theoretical contributions, the anticipation and reflection of a possibility of use, or is it yet another commodity, that is, another example of the "commodity-determined form of social relations" (Postone 10) prevalent in academia as it is prevalent in every other labor sphere?

The question could be dismissed as irrelevant. It could be thought that if social relations are necessarily commodity determined, then no new, or new/old, theoretical stand could be proposed that did not always already incorporate the commodity form through its own self-projection. At the same time, it might be opportune to linger with the question in this particular case, to the extent that the proposal for communism, or for neo-communism, has to do with suspending the commodity form as the determining referent of social relations. This chapter will do just that: it will attempt to read Jodi Dean's *Communist Horizon* and Bruno Bosteels's *Actuality of Communism* against the background of their own presuppositions, with a view to asking whether they succeed in establishing what they ostensibly aim to establish: that they announce a genuine possibility of use (critical use, political use) that will break through the impasses and limitations of so many other theoretical or theoretico-political positions, which they variously criticize as thoroughly captured by, respectively, "democratic drives" (Dean) or "speculative leftism" (Bosteels).

I will not proceed with an extensive review of the two books, partially because there is much in them I agree with, and partially because I do not have enough space merely to celebrate their readings of, say, contemporary political ontology, Slavoj Zizek's notion of the political act, or "the nonhistorical and apolitical condition of politics itself" (Bosteels 137) in Bosteels's book, or of the party form in politics ("a politics without the organizational form of the party is a politics without politics" [Dean 19]), the analyses of "communicative capitalism," the "presentation of "the people as the rest of us," or the notion of "present force" ("whereas the Right treats communism as a present force, the Left is bent around the force of loss, that is, the contorted shape it has found itself in as it has forfeited or betrayed the communist ideal" [53]) in Dean's. Instead, I will focus on specific critical points of disagreement, with a view to making a contribution to the discussion they themselves propose. Before getting to them, I must preface at some length.

Let me anticipate by saying that "democratic drives" and "speculative leftism" are strongly polemical terms that Dean and Bosteels, respectively, use to demarcate their position from some netherworld of what they consider more or less desperately erroneous opinions. A secondary but nevertheless significant (to me) strain of my intention in this chapter is perhaps not so much counterpolemical (in the sense that I would like to argue back and eventually disagree with the assessment of the critical antagonisms they locate) as it is only clarifying in nature. Fighting the general confusion in the academic-theoretical enterprise is something we never seem to do enough of—perhaps because there are hidden rewards to the confusion

itself, allowing us to proliferate our position-taking within a sea of ambiguous conceptual determinations and diffuse constellations of sympathies
and antipathies, above all in the political terrain (which is the only terrain
Dean or Bosteels care to occupy).

I will use as a critical prop Fredric Jameson's "Political Conclusions,"
the last chapter of his book *Representing* Capital: *A Reading of Volume One*,
to keep within the horizon of Marxist or communist presuppositions. In
turn, something in Jameson's argument will enable me to pursue my reluc-
tantly quixotic process of theoretico-political clarification vis-à-vis another
strand of thought relevant to my field of endeavor, namely, the decolonial
critique of domination (with which Dean and Bosteels may have issues in
part similar to my own). My contention will be that the decolonial option
is for circulation rather than use and, as such, is a prepackaged commodity for compensatory consumption, a *pharmakon* whose auto-immunitary,
poisonous side we ignore at our peril. This detour is necessary to my overall argument, since Bosteels's book ends by offering a strong endorsement
of Álvaro García Linera's Marxist-indigenist project for Bolivia as a precise example of what his proposal for a "communism of communisms"
might mean, and one, furthermore, that emphasizes "the emancipatory
potential coming from the extremities of the capitalist body" (257). Let me
demarcate García Linera's project from the decolonial critique of domination, which Bosteels also does, even if not very explicitly: García Linera
is a Marxist philosopher who works for the possibility of an integration
of indigenous demands into a fully universalist, communist project. And
yet he does it in ways that are only questionably communist or even neo-
communist. I will not be able to approach that subject in this chapter (I
have done it elsewhere).[1] But my detour through the decolonial position
fulfills the interest of clarification I referred to above.

II

We might disagree, but we need to take seriously (as opposed to thinking
that he cannot possibly mean it) Jameson's contention, speaking as a
Marxist, that political theory, which is "always in one way or another constitutional theory" (139), and therefore the very concept of democracy, are
"decisively disabled" by the introduction of money, first, by Locke and,
later, capital (140): "With the emergence of capital, then, a host of the traditional categories of constitutional thinking become unserviceable, among

them citizenship and representation; while the very idea of democracy as such—always a pseudo-concept and for most of its historical existence in any case a term of opprobrium—becomes a misleading illusion" (140). To that extent, he says, Marx's mature thought as elaborated in *Capital* does not offer any political conclusions. Or not at the theoretical level, as there is a "tactical or strategic sense" of politics in which "Marx . . . was also a political genius, and . . . (like Lenin) 'thought politically' all the time and always had a keen eye for the political possibilities of any given situation or conjuncture, in that also very much like Lenin himself" (143). But our enthusiasm wanes when Jameson declares that, therefore, "both were pre-eminently and in the best sense of the term opportunists: and that both, in keeping with Machiavelli's teaching and example, were capable of the most astonishing turns and reversals, and placing the value of the concrete analysis of the situation or conjuncture higher than faithfulness to any preconceived principles" (143).

We are all, I suppose, for a-principial or an-archic thought, and we all hate preconceptions, but one needs to wonder whether opportunism, even in the best of senses and with the best of intentions, is truly a-principial and nonpreconceived or rather the very opposite of it.[2] "Placing the value of the concrete analysis of the situation or conjuncture higher than faithfulness" to a cause means exactly that a more or less disavowed principle of self-advantage creeps in as the right justification for action or reaction. In other words, in Jameson's formulation, we are not even in the Machiavellian realm of means justified by ends, which can hardly be classified as opportunism, unless ends are immediately conceived of as self-serving. The problem here is not a trivial one, and it has haunted actually existing communist politics for most of the twentieth century and counting: from the political position Jameson opens up, saying in effect that there is no other available, one must conclude that the true political struggle, at least within capitalism ("surely there has . . . been a long history of political invention under socialism" [141]), and as we await its final crisis and the advent of the association of free producers, consists of always looking for one's advantage, perhaps including the advantage of one's comrades (so that we can turn our personal position into a collective one), insofar as they don't go silly, or become inconvenient, interfering with my advantage, in which case they will have to be removed from the scene, if I can afford it, and whatever it takes (actually, a position that has a very sinister but well-known track record in the history of the Left). The previous renunciation or dismissal of democracy as a pseudo-concept and misleading illusion seems to confirm it. I don't see the humor in the strong association of communism and opportunism.

The question is then worth raising as to whether Jameson is not falling, on this particular point, *contra* Marx, into a regression toward the notion of "private property" that he affirms threw a monkey wrench into and made unserviceable any political theory in Locke's time: "The intervention of this foreign body [money] into a system of abstractions that are formally unable to accommodate it or to theorize it means that political theory—constitutional theory—is no longer able to function autonomously; and the name for that moment is 'private property'—a reality utterly recalcitrant to constitutional construction" (140). Opportunism, in effect, incompatible with democratic thought, is only acceptable once one considers the political realm either nonexistent (a "misleading illusion") or exhaustively contained by the notion of the world as private property, whether the latter is personal or collective, held in my own name or in the name of the party, and so forth.

Jameson does not clarify whether "private property" holds the same relationship with capital as it does with money. But Moishe Postone has attempted to reconstitute Marxism otherwise, still on the basis of Marx's *Capital* but against what he considers a mostly outdated Marxist tradition, as a theory "that must be based on a conception of capitalism that does not conceptualize the most fundamental social relations of that society in terms of class relations structured by private ownership of the means of production and the market" (7). It is not private property that defines capitalism's specificity, but rather, in Postone's terms, the commodity or the commodity form, which, as a category of social practice, "is a structuring principle of the actions, world views and dispositions of people" (8). The commodity is abstract labor, and it is abstract labor that determines social interdependence in capitalism as "the domination of time" (10). If so, then it is not private property that conditions, or ruins, the very possibility of political action in capitalist conditions: "Marx's mature theory of social constitution is not one of labor per se, but of labor acting as a socially mediating activity in capitalism. This interpretation transforms the terms of the problem of the relationship between labor and thought" (14), and allows for "a fundamental rethinking of the nature of capitalism and of its possible historical transformation" (15) "inasmuch as it analyzes not only the inequalities of real social power that are inimical to democratic politics, but also reveals as socially constituted, and hence as legitimate objects of political debates, the systemic constraints imposed by capital's global dynamic on democratic self-determination" (16).

We can, therefore, according to Postone, engage in democratic politics in an attempt to undo or loosen up the domination of time through the social mediation of labor, which remains the goal of what I would consider a good Marxian politics within, but necessarily also beyond (whenever or wherever there is a beyond), capitalist rule. There is a disagreement here that will reveal its fundamental importance, I think, as we move into the core of Jameson's "Political Conclusions." The latter are prefaced by a reference to Karl Korsch's "two fundamental languages" of Marxism, namely, "the 'objective' description of the historical process as a development of the productive forces and the 'subjective' description of history as class struggle are two independent forms of Marxian thought, equally original and not derived from one another . . . they are to be applied singly or together to the conditions of each given position" (quoted by Jameson 142). So Marxists have a choice, and they can emphasize the systemic constraints in capitalism or choose the vindication of political agency. As to the latter, the problem is that it is "liable to produce a dangerous voluntarism in which the subjects concerned lose any sense of the massive power of the system and are prepared to fling themselves into hopeless struggles and inevitable martyrdom" (144). As to the former, "it should be clear that it encourages fatalism . . . the passive cynicism of the lack of alternatives and the hopelessness and powerlessness of the subjects of such a system, for whom no action is possible or even conceivable" (145).[3]

Predictably, given his views on politics, Jameson prefers the systemic emphasis, while conceding that "it is not at all clear that we are in a situation of massive systemic stability, without any possibility of agency or action" (145). It is, however, the absence of any clear guidelines for anti-systemic action, and the resulting "general confusion," that prompt Jameson's choice and, therefore, what comes to be Jameson's dual corollary to his book: in the first place, "the lesson that capitalism is a total system . . . is designed to demonstrate that it cannot be reformed, and that its repairs, originally intended to prolong its existence, necessarily end up strengthening and enlarging it. This is then an argument against what used to be called social democracy," whose "vocation" is "to keep the total interests of capitalism at heart and to maintain its overall functioning" (146–147). The second conclusion moves beyond negation and supplements Korsch's two fundamental languages with a pair derived from Louis Althusser: "the tension between the categories of domination and of exploitation" (149). Jameson unequivocally chooses exploitation as the useful one, since domination appears as the secondary result of the structure of exploitation and "also the mode of its reproduction rather than of its production" (150).

It is interesting that Jameson selects anarchism as the holder of the antithetical position, that is, the position that privileges domination as a hermeneutic category for political action. Jameson names this option "an essentially moral or ethical" one, "which leads to punctual revolts and acts of resistance rather than to the transformation of the mode of production as such" (151): "the outcome of an emphasis on exploitation is a socialist program, while that of an emphasis on domination is a democratic one, a program and a language only too easily and often co-opted by the capitalist state" (150). So, finally, Jameson comes back to politics through his militant assertion that it is through an emphasis on the modalities of exploitation under conditions of globalization, which produce massive unemployment, hence the disenfranchisement of life now turned into "naked life in all the metaphysical senses in which the sheer biological temporality of existences without activity and without production can be interpreted" (151). It is a focus on global unemployment, as the specific aspect of the domination of time in globalization, rather than some other "tragic pathos," that can recommit us "to the invention of a new kind of transformatory politics on a global scale" (151).

I endorse the cause of a transformatory politics on a global scale, and I think it should be pursued, to the extent of our ability, through a critique of exploitation *and* domination, for the sake of a democratic future rid of the fundamental theft of time that determines or is conditioned by capitalism's innermost structure. That might make me a communist or not—I suppose this is merely a terminological issue. Jameson himself concludes his book, as we just saw, appealing to a "new kind" of transformatory politics, which is clearly a rejection of old communism in terms of tactics and strategies. But communism can surely reinvent itself, and the reinvention should include abjuring from its undemocratic past. Old communism's massive opportunism, its arrogant dogmatism in thought and practice, its reification of thought, both assumed and pursued in blind fidelity to the demands of despotic leadership—those are means we would not want and ends we should despise. So there is much I agree with in Jameson's argument, but I take exception to the cavalier dismissal of democracy, which for me should not just be an instrument but the very end of the transformatory politics he himself recommends. Even if we accept Jameson's determination of what has been called social democracy as a finally counterproductive structuration of political life under capitalist conditions (all the while better than its alternatives, all things considered), there can be no good revolutionary horizon that does not at the same time incorporate and seek a deep democratic habit whose coming into existence would itself be revolutionary, if not the very justification of revolution itself, and that needs to be prepared in thought as well as in personal and professional practice, since it cannot be prepared anywhere else. From what we can see, this is easier said than done.

I also agree with Jameson's emphasis on a critique of exploitation rather than domination. Jameson's explanation of his position is understated for obvious political reasons, but I suspect it is not just anarchism as such that is targeted, but much of what goes under the name of identity thinking and postcolonial studies as well. His only indication in this regard is the following rather cryptic comment: "'Imperialism' is indeed a useful conceptual space in which to demonstrate the way in which an economic category can so easily modulate into a concept of power or domination (and it is clear that the word 'exploitation' is itself scarcely immune from such slippage either)" (151). In any case, it is rather misleading in today's political context to claim that it is the anarchists who primarily privilege domination; it is rather the full array of postcolonialists and identitarians. But perhaps there would be a certain risk in stating the latter, which is not totally all right from an opportunist's perspective. In the next section of this chapter, and still in preparation for what I would like to say on Dean's and Bosteels's books, I will attempt to make clear why much domination critique is insufficient, misleading, and therefore unsatisfactory from the point of view of any conceivable "transformatory politics on a global scale." I will focus on a single essay by the Puerto Rican sociologist Ramón Grosfoguel, as it sums up the dominant strand of anti-colonial thought (both postcolonial and identitarian) for Latin America at present.

III

The Grosfoguel article in question is entitled "La descolonización de la economía política y los estudios postcoloniales: Transmodernidad, pensamiento fronterizo y colonialidad global" (The decolonization of political economy and postcolonial studies: Transmodernity, border thinking, and global coloniality), and it was published in *Tabula Rasa* in 2006. It is a useful essay given its summary focus—it wants to be a recapitulation of the decolonial position. But it is also useful because of its (relative) quality—it bears saying that decolonialism in general, that is, the style of thought named as such, over-relies on declamatory rhetoric and the production of inspirational blips, and is not sufficiently concerned with the requirements of strong argumentation. Grosfoguel's essay is perhaps a cogent summary of the position at its presumable best.

It starts by summing up Walter Mignolo's introductory essay to the first issue of the journal *Nepantla: Views from South*, glossing some of what had transpired at the "Cross-Genealogies and Subaltern Knowledges" conference at Duke University in the fall of 1998. Mignolo presented there something that Grosfoguel totally endorses, namely, the necessary splitting of the Latin Americanist intelligentsia between the so-called postmoderns and those who, within a matter of years, would come to denominate themselves "decolonialists." For Grosfoguel, who was a participant at the conference, what was determinant was the open gulf between what he perceived as a numerically dominant presence of individuals (I suppose I was one of them) whose work or words were imbued with or contaminated by "European thinking," which made them all complicitous with the intellectual parameters of the so-called area studies apparatus in the US academic system, and the presence of a smaller number of righteous thinkers who of course found themselves in a position of resistance. The first group of participants "reproduced the epistemic schematics" (Grosfoguel 19), that is, the habitual imperialist and Eurocentric state of affairs, on two main grounds: they appealed to Western thinkers, such as Jacques Derrida, Antonio Gramsci, Michel Foucault, or Karl Marx, over against "racial and ethnic perspectives from the region." And they "produced studies on subalternity rather than studies 'together with' and 'from' subaltern thinkers and movements" (19). Never mind that Indian subalternism was also a reference for this group (Ranajit Guha, Gayatri Spivak, Dipesh Chakrabarty), since for Grosfoguel, Indian subalternism was equally guilty of privileging an exclusively Western epistemology, which meant that the radicality of their critique was constrained within the circle of Eurocentrism. Grosfoguel tells us he could only feel "unsatisfaction with the project" (19), giving us, by the way, perfect confirmation of the purity of his Latin and Puerto Rican being in some secret and tellurian vein. A minor concession is that at least the Indian critique of modernity was attempted "from the global South," which made it morally superior to a critique from "the global North," which is all the Latin Americanist subalternists (other than the righteous ones) managed or were managing to do (19). Grosfoguel's conclusion is that, under such conditions, it was necessary to attempt a thorough "decolonization" of everyone: subaltern studies, postcolonial studies, postmodern studies—which, of course, he courageously undertook to do.

So, according to Grosfoguel, a proper Latin Americanist, in order to do Latin Americanist work, should not use sources that are alien to the Latin American region, though with a radical, looping-the-loop caveat: those proper sources should not just be Latin American but should in fact themselves emanate from "ethnic and racial" sources other than European ones (19). Thought is just pure originary or postoriginary location, and location is pure self-determination: for a subaltern, Eurocentric-resistant position, nothing that does not come into being as thinkable from the sources of the non-European tradition should be thought, and nothing without an indigenous, or at the most afro-indigenous, certifiable provenance should be taken into account. Grosfoguel is still echoing Mignolo, who in his introduction to Rodolfo Kusch's *Indigenous and Popular Thinking in América* offered perhaps the clearest (and most brutal, except that decoloniality is already a form of brutal thought) formulation of the prescription: "If one is of European descent in América, one has two options: the imperial one, following European ideas, subjectivities, and global designs, or the de-colonial one. But the de-colonial option is not just joining Indians and Afro descendants in their claims and protests. It is to embrace their epistemology, thinking through their categories" (xx). So it is not just hapless Latin Americanists who should be decolonized, but also all Latin Americans of European descent—and decolonized, first of all and primarily, from themselves, which throws a curious little wrench into the locationalist principle (perfectly unnoticed by Grosfoguel, of course): since one is always somewhere, even the Latin Americans of European descent are somewhere, but they are out of luck, because their somewhere is, by definition, always necessarily misplaced, always necessarily to be dismissed. We are not far from the insinuation of a Maoist-style necessary collective reeducation at a continental level, which no doubt remains an essential part of the decolonial dream.

Grosfoguel goes on to establish that thought only ever happens (from) somewhere, which phenomenon deserves two distinct names: the first name is "geopolitics of knowledge," meaning that, as soon as you speak, you speak from the earth ("geo-"), from your place on earth, tellurically, rootedly; and the second, clumsier name is "corpopolitics of knowledge," which adds the dimension of corporeality to the earthly one: you speak not just from an earth, but also from a body. The proper name should therefore be "corpo-geo-politics," except that such a term would invite infinite self-proliferation: "corpo-geo-sexo-neumo-raciopolitics" would be even more appropriate, and so forth. But the point Grosfoguel is making, perhaps counterintentionally, is that one only ever speaks from power, from empowerment, great or small, and there is no way out—power, much or little, understood as self-legitimation and self-grounding, is the irreducible condition of locationalist thought. Westerners, for instance, are also necessarily locationalist thinkers, speaking always and everywhere from power, except that the self-claimed power of the Westerners is a power of domination that hides itself as such, seeking shelter in some kind of "zero point" or "God's eye" (2). Westerners speak from God's eye because their position of enunciation, as power, claims universal power, that is, infinite power.

The dialectical turn here will have implications: power is the irreducible condition of speech, but the supreme power is the forgetting and negation of locationalist speech by virtue of its subsumption into infinity as proper location: which of course (perhaps with a little help from military and economic instruments) establishes simultaneously the sheer, naked force of Eurocentrism and the absolute epistemic privilege of nonforgetful locationalist speech as such. Decolonialists are those who refuse to indulge in the negation and forgetting of location as the primary resource of thought, insisting that one only ever speaks from a concrete earth and a concrete body, and thus exposing Western thought to its own disavowed abyss. The decolonial critique of Western thought thus consists of the fact that Western thought suffers from the imaginary malady of hypostatizing its own location as universal, through some grounding hyperpower whose paradoxical result is the forgetting of the necessary concretization of location. Hence, Grosfoguel says, its essential imperialism, through an "eye-of-God" dimension—"theophthalmic," we could say—naturalizes European thought as the very norm of thought. Through this, the European thinker becomes, in every case, a parody of himself or herself, a disgrace, really, and must be reeducated, particularly in the case of European thinkers who do not make Europe the exclusive object of their reflection, for example, us nondecolonial Latin Americanists of the postmodern kind.[4]

The locationalist dimension is one of the two features that have made the fortune of the decolonial option in recent times. It promises a radically dehierarchized, decentralized, horizontalized reception of subaltern (that is, non-Eurocentric, or non-Occidentalist) perspectives, where everybody can claim the radical authority emanating from singular position, whatever it is, and speak from it without even having to worry about critiques from any kind of Western thought, which by definition one should never take up. The common denominator is merely the common shared antagonism, the creation of an enemy, called imperialism, particularly or eminently the imperialism that cannot think of itself as such (but the decolonials always know). The clear identification of an antagonistic pole—the allegedly monologic eye-of-God perspective of Western demeanor, knowledge, and critical theory—has the attraction of a neat division of the political field (within the so-called geopolitics of knowledge) into friends and enemies, à la Carl Schmitt, without, however, imposing on the friends any conditions other than those associated with subaltern provenance: they must be who they always already are and speak only from there, provided a purity has been kept. Particularisms and pluralism are celebrated without restrictions in the name of the accomplishment of something rather laboriously called a "radical anticapitalist, pluriversalist, decolonialist diversality" (44), which would supposedly provide a good resource for comparing notes and preparing a strategy. The strategy is to be prepared for the purpose of the substantiation of a "transmodern, decolonial socialization of power" (13), Grosfoguel says, taking a hint from Aníbal Quijano's notion of the socialization of power, which then constitutes the proper revolutionary-utopian horizon for the adepts of the coloniality of power: "This would imply a certain form of self-administered, global, democratic organization that would function as a global collective authority in order to guarantee justice and social equity at the world scale. The socialization of power at the local and global levels would imply the formation of a public authority outside state structures and against them" (43). It does sound banally utopian, as well as problematic and rather precarious, but that has never stopped any decolonialist.

But the second element of the good fortune of the decolonial option today can only be mediately derived from the first. From radical locationalism we can indeed establish the necessary rejection of any universalist and monologic position, but it is not clear to me how one can move from that rejection to the postulation that Eurocentric monologic universalism, through its eye-of-God perspective, was able to establish universal domination through the simultaneous imposition not of one rule of domination but of many: Grosfoguel counts fourteen on the basis of a little apologue, which hellishly runs: "A heterosexual-white-patriarchal-Christian-military-capitalist-European man arrived in America and established simultaneously in space and time several mutually imbricated global hierarchies that for clarity's sake I will enumerate as if they were separated from each other" (25). They range from full-blown capitalism ("a particular social class formation where a number of forms of labor ... will coexist as a source for the production of surplus value through the sale of commodities in order to obtain benefits in the world market" [24]) to sexual regimes, to racial regimes, to gender regimes, to knowledge regimes, to linguistic domination, to aesthetic domination, to global communications domination, to ageism where the ages between sixteen and sixty-four years are privileged over any other age. The European fellow visited many kinds of monologic evil on an apparently dehierarchized, self-possessed, and fully democratic set of social formations. What does not seem to be subject to debate is whether he did it on not just culturally pure, but previously dehierarchized, self-determined, pluralist, and fully democratic social formations. The apologue is missing one leg.

He lists a few more regimes of evil and monologic terror, but the point being made is that domination is not merely the result of the establishment of an economic regime, from which everything else would ensue: exploitation does not explain domination, and domination does not mechanically derive from exploitation. Domination is not for decolonials the secondary consequence of an economic organization of the social in view of massive extractivism and theft. Cultural domination does not simply take priority over exploitation, but rather economic exploitation is merely a variety of cultural domination, which is the true and essential European design. In fact, according to Grosfoguel's definition of Quijano's "coloniality of power," "the idea of race and racism becomes the organizing principle that structures all of the multiple hierarchies of the world system" (26). So we are now back into a kind of monology, not economic but racial, and there is in fact a powerful reductionist principle at work in decolonial ideology, which is that of racial domination over and above anything else. In fact, conceivably (nay, necessarily, according to the doctrine of the coloniality of power) capitalism itself, and mysteriously also sexism, would or could be reduced to their intrinsic racial principles, that is, to the principles that structure racial domination as the very truth of the European world spirit.

So, locationalism, on the positive side, and anti-racism, on the negative or critical side, could be taken to be the two forms of truth that the decolonial option pushes as its own brand of anti-systemic struggle in view of a global transformatory politics. This is a form of domination critique that can hardly be associated with anarchism, particularly if we are to believe, with Jameson, that anarchists are also "people of the Book, acknowledging *Capital* as their fundamental text" (150)—that is patently not the case for decolonialists, whose relationships with any books are in general vague and distant. In fact, one of the secondary, but by no means unimportant, problems decoloniality confronts (it is simply removed from the forefront of discussion) is the problem of running into any number of subaltern "positions of knowledge" that seem to invoke the very opposite of democratic anarchism, and veer, rather, into the authoritarian side of things. In any case, given the strong reliance on blanket prescriptions and proscriptions regarding not just thought but the mere opinions of decoloniality-inspired believers (and a distinction should be made between decolonials and the people whose truth they claim to affirm), anarchism is clearly not a part of their intention.

But let us say that decoloniality as such could be conceptualized as a democratic critique of domination, even if it should then endorse, in and by principle, positions that would themselves indulge in domination of the human by the human simply because they have genuine subaltern, locationalist provenance, and some kind of cultural cachet; the fact remains that decoloniality finds its absolute limit at the time of accounting for the production of domination, which lamely becomes, in their minds, simply the product of the extrapolation of European racism (and the thirteen other things in Grosfoguel's list) onto non-European latitudes. That, to understate the case, is idealist historiography at its most extreme. Domination includes exploitation means that exploitation would cease if people would just learn to behave in a nonracist manner, which perhaps only Quijano's "public authority" could teach them or enforce. Except, of course, for the good work decolonialists are already doing. The suspension of racism, decolonials seem to claim, would by itself bring down the structure of economic exploitation and would magically bring down capitalism.

I do not mean to deny the importance of a critique of cultural domination for the advancement of democratic struggles, but I believe, with Jameson, that a critique of domination is at best only a critique of the mechanisms of reproduction of economic exploitation rather than of its production. Hence, decoloniality can only ever succeed, even as a global ideology, as an ideological commodity, fit for circulation, even earmarked for extraordinary circulation as a compensatory mechanism for the neoliberal crisis. Who will disagree with the truisms that the obscure dominators come to us as if from the eye of God, theophthalmically, and that they wage a personal war on each and every one of us (provided we are not one of them), which, why not, can be conceptualized as a race war? Even Freud's President Schreber felt the rays of God taking him from behind at every moment of his life. The problem is not the intuitive truth of cultural paranoia, always available, and perhaps at the same time always already right. The problem is that cultural paranoia will not accomplish, perhaps does not even mean to accomplish, the transformative turn in global things that would be associated primarily with an end to the economic domination of time, of each and every one's time, which is only another name for exploitation under the commodity form of abstract labor. At the limit, decoloniality pursues a strategy of delinking, since separating from European racial domination is primary, and there would be nothing specifically wrong with a social-democratic capitalism, or with some other form of economic production more closely connected to non-European history, provided it is orchestrated through, say, Afro-indigenous hands (or through decolonialist hands that themselves only feel the world through Afro-indigenous categories, if we can believe them). The possession of the means of cultural and economic production is the dominant goal here, and not their intrinsic quality. In other words, it is not so much a matter of expropriating the expropriators as it is of racializing the racists, and making them feel the burden of subaltern history.

Take the case of Simón Yampara, not necessarily a decolonialist, but rather a Bolivian indigenous leader whose contribution to the high-level discussions held in the Bolivian vice presidency—in the presence of Álvaro García Linera and other prominent Bolivian intellectuals, indigenous and nonindigenous, and with a number of European and North American leftist or communist intellectuals also present—and sponsored by the Fundación Banco Central in La Paz in August 2007, might help us understand the complexity of the problematics raised by decoloniality itself. Yampara said: "We see that today, in Bolivia, political expression does not help us exit the right-left polarity. We the Aymara, the Quechua, the *kollanas* are neither right nor left, neither in thought nor in ideology, but they make us believe we are, and then, occasionally, we are hiding ourselves. That is why we must ask: who are we? . . . We are used to thinking about dawn and dusk, about *urin*, *aran*, and *taypi*. But the other logic makes us think in terms of thesis, antithesis, and synthesis. There is a problem when we compare synthesis and *aypi*. . . . I want to escape the mental colonization of Marxism. Marxism marks for us the second era after Christianity, it came to colonize our mind, the mind of the *kollanas*, the mind of that which is called the indigenous, the Indian" (Negri et al. 170–171). We can dismiss Yampara's position, but it would be hard to persuade him that Marxism would be better for him than his insistence on indigenous thought categories. Dismissal, however, would be less than democratic. But the real issue is neither the acceptance nor the rejection of radical differends such as Yampara's for global or even local political work. Let us posit radical respect, hence acceptance of the differend as such— this would mean an acceptance of an altogether different understanding and conceptualization of politics. What can we be expected to do about it?

The point is, decolonialists would find their hands tied. According to the locationalist principle, Yampara's claim to political truth—even if his political truth is mostly negative, and consists in an exodus from politics as such at the national level in the name of radical decolonization—which includes every endorsable principle of subalternist locationalism, would have to be conceded epistemic privilege. From that perspective, no one would be in a position to propose an alternative: a preference for leftist politics, say, in the face of Yampara's demand, would already include inexcusable, extraordinary violence. Indeed, decolonialists would not even be authorized, under their own principles, to engage in any discussion with Yampara: what kind of discussion could be conceptualized as anything other than an attempt at imperialist, Occidentalist imposition? Yampara has made a demand—a demand, in effect, for noninclusion—that remains fundamentally outside any possibility of critical interrogation. As no kind of translation or transcodification could take place into a language not already contaminated by cultural imperialism, it can only give rise to acquiescence or silence. Everyone in the audience could only learn to think through the indigenous categories just presented, transpose himself or herself into them, or hold his or her peace. No negotiation is possible that is not of a condescending, patronizing, or at best compromising sort. This is the point at which decoloniality runs into its own failure: when circulation stops and use cannot take place, when the *pharmakon* triggers an unpredictable proliferation of side effects, and a kind of autoimmunity sets in with a view to the end of politics through ethical collapse. Neither Right nor Left nor anything else: is that all we can hope for?

IV

Not according to Jodi Dean or Bruno Bosteels, who, placed before Yampara, would already, plausibly, be thinking of either democratic drives or speculative leftism. Or we can take Jameson's terminology and speak of a (non-)politics of the tragic pathos, whose only use, beyond circulation as use, is compensatory "democratic" enjoyment. I think this is the proper framework to offer my reading of some aspects of both Dean's *Communist Horizon* and Bosteels's *Actuality of Communism*. Even if Dean's book was published in 2012, as opposed to Bosteels's, which was published in 2011, Bosteels's book includes a number of references to Dean's, based on his use of the typescript. And Dean's book quotes Bosteels on several key occasions. We might assume, perhaps a bit reductively, that both books share an apparently similar horizon, and that they are in fundamental agreement with each other—the specific variations consist in their diverse analyses and subject matters, which perhaps authorize me to attempt a somewhat interlaced reading of both texts.

Bosteels's book starts and ends with references to the powerful political impact of Álvaro García Linera's work, both theoretically, through his books and articles, and politically, through his participation as vice president in Evo Morales's government in Bolivia. The first reference comes in the form of a quotation from Étienne Balibar's "Remarques de circonstance sur le communisme" (Circumstantial remarks on communism; 2010), who mentions García Linera in a footnote in the context of an important discussion of what "communism" might mean today:

> I propose to invert, in some way, the aporia of communist politics as the dialectic of a "State-non-State," by seeing in it not so much a supplement of radicalism in socialism but rather a paradoxical supplement of democracy (and of democratic practices) capable of altering the representation that the people make for themselves of their own historical "sovereignty": another interior (or rather, an *interior alteration*) of populism, or the critical alternative to the becoming-people of anti-capitalism as well as, in certain historico-geographic conditions, of anti-imperialism. (Balibar, quoted by Bosteels in *Actuality* 13)

That communism should then mark the place of a democratic supplement to leftist struggles today, a necessary precision nevertheless, does not seem to me to matter as much as Balibar's statement that communism is a critical alternative to the becoming-people of anti-capitalism/anti-imperialism: an internationalist alternative to populism, then, a change at the core of the populist movement, and therefore, in my view, an alternative to any politics or nonpolitics of the tragic pathos. It is in that sense that I am not entirely certain Balibar would welcome Bosteels's idea that we can have a "communism of communisms . . . beyond the endless polemics, the bitter self-criticisms, and the vicious internecine strife that continues to divide the Left more efficiently than the Right could ever hope to accomplish" (Bosteels, *Actuality* 18).

A certain unification or agreement is then called for by Bosteels, and it would be named "communism." There are difficulties in approaching that posited or necessary common horizon at the very level of understanding, let alone action, let alone results. Bosteels, although aware that there are other obstacles, focuses on what he calls, following formulations by Jacques Rancière and Alain Badiou to which he gives his own spin, "speculative leftism":

> We could . . . call "communism" the ensemble of struggles, desires, and impulses that aim to exceed the parliamentary Left with its predictable oscillation between enthusiasm and betrayal. This excess is not just an ideological deviation, it is also the repeated beginning of a necessary drive toward continued emancipation. In fact, communism acquires much of its strength precisely from immersion in this excess, which in many regards may well be the very source of its political actuality. However, insofar as the ensemble of struggles, desires, and impulses to exceed the parliamentary destiny of the Left may also appear to sidestep all questions of mediation except to posit that everything must be invented from the ground up, the ensuing definition of "communism" often becomes indistinguishable from another kind of "leftism," namely, "speculative leftism." (23)

Speculative leftism is then seemingly to be considered not a part of the "communism of communisms" he has invoked, but rather, specifically, its inner limit and deconstituting possibility. If Badiou says "we can term speculative leftism any thought of being which bases itself on the theme of an absolute commencement" (quoted by Bosteels 26–27), it is because speculative leftism proceeds on "theoretical operators" (25) that call for a purity never granted to concrete politics as such. To that extent, there will be no communism, and no communism of communisms, without "a certain degree of duplicity and impurity" that "must be preserved in the articulation between the old state of things and the new emancipatory truth" (29). If communism is to be the new emancipatory truth that "allows for the historical inscription of politics in a concrete situation" (30), then speculative leftism is what blocks such historical inscription by turning away from the realities of power and the state, indeed of history as such, through a "philosophical appropriation" that reabsorbs the political and leaves it no way out (33). The culprit must of course be named deconstruction. Through "half a century" of it, Bosteels says, "we have grown accustomed to the retrieval of communism as an element of ghostly spectrality, without the threat of its manifesto-like realization, or to the repetition of communism as an ever-present but always untimely potentiality without actuality" (34).

We are already in dense waters. Whether deconstruction is the proper name of speculative leftism or the other way around, the fact remains, for Bosteels, that what we are dealing with is an obstacle to the earthly manifestation of a new emancipatory truth represented by (neo-)communism. But the obvious question comes up: suppose we remove the obstacle, suppose we deconstructionists and speculative leftists agree to remove ourselves from the scene, inconvenient or silly as we might have come to see ourselves, would there not be a legitimate suspicion that the removal of the obstacle would leave that truth of emancipation free to enter its necessary catastrophe and ruin? What is the historical inscription of politics into a concrete situation if not the historical inscription of politics into its own obstacle? The dream of removing the obstacle may well be duplicitous and impure, but surely not in the sense intended. It is the dream of a seamless adjustment to the real as it is, a purportedly anti-utopian eyeball-to-eyeball confrontation that may nevertheless hide unsuspected heights of heroic utopianism. Read, from that perspective, the following concluding lines to Bosteels's "Introduction": "The notion of actuality as used in connection with communism presupposes the immanence of thought and existence, going so far as to accept the much maligned identity of the rational and the real, not as a dogmatic given guaranteed by the objective course of history, but as an ongoing and open-ended task for politics" (39).

There is no appeal to the objective course of history, that is, to the old truths of historical materialism—nothing so gross. Instead there is an appeal to the fact that, free from the merely theoretical obstacles of a doggedly deconstructive speculative leftism that conspires for an absolute commencement of being outside history, the path, ongoing and open-ended, will be open for the reciprocal incarnation of the rational and the real, and communism will be shown to be, not a utopian or otherworldly Idea, but rather, much more ambitiously, "something that is always already here, in every moment of refusal of private appropriation and in every act of collective reappropriation" (39). Indeed, there is no need for any new commencement if we discover that what we have been seeking has been with us all the time. But has it?

We may be able to get a deeper glimpse into what is at stake in these moves if we now turn to Jodi Dean's conceptualization of "democratic drives." I will simply define the notion as her version of speculative leftism, as indicated by the footnote where Dean prepares her critique of "some on the Left" (the "melancholy Left") by referring to Bosteels's "definitive discussion of the theoretical tendencies characteristic of this 'speculative left'" (54n14). The word "definitive" is definitive: Dean thinks there is no appeal to Bosteels's determination of leftist antagonists, so she will simply elaborate on it. But her elaboration takes the shape of a denunciation of leftist democratic "drives" that inverts Bosteels's diagnosis of communism as the retrieval of what is always already there. For Dean, it is democracy that is always already there: "The Left repetitively invokes democracy, calling for what is already there. These invocations of democracy take on a pattern that Lacan describes via the psychoanalytic notion of drive. Like desire, drive refers to a way that the subject arranges her enjoyment (*jouissance*). With respect to desire, enjoyment is what the subject can never reach, what the subject wants but never gets—*oh, that's not it*. Drive differs in that enjoyment comes from missing one's goal; it is what the subject gets, even if she doesn't want it" (65).

Desire is communist, democracy is merely enjoyment. The corollary, then, is that "the Left is stuck in democratic drive as the actuality of its suppression of communist desire. In each instance, communism names that in opposition to which our current setting is configured, the setting within which contemporary capitalism unfolds" (69). To be stuck in democratic drive is to obtain your political enjoyment in a sort of dirty way, duplicitous and impure, through a constant rejection of what is already there, a constant denunciation of what arrives, a constant (but this constancy hides a fundamental inconstancy) disavowal of the truth of a communism that now emerges, not just as the proper goal of desire, but *really* as the other side of our own stupidity. What seems strange, from the point of view of consistency with Bosteels's determinations, is that, to the extent that "our setting" is configured in that particular way, nothing short of a new commencement would seem to be capable of bringing us closer to the center of our being, to the core of our desire. That new commencement, that is, the other side of the "setting within which contemporary capitalism unfolds," is communism, which now appears as the immanence of thought and life, the accord of subject and experience, but for which we would have to remove (or to have removed) the obstacle of the drive, in the understanding that every drive, whether it be called democratic or not, is always associated with the death instinct. What might enable the Left to move past its impasse, which consists in viewing "the lack of a common political vision or program as a strength" (54), what might enable the Left to reach communist unification, is the removal of the obstacle understood as a removal of the melancholic drive, which Dean analyzes at length in her chapter 5, to which I will turn in a minute.

But first let us go to Bosteels once again, since his discussion of the "Ontological Turn" in leftist thought is a clarifying presentation of what might be in play in the disputes or disagreements concerning the relationship between drives and desires for the political subject. Bosteels has astutely taken the problem to its source, by noting that the polemic between "speculative leftists" and "actual" communists in part refers back to an experience, or lack thereof, of the coincidence of thinking and being. He notes that while "most radical ontological investigations would seem to start from the nonidentity of being and thinking" (50), the delinking or unhinging of those two dimensions "has profound consequences for politics precisely insofar as what disappears is any necessary linkage connecting the paradigm for thinking of being to practical forms of acting" (51). Bosteels obviously would like to bring about a new thought of the identity of thinking and being, since for him the very possibility of an "actuality of communism" hinges on it. As a consequence, what Bosteels proposes is the inversion of leftist ontology into a new theory of the subject. His "ontology of actuality" (59), on which depends his proposal for the actuality of communism, is premised on the possibility of the renewal of a theory of the subject that, he thinks, speculative leftist options have "barred or blocked, put under erasure, or kept at the level of sheer virtuality, or of potentiality without actuality" (53).

Accordingly, "the defining polemic behind the current ontological turn in political philosophy—what we might call its principal contradiction or its fundamental line of demarcation—depends not so much on the elaboration of a leftist ontology in one way or another as on the possibility of a leftist . . . theory of the subject" (53), which speculative leftists seemingly attempt to dismiss. "Can emancipatory politics today still take the form of militant subjectivization, or should the deconstruction of metaphysics also include all theories of the subject among its targets? Is every subject necessarily enmeshed in the history of politics as a history of sacrificial violence, or can there be a form of subjective fidelity to the very traumas and anxieties that bear witness to those vanquished and sacrificed?" (73): this is the question, but it is not a question whose answer Bosteels engages with directly. Rather, the answer, in the context of what follows, appears as what is preempted by the positing of a militant subject of communism (see Dean 35 for a definition of communism as a "politics of a militant subject"). It seems easier to set up an opposition between "philosophical radicality" and "political effectiveness" (Bosteels 128), for which all the arguments about speculative leftism and the actuality of communism have been preparing us. Political effectiveness, by definition, depends on the resolute actions of a militant subject of the political (which is something I do not suppose anyone disputes, as far as it goes), but, on the other side of the polarity, "philosophical radicality" is guilty of a thorough depolicitization, unless it has to bear the burden of a reactionary politics against politics: if "philosophical radicality" is to be privileged, "this does not signal a loss or a defeat so much as it is the inevitable outcome of a willful act of renunciation: a will not to will. In the end, [Moreiras's] is a strange kind of passive decision, or a decision in favor of passivity and inaction, this being the only remedy against the deafening calls for political effectiveness and activism" (128).[5]

Of course, Bosteels and I do not have to agree, and what matters now is not self-defense, but rather showing how rather surreptitiously in Bosteels's text a naturalization of a militant subject of politics takes place through an appeal to political effectiveness. But he is not alone, and this is the equivalent move in Dean: "Continuing in the flow, persisting in the repetitions of drive, we over and over reconstitute capitalism's basic dynamic, perhaps generating 'the possibility of another organization of social life' but also and at the same time hindering 'the possibility from being realized'" (155). Speculative leftists and subjects of the democratic death drive bear a large responsibility, almost doubled, it seems, as they are charged simultaneously with glimpsing different worlds and preempting their coming into being—which is precisely what the properly informed militant subject of actual communism, immersed in flexible politics, aloof from any kind of philosophical radicality, free from any thought of tabula rasa and absolute commencement, and with a clear eye open to infinity, could never bring himself or herself to do.

For Dean, the subject of communism would naturally be the subject of desire, as opposed to the destitute subject of drives. Showing this is the purpose of the chapter called "Desire," which is prefaced by a previous excursus on Slavoj Zizek on drive and desire. Desire is of course not perfect: "Desire is always a desire to desire, a desire that can never be filled, a desire for a *jouissance* or enjoyment that can never be attained. In contrast, drive attains *jouissance* in the repetitive process of not reaching it. One doesn't have to reach the goal to enjoy. Enjoyment attaches to the process, thereby capturing the subject. Enjoyment, no matter how small, fleeting, or partial, is why one persists in the loop of drive" (102–103). But the perfect identification of the possibility of communist desire does not depend so much on the inadequacies of Lacanian desire as such; it is rather, as in the case of Bosteels's political effectiveness, a function of the problems that exist in the opposite number. Hence, says Dean, quoting Zizek, "although [in desire and drive] the link between object and loss is crucial, in the case of the *objet a* as the object of desire, we have an object which was originally lost, which coincides with its own loss, which emerges as lost, while, in the case of the *objet a* as the object of drive, the 'object' *is directly the loss itself*—in the shift from desire to drive, we pass from the *lost object* to *loss itself as an object*" (103), which is what makes it paradigmatic of the functioning of a certain Left that Dean, following Wendy Brown, will call the "melancholic Left." The melancholic Left is no better—rather it is the same as—the speculative Left: it is not that they are looking for something they cannot find. Rather, they are desperately fixated on loss as object, which makes them not just politically inefficient, but in fact all too efficient in their hindering the proper final advent of the lost object of communism. Hence, they perhaps need to be removed, as an obstacle does, or treated or reeducated or persuaded, if we prefer to be less forceful. But presumably they should not be left alone. We seem to be beyond deconstruction here, and the range of denunciation now covers a full range of democratic fixations.

Dean, however, does not agree with Brown on the characterization of what might just constitute the defining characteristics of the melancholic Left. Where Brown's left melancholy is "more attached to a particular political analysis or ideal—even to the failure of that ideal—than to seizing possibilities for radical change in the present" (160–161), Dean's melancholic Left represents rather "a phenomenon of bourgeois decomposition" (Benjamin, quoted by Dean 159) that should be understood through Sigmund Freud's 1917 paper on mourning and melancholia, for Dean "the most valuable aspect of Brown's analysis" (163). The melancholic is of course caught in the death drive. "The patient represents his ego to us as worthless, incapable of any achievement and morally despicable; he reproaches himself, vilifies himself and expects to be cast out and punished. . . . He . . . has lost his self-respect and he must have good reason for this" (Freud, quoted by Dean 164–165). Freud's account of those reasons has to do with the splitting of the ego—the subject, by hating himself, actually hates his narcissistic identification, the other he lost. "The answer to the question of the subject's loss of self-respect turns on the object: it's the internalized object who is judged, criticized, and condemned, not the subject at all" (Dean 167).

We are in the realm of the drives: the melancholic feels loss itself as an object, and is passionately attached to it. It is an explosive mechanism politically—through that kind of attitude, communism will never come. For Brown, the melancholic attachment of the leftist has to do with some "loved and lost object that promised unity, certainty, clarity, and political relevance" (Dean 169), which is bad enough. But Dean is not happy with that explanation: "Brown suggests a Left defeated and abandoned in the wake of historical changes. Benjamin [Brown bases her essay on two texts by Benjamin, not just Freud's paper on mourning and melancholia] compels us to consider a Left that gave in, sold out" (171). We now have a Left that "has given way on the desire for communism, betrayed its historical commitment to the proletariat, and sublimated revolutionary energies into restorationist practices that strengthen the hold of capitalism . . . It sublimates revolutionary desire to democratic drive, to the repetitive practices offered up as democracy" (174). This is a tough and merciless diagnosis, but what I find more significant about it is not its toughness, but rather its scorn for democratic drives, which are here presented as the useless (or worse) sublimation of properly robust communist desire turned unattainable. The Left melancholic is doubtless a poor sap who has gone under and can no longer tell sick *jouissance* from healthy pleasure.

We might be forgiven for raising some suspicion about this all too helpful structure, particularly as we note that, following the rhetorical pattern that we saw before, communist desire only shines by default, in opposition to pathetic democratic drive. At the time of theorizing it, in effect, Dean abruptly abandons psychoanalysis and moves immediately into the notion that "communist desire is a given. What Negri positions within the totality of capitalist production in the present, Badiou positions within the eternity of the philosophical idea" (181). Like a political effectiveness that becomes constituted as such through the very condemnation of philosophical radicality in Bosteels, in Dean communist desire is a function of the failure of democratic drives, its other side, since there must be a proper desire that we betray in the drive, and it needs no justification but only celebration. It is, as we know, only ever the other that must undergo analysis. The problem is that, in this structure, in the same way the Hegelian master needs the serf, we need the neurosis of the other to posit our own normality, we need the melancholy or speculative leftist, in their miserable deprecation, in order to shine forth as the righteous one. Removing them from the scene, to mention a problem raised by Marx, is a little like removing the fetters capitalism places on production—we risk the possibility that production stops without its fetters, in the same way that I would no longer ever be hungry if I could eat all the time. But it is not clear that the mere arrest of production, the scorn on philosophical radicality, or the defenestration of the melancholy could bring communism into its transparent actuality. Dean and Bosteels, however, propose nothing else.

V

I started this chapter wondering whether *The Actuality of Communism* and *The Communist Horizon* made a persuasive case in terms of announcing a genuine possibility of communist use that would break away from the impasses and limitations of melancholy or speculative leftisms. The announcement of clear and present communism in Bosteels and Dean is shadowed by their reliance on the need to overcome the inner limits that hard-headed fellow travelers place on themselves, hence on everybody else. This is a political path that does not match Jameson's Althusserian alternative between exploitation and domination, or the decolonials' dichotomies between the West and the rest. The enemy here is an internal fold in the people, and there is no properly political solution to this problem other than the solution of critique and persuasion, which may be hard going. As a result, neither the actuality of communism nor the overwhelming presence of the communist horizon is given either political or intellectual necessity—both are to a certain extent enthusiastic prescriptions (done with great flair and talent, it goes without saying), written for a public that has already been convinced—at least for the most part. Both projects, unless it is the same project, pursue a political will toward a communism that is ambiguously defined as a commitment rather than a mode of production or a particular constitution of the social, and fall therefore on the subjective side of Karl Korsch's equation, the one that Jameson takes up, in terms of the two fundamental languages of Marxism. They present their project, not as a result or an inducement of democratic struggle, but rather as the supersession of democratic struggle in favor of another constitution of political militancy that is somewhat redundantly characterized as communist militancy: a new manifestation of historical truth that is at the same time always already with us, as some other side of the real that paradoxically indexes the really real, if only we could remove the internal fold in the people themselves. Surely a critique of exploitation (witness the analysis of communicative capitalism in Dean or the chapter on García Linera in Bosteels), rather than of cultural domination, is the focus of their intended praxis, which is also clearly placed in favor of the invention of transformatory politics on a global scale.

This is perhaps the time to establish an uncertain difference between Bosteels's and Dean's positions. In his conclusion, Bosteels restates his position in favor of a "communism of communisms," but this time he does not fall so hard on speculative leftism.[6] On the contrary, he says: "There is room for a communism of communisms in which speculative leftism is not just the symptom of a maddening desire for purity but also serves as a constant source of revitalization for communism" (283). It is a bit condescending, perhaps counterintentionally, but it is something of an offer for conversation, and Dean may share the conviction that her democratic melancholics might also have something critical to offer to an all too enthusiastic political affirmation, although I have not been able to find it explicit in her book. In any case, this late refusal of demonization is welcome, although any future conversation would have to take into account words published by Bosteels only a year later, in the "Translator's Introduction" to Alain Badiou's *The Adventure of French Philosophy*. There Bosteels says, still speaking about the "philosophical radicality" he chastised in *Actuality*: "While it once had the critical virtue of fending off the twin errors of blind dogmatism and empty empiricism, 'finitude' has today become a dogma that risks keeping the empirical from being internally transformed. And conversely, 'infinity'—which was once, in its virtual rather than its actual form, inseparable from the idealist vagaries of theology—is perhaps the only materialist answer to the jargon of finitude today (provided, of course, that we understand what this implies for the definitions of 'materialism' and 'idealism')" (xxvii–xxviii).[7] But, if infinite communism needs to be defined as "the only materialist answer" to a "dogma" that consists in stating the rather undogmatic necessary finitude of human existence, it is hard to see how those of us speculative maniacs (the text makes clear that we are the endorsers of the finite) might still be able to serve as interlocutors— perhaps speculative leftism keeps communism vitalized by offering a distinct target of disqualifying attack, so that there is no need for removal? But that is hardly the interlocution one would welcome, and one starts to think that Bosteels at least may have also fallen into the error I suggested for Jameson: that there is in him a certain slight regression into a conception of the world of thought as private property for the communist materialist. But communists do not own communism, in the same way that democrats do not own democracy, and they have no business keeping the rest of us away from the parameters of acceptable leftist discourse, whether in the university or elsewhere.

Bosteels's last chapter is on the work of the Bolivian thinker Álvaro García Linera. He starts it in reference, once again, to Wendy Brown's article on the melancholic Left, to which, he says, we must offer an alternative. García Linera, not just as a thinker but as a thinker whose political practice is energetic and consistent, and has been so for many years, is no less than the example of such an alternative, and Bosteels brings Dean into the picture here as well when he affirms that both his and Dean's notion of the communist horizon is taken from García Linera's phrase "The general horizon of the era is communist" (226): "Jodi Dean explains in her own riff on the notion of the communist horizon that she also borrows from García Linera. 'We can lose our bearings, but the horizon is a necessary condition or shaping of our actuality. Whether the effect of a singularity or the meeting of earth and sky, the horizon is the fundamental division establishing where we are'" (Bosteels 228; Dean quoted by Bosteels).

I am not a believer in such a clear orientation for our actions. Or rather, it is because I am not a believer in any kind of given or preposited horizon for action (to that extent, I follow Jameson's determination of the "objective" system of capital), and because I believe in no grounds of legitimacy for political praxis other than the tenuous legitimacy that follows from the absence of any legitimacy coming from anybody else (which seems to me the best argument to be made in favor of a radical, even illegitimate or savage, democratic practice as praxis and habit of thought), that I would express my doubts regarding the inevitability or the actuality or the substantiality of communism as a horizon, albeit in a new historical form. This may sound anarchist, but in any case anarchism, *contra* Jameson, does not have to result solely in critiques of domination or in punctual revolts and social democratic programs easily co-opted by capital. In the meantime, if what is proposed is a theoretico-political alliance for a movement toward the abolition of the present state of things, for the sake of a democratic future that might conjure away the domination of time, I will be happy to be a part of it. I have never suffered from paralysis or undue passivity. In fact, I have never stopped being bothered into action, in my own limited way, by the forms in which those reasons for melancholy Brown, Bosteels, and Dean decry keep coming back to us. Or, rather, unfortunately, at us, through their very theorizations.

Chapter 7

TIME OUT OF JOINT IN ANTONIO MUÑOZ MOLINA'S *LA NOCHE DE LOS TIEMPOS* AND *TODO LO QUE ERA SÓLIDO*

> Over three years awaiting the irruption of disaster, even since he saw in
> Berlin the parade of the men with brown shirts and torches setting the pace
> on the shining cobblestones, and when finally it came it found him dis-
> tracted, dozing on a rocking chair in the heat of the August afternoon, in
> slippers, with his collar unbuttoned, open shirt, as drowsy by sleep that it
> took him a while to understand these methodical men who did not raise their
> voices, did not wear the attire of *milicianos* and had no sinister rifles were
> probably going to kill him.
>
> ANTONIO MUÑOZ MOLINA, *La noche de los tiempos*

I

The texture of historical life belongs in the very fabric of the present, but
we are so familiar with old notions of historicity based on a linear understanding of time that only the rare author, a literary one for the most part,
can undermine our laziness and force us to take a new and usually disturbing look. In his article on *La noche de los tiempos*, Angel G. Loureiro
refers through his very title ("En el presente incierto") to Muñoz Molina's
powerful exercise in another kind of historical memory: an attempt to
undo old and new pieties in the name of a difficult use of imagination
toward an alternative understanding of historical temporality. But it is
not so much the uncertain present as the future ("the first gray light of
the first day of her trip, of an immediate morrow she cannot glimpse and
I can no longer imagine, her unknown future, lost in the great night of
time" [*Noche* 958; my translation here and throughout]). It is a future that
may or will have been dislocated and terminally compromised by something we did or did not do, something I did or not, something they did,
either intentionally or distractedly, confidently or fearfully, hurriedly or

with all possible deliberateness and slowness: such is the "night of time" that gives a title to Antonio Muñoz Molina's 2009 novel. And yet 2009 was still a relatively good year, when people could still afford some distraction: those were still good times in Spain, before the full onset of the current economic crisis, the increase in unemployment, the collapse of the real estate market, the closing down of thousands upon thousands of small businesses, the Catalan move toward independence, and so many other ominous signs of an uncertain future. Muñoz Molina was already anguishing about a fall, premonitorily—if, that is, we accept the notion that his 2009 novel about 1935–1936 is directly allegorical of the Spanish present.[1] The allegory would be given a more literal embodiment in *Todo lo que era sólido*, from 2013. My attempt in this chapter is to establish some links between the two works, with a view to saying something that might, I hope, move beyond establishing a mere thematic sequencing.

In fact, *Todo lo que era sólido* is prefigured in the 2009 novel, in some precise paragraphs. The title sentence ("everything that was solid") comes up almost verbatim ("As disconcerting as the ease with which everything that seemed solid collapsed in Madrid in the course of two or three days in July was his own ability to adjust without complaint or much hope to this state of transition" [541]), but more important, at the level of anticipating the themes of *Todo lo que era sólido*, is perhaps the following paragraph: "I would have wanted to know at what point disaster became inevitable, when the monstrous started to seem normal and gradually became as invisible as the most common actions in life; when the words that encouraged crime and that nobody believed because they were monotonously repeated and they were only words became crime; when crimes started to become so habitual they already formed a part of public normality" (329). This paragraph would have been common to the structure of both works, even if it does not literally appear in the later one. The peculiar antiheroic hero in *Noche*, Ignacio Abel, whose temporal absorption, that is, whose inability to establish a certain focused relationship to his own temporality leads him into any number of moral errors, lives temporal disjunction as a torment: "Humiliated by his own impotence, he was intent on imaginarily changing the course of the past: by himself, debating with ghosts, altering his own actions and those of the people he knew and even those of public life characters, rebelling against his own blindness and getting belatedly embarrassed about it, fervently disagreeing with someone he had not wanted to challenge a few months earlier" (335). It is the same temporal disjunction that prompts the peculiar pathos of *Todo lo que era sólido*,

where it is always a matter of a retrospectively unavoidable but nevertheless guilty distraction: for instance, "What started to happen in the mid-
1980s without anyone noticing or exposing it is that at the very same time
public institutions began to have access to a lot of money, effective con-
trols on the legality of political decisions vanished" (42).

The novel, and perhaps both works, knows at some level of its textual
unconscious that even a vigilant awareness, an impossible lucidity (such
as the one Rossman pathetically embodies in *Noche*), all of it would have
been in vain and for nothing, as one cannot rebel against necessary disaster without becoming something of a clown and an outcast in unpro-
phetic times, which would make for an inefficient rebellion. And yet the
novel, and perhaps also *Todo lo que era sólido*, is helpless to avoid rebelling against the impossibility or the inefficiency of rebellion. I think the
latter is the main textual mechanism for the composition of both *La noche
de los tiempos* and *Todo lo que era sólido*—a statement that could have as
a corollary the idea that the historical situation depicted in both texts is
the pretext or merely overdetermines a deeper existential preoccupation
that may have an altogether different rank: the rank of an obsession or
lost object that organizes and sutures the very possibility of writing. I do
not think Muñoz Molina is attempting to offer, or proffer, in either of the
texts, what would amount to a simpleminded call for a more alert, voluntaristic subjectivity: his protagonist, as well as the narrator in *Todo lo
que era sólido*, suffers from a subjectivity that cannot quite find the road
to effective agency, not even retrospectively. It is this gap in subjectivity,
experienced and recounted as such, that makes the writing both possible
and necessary.

Indirect confirmation might be the interlacing of a love story with
the more substantial political ploy in *Noche*. Abel's untimely and adul-
terous affair with a North American student, Judith Biely, apparently
loosely based on Pedro Salinas's affair with Katherine Whitmore, which
led Salinas indirectly to his position as professor of Spanish Literature at
Wellesley College during the civil war years and beyond, is at the same
time Abel's redemption and his doom, his final displacement and disloca-
tion: his love, which he is not free to reject, will be responsible for some
of his worst betrayals and desertions. After all is said and done, after the
end of the novel and its story, Abel's fate as a broken man (broken not because he fell in love with a woman who made herself available but was
not his wife, not because he was overwhelmed by political events, and not
because he was disappointed in his conventionally progressive views of

human nature or in his lifelong professional expectations; rather, broken because he deserted his family at a time of war and because he allowed somebody to face a terrible death, breaking his word of honor in the process: a broken man indeed, beyond redemption) is not to be distinguished in essential terms from that of Dr. Santos, another fictional character in the novel, a Spanish professor at Burton College, and perhaps a summary of so many of us: "the odious avalanche of obligations, the unacceptable normality it would cost so much to get used to, even though he would be slowly abducted by it, subjected to its charms, habituated to his daily dosage of delays, expectations, and routine, one among so many displaced European professors, speaking English with a strong accent, fearful and rather stuck-up, excessively ceremonious, impatient to please, to obtain a certain safety that would compensate them for what they had lost, dressing with a formality impregnable to America's clothing casualness, waiting for letters from family dispersed around the world or disappeared without a trace, far from the reach of any queries" (955).

We should read in this commentary on a future Abel modeled on Dr. Santos not just a swipe against expatriate professors in North American universities, but a reflection on all inner exiles, all of those whose life has undergone a more or less traumatic experience of displacement, of defeat and loss, whose outcome, which can of course always be more or less productive notwithstanding, can never retrospectively compensate for the promise of the pretraumatic past: alienated life, dislocated life, damaged life, none of it capable of surmounting disorder.[2] In the meantime, we can dream on regarding the possibility, always already missed, hence even more painful, of a particular instant of redress, an instance of absolute justice, as it were: "Things are always about not to happen, or to happen otherwise; they approach their consummation very slowly or very rapidly or they veer toward its impossibility, but there is an instant, only one, when they can still be helped, when what is about to be lost forever can be saved, when the coming of disaster and apocalypse can be detained" (330). The possibility of seizing the occasion, in a voluntaristic act of timely decision, can never be disregarded in advance, hence its fateful character—but it should also be noted that neither can it be planned for. And people cannot be educated into putting it into effect.

Who could, in any case, seize the occasion for correct and decisive action in historical situations that, as the novel says repeatedly, leave no place for "people like us"? What people? People like Abel's old professor, Karl Rossman, a Berlin Jew now exiled in Spain who would be gratuitously murdered by Spanish communists in September 1936. And people like Abel himself, or some other members of the set of characters in the novel: José Moreno Villa, or Manuel Azaña, or the indefatigable Juan Negrín. "There is no place for people like us," says Rossman (353). And Negrín will say: "They hate people like us. Those who do not believe that by scorching the present world a much better one will become possible, or that through destruction and murder justice can be brought in" (445).

This is a direct reference and perhaps a personal homage to Manuel Azaña's 1939 testimonial text *La velada en Benicarló*. The latter was written in the early spring of 1937, in Barcelona, before the street struggles that ended the hegemony of the anarchists and nationalists in the Catalan area and gave the Republic a fighting chance of organizing the war effort against the anti-Republican insurrection, and it is a book that helps place both *La noche de los tiempos* and *Todo lo que era sólido* within their willed dramatic setting. In the "Preliminar" to his text, Azaña talks about a "drama" that goes well beyond the war and whose presentiment "has carried some persons' spirit desperately to touch the bottom of the nothingness" (33). It is because "for men like us the world is coming to an end" (35) that a compensatory reflection emerges according to which "in Spain two ferocious sides attempt to destroy each other. Neither can dominate the other. When this is recognized and the war is over, those who kept away from it and have made reproaches to both sides will take charge of governing the country" (37).[3] The Republicans in dialogue in Azaña's text may state, in the abstract, that the problem can be reduced to "a problem of freedom, of reason, of human dignity. That of implanting a tolerable regime, tolerant, that would result in a more intelligent State, closer to the social morality of our time, taking better advantage of the value of men and respecting freedom of judgment" (70–71), but such a possibility flies in the face of a historical destiny that has turned Spain into a country where

> for many Spaniards it is not enough to believe whatever they want: they take offense, they are scandalized, and they rebel if the same freedom is given to others who think differently. For them, the nation consists of those who profess the same orthodoxy they do. A nation thus understood must be cleansed through tremendous amputations. The territory is less important. The spirit of a nomadic tribe, of a chosen and mystical people. The cross, curved or not; the half-moon or any other emblem (also the hammer and sickle), shining in a burning sky. Everybody submissive. A pilgrimage in the desert and the arrogance of saying: I have no enemies anywhere within the horizon. Thus speaks

the national spirit in this great case and let other values taken as primordial perish or be endangered. (86)

This is not Muñoz Molina but Azaña speaking, although Azaña is part of the intertext in *La noche de los tiempos*. The *we* that Muñoz Molina partially endorses, and wants to endorse partially, and that in a crucial conversation at the end of the book (a difficult, painful conversation that seals the lucidity that comes, perhaps, sometimes, once everything solid has vanished into thin air) takes Abel, lucidly rather than pessimistically, to jeopardize the very continuation of Judith's love for him (902–915), is a *we* that sees itself able to "continue whatever in Spain has been independent thinking and freedom of spirit" (Azaña 86), but it is also an empty and precarious *we* that the novel itself never ceases questioning. It is reasonableness as such and dignity as such, hence the very possibility of timely and decisive action, which are always already under siege through distraction and occupation, if not through Machiavellian *fortuna*, through the imponderability of fate, or through the pressure of a certain social necessity or usage, the Anaximandrian *kata ton khreon* that undoes both justice and injustice and dislocates the order of time as it sees fit, beyond, even, if perhaps through, human agency.[4] The Abel that is desperately nursing his wounds at Burton College can no longer believe in any empire or promise of reason, and he finds himself "more deluded than any of them [the others]" (933): "He said that what was most astonishing to him was to have been so wrong, in everything, especially about those things he felt most certain of; to have relied on the solidity of everything that went under from one day to the next, without drama, almost without effort; to have been so wrong about himself" (932–933), which of course takes the *we* to the abyss of its own disaster. Abel, like any of us, has never been in control of anything.

II

"Everything that was solid" refers to Karl Marx and Friedrich Engels's 1849 *Communist Manifesto*. In the translation favored by the www.marxist.org/ archive, which is Samuel Moore's 1888 translation, supervised by Engels, the paragraph reads:

> The bourgeoisie cannot exist without constantly revolutionising the instruments of production, and thereby the relations of production, and with them the whole relations of society. Conservation of the old modes of production

in unaltered form was, on the contrary, the first condition of existence for all earlier industrial classes. Constant revolutionising of production, un-interrupted disturbance of all social conditions, everlasting uncertainty and agitation distinguish the bourgeois epoch from all earlier ones. All fixed, fast-frozen relations, with their train of ancient and venerable prejudices and opin-ions, are swept away, all new-formed ones become antiquated before they can ossify. *All that is solid melts into air* [my emphasis], all that is holy is profaned, and man is at last compelled to face with sober senses his real conditions of life, and his relations with his kind. (http://www.marxists.org/archive/marx/works/1848/communist-manifesto/ch01.htm)

The more modern translation by Terrell Carver reads a bit differently, and the phrase corresponding to the German *Alles Ständische und Stehende verdampft* is rendered as "everything feudal and fixed goes up in smoke" (cf. Marx, *Later Political Writings* 4). Even Carver's translation hardly does justice to the German phrase, in which *Ständische* does not just mean feu-dal, but rather embodies a reference to a dissolution of a certain traditional order that should, however, be perceived not just as emancipation but as a direct consequence of the increasingly thorough subjection of life to the principles of market equivalence and capitalist rule—which in Spain the neoliberal order radicalized even under socialist governments. The gradual transition from a peripheral capitalism to a full-blown one under conditions of integration to the European Union made Spain undergo ver-tiginous social change starting in the 1980s. Surely that change was not uniformly negative, and it benefited large segments of society: "Nothing mattered too much insofar as there was money. Nothing really mattered" (Muñoz Molina, *Todo* 204). But its drastic quality imposed a number of modifications on the very texture of ethical life—while there is no reason to idealize former ethical structures, what Marx and Engels call attention to is the disruptive quality of capitalist revolutionizing as such, particu-larly, I might add, when the very ground of such revolutionizing (the influx of financial capital) is taken away suddenly, as happened at the inception of the recent crisis. There is no doubt that all of this is marked in Muñoz Molina's choice of title for his book.

And yet another famous Marxian paragraph is probably just as appo-site. I am referring to the passage from *The Eighteenth Brumaire of Louis Bonaparte* that says:

Men make their own history, but they do not make it just as they please in circumstances they choose for themselves; rather they make it in present circumstances, given and inherited. Tradition from all dead generations weighs like a nightmare on the brain of the living. And just when they appear to be revolutionizing themselves and their circumstances, in creating something unprecedented, in just such epochs of revolutionary crisis, that is when they nervously summon up the spirits of the past, borrowing from them their names, marching orders, uniforms, in order to enact new scenes in world history. (Marx, *Eighteenth* 32)

If my initial hypothesis regarding the contemporary inspiration of *La noche de los tiempos* were correct, then we would have to assume that Muñoz Molina was already intent upon exploring and intervening in the phantasmatic fabric of the spirits of the past, not to engineer historical change, but rather to dissipate, preemptively, some of the ghosts whose marching orders had come to them from a number of suspicious agencies. The repeated call for reality checks in *Todo*, the animosity against delusion in any of its forms, has a direct antecedent in the extensive confrontation with the circumstances surrounding Ignacio Abel's life in the Madrid of 1935–1936, which forms the very structure of the novel as such.

Todo lo que era sólido is not content, however, with the denunciation of either the phantasmatic, that is, haunted if forgetful, haunted because distracted, character of the Spanish present (there is no pretense that the current crisis can or should be compared to the one that led to the Civil War in view of anything like some permanent structure of Spanish history) or with the protest in view of the apparent dissolution of everything traditional that should have been left in place. It does call for a "civic rebellion" (245) that would presumably follow the notion that it is only once everything old has gone up in smoke that men and women are perhaps offered a chance, rather than be forced, as Marx and Engels claim, "to take a down-to-earth view of their circumstances, their multifarious relationships" (Marx, *Communist* 4). Muñoz Molina does call for a "serene" (245) settling of accounts with the Spanish present through no particular emphasis on hauntology and no overdue and overdone attention to historical memory, but rather in view of the need to come to terms with what is possible, necessary, reasonable, and commensurate with the imperative to avoid a recurrence of historical disaster. But his words are sufficiently harsh to let everyone know that it is precisely historical disaster that has been banally courted through the particular distraction of Spanish political and social life in the last thirty years or so.

"I could not find anything to set eyes upon that was not a remembrance of death" ("No hallé cosa en que poner los ojos que no fuera recuerdo de la muerte"), says a famous sonnet by Francisco de Quevedo, who is certainly not one of Muñoz Molina's favorite writers. And yet it is difficult to avoid thinking of it as one reads into the darkness of Muñoz Molina's account, notwithstanding the strong comic flair of many of its pages. For Muñoz Molina, the current financial crisis is not exactly a crisis that fell upon the Spaniards as if from heaven: it is also a crisis created and propitiated by any number of defects in Spanish political and social life, which the book exposes, hence it is a crisis that falls directly into the Marxian dictum that men create their own history even if in conditions not of their own making. Muñoz Molina argues in favor of a new traumatic awakening that can perhaps be reconducted, not, as in Abel's case, toward displacement and exile, abstention and remorse, but toward a civic rebellion that can produce not just new social hope but also, beyond hope, a sustained future along Azanian lines of liberty, reason, and human dignity: "great transformations," he says (235). They are possible, perhaps necessary, which does not mean they will take place. Muñoz Molina understands the difficulties. My interest is not in rehearsing or repeating his lucid analysis regarding the contemporary crisis, or even his proposals for political reform (see 245–246), which I largely share, but in detecting a pattern in the proposal itself with which I cannot help but identify, once it is made explicit.

The epigraph to *Todo* is a sentence from Joseph Conrad's *Lord Jim*: "It is extraordinary how we go through life with eyes half shut, with dull ears, with dormant thoughts." How could it be otherwise? There is no choice if we want to move forward without excessive anguish, as too much lucidity weakens or destroys. And a lack of memory is also resistance to lucidity, which is only another form of lucidity, albeit of a more pragmatic kind. It protects against traumatic experiences or wards off obsessions such as the one that seems to be at the very heart of the book, which we can, perhaps reductively, cipher in the following sentences: "What had been very valuable all of a sudden was not worth anything" (18); "There is no longer anything that can be taken for granted" (233), or "What we have is much more singular and fragile than we thought" (233). Yes, everything melts into air or goes up in smoke. Muñoz Molina is ostensibly referring to the economic crisis of the last few years, which has led the country into a social precariousness unknown for the last few generations, and which has brought on the most radical and dangerous political crisis since July 1936 (the Catalan challenge for independence). We can think, or sense, that Muñoz Molina's own mortality is also at stake in these fretful reflections, and from it comes a felt need for a settling of accounts and a clear political word, as we will see. But I must detour for a moment to some considerations that are part of the reason for this chapter's presence in this book.

I share birth year and initials with Muñoz Molina, but I spent my early youth in Barcelona, whereas he spent his in Madrid. He mentions his proximity to the Communist Party during his years as a student at the University of Madrid during the 1970s, although he never became a militant or a party member. Like him, as a student at the University of Barcelona, I was invited to request membership in the Partit Socialista Unificat de Catalunya (PSUC), that is, the Catalan Communist Party, which I rejected without a great deal of anguish, as, in all my naïveté and through my acquaintances, I had already started to suspect and resent a number of authoritarian habits or gestures in party members that I disliked. I wanted to militate in no party. In those days in Barcelona, but not yet in Madrid, where things would develop in similar directions a bit later, a certain anti-Francoist libertarianism was far more attractive—we called it the *rollo*, and it was the antecedent of what in four or five years would start to be known as the *movida* in Madrid and the rest of Spain. We spent many of our nights at El Café de la Ópera, Zeleste, or El Elefante Blanco, or at the Jazz Colón, discussing Deleuze and Artaud, Nietzsche and García Calvo, hitting still-illegal hash joints, and speaking a bit excessively about sex, never mind politics. My friends were all anti-Franco, but they could not stomach the Communist Party, or Catalan nationalism, or those other young fellows who a few years earlier might have become nuns or friars or Opus Dei members but who, now, left to themselves, would transmute into members of pro-Chinese or pro-Albanese fringe groups. But my friends also disliked the so-called *ácratas*, whose disarming good faith and unfathomable gullibility would have made even St. Francis suspicious. These peculiar anarchists also had poor taste in music. We were, however, close to the Assemblea de Treballadors de l'Espectacle, which had formed a cooperative in the Saló Diana, a shelter and temple where everything that mattered to us beyond the street itself happened and could happen at any time.

It was around the time that I was invited to join the PSUC that the Assemblea organized three days of a cyclical and continual performance of José Zorrilla's *Don Juan Tenorio*, in the Mercat del Born. As the party went on, all of us became conscious of the generational and personal importance of what was happening—or at least I remember it that way, no doubt retrospectively assigning to a single event what was more likely an accumulation of experiences lasting several years, for me the crucially formative years of the first Spanish transition. But those were nevertheless three intense, intensely joyful days. At some point during their course, we learned, through a kind of anticipated mourning that was also an awareness of the limit of our own physical capacity, that they would not come back, that they were unique and fleeting, and that they had given us access to, and had perhaps at the same time closed or foreclosed, a form of experience after which it would be difficult for any political experience on offer to seem anything but compensatory, a mere reflection at best. In hindsight, but I think we knew it then, the Born *Don Juan* marked for us, in Barcelona, the limit after which the narrative of the Spanish democratic transition would have to be told according to a logic that could only start in *desencanto* ("disenchantment" or "disappointment"). We used that word before it became popularized in Jaime Chávarri's film *El desencanto* (from 1976, but it had an intense life that made it seem new for three or four years), which certainly became a cult film and a work of reference for us. And *desencanto* became the reverse of a number of infrapolitical experiences whose intensity would have exceeded everything political.[5] Or else I could say that such experiences—the end of Francoism, the beginning of our adult life, the promise and excitement of an overdetermined youth, but also the contradictions and the hypocrisies of so much that we were seeing, starting with the pathetic life of a university already controlled by nominal democrats and less than democrats of various anti-Francoist adscriptions—forced a mourning for a promise of a life more political than politics, a life that made politics pale. For me personally, it would eventually mean that I had to leave Spain, since I was unable to find a productive place—in 1978, 1979, 1980—in the concrete life of the country. It was not written that I would find it in any other country, but that is another story.

Muñoz Molina refers emphatically in *Todo lo que era sólido* to a similar temptation to leave in the same years. But he decided to stay, perhaps only because he was called to military service and ended up finding a job as an administrative assistant at the Granada City Hall. It is then that his book starts, only to move into the narration of a second beginning that happens thirty-two years later. Muñoz Molina, as he tells it, takes notes in New York, when the news reaching him from Spain, as published in the North American newspapers, made it seem as if a great transformation were in the works. But what is he taking notes about? "In almost every city one of the main squares was filling up with people demanding radical change in political life, people that belonged to no party, that did not support the usual forms of demagoguery with which every political class had become accustomed to lull or corrupt their constituencies" (235). Not until almost the end of the book does Muñoz Molina reveal the real engine that prompted its elaboration, or made it seem necessary:

> People settled in the squares and would not leave. Over the phone the rumor of the multitude sounded like a sea. I would speak on the phone with one of my sons who was at the Plaza del Carmen in Granada. I would speak with another son camping in Puerta del Sol in Madrid. From so far away [Muñoz Molina is spending the academic semester in New York] the clamor of so many was startling and brought on a particular kind of nostalgia. It was good to have left, but now it was necessary to return as soon as possible in order to see with my own eyes what was going on. It was as if the simulacrum had broken; as if something that had kept on without change for so long could no longer last. And it seemed that people, most of them young or very young, were for the first time refusing to continue to play as secondary actors in the great corrupt production of Spanish politics. They said very concrete things and also things that were too abstract; they formulated reasonable projects and also disasters dressed up in poetic language; but that mixture has been present at the beginning of all the great transformations. (235)

Astute commentators such as Sebastiaan Faber express disappointment that Muñoz Molina did not discuss the 15-M movement in more detail ("he does not devote more than two pages to the *indignados*," says Faber [3]), but it seems to me that those two pages are decisive through their very restraint.[6] Muñoz Molina, not by chance but in the very structuration of his work, of its deep tendencies, including its thorough critique of subjectivist voluntarism (although I understand and share the critique Faber makes that some pages in *Todo* seem to elide the deeper position and seem naïvely to call for a renewal of voluntarism, it is also fair to remember the genre of the book, which was written to have a direct impact on political consciousness and action), understands that he can only help out or contribute in preparing the work of a new generation. Muñoz Molina has been establishing his discourse to clear the ground for a "great transformation" in Spanish politics whose protagonists, if it were to happen, would be his children, both of them active supporters of the 15-M movement. It is indeed the narration of a historical moment when everything that seemed solid has gone up in smoke almost overnight, but thanks to it, people, and especially the younger people, are thrown into the possibility, which remains only a possibility, of making history even if under conditions not of their own making. Every element of the book moves in that direction—in the direction of the establishment, or rather, of the visibility and necessity, of such a possibility.

Muñoz Molina himself does not promote a revolutionary transformation in the conventional sense, as others may have done at the time and perhaps still do. That is his choice and his style. Rather, he personally prefers to aim for a thorough cleaning of the country's stables, from a position that he calls "accepting reality" and "refusing delirium" (227). This is, after all, the encounter Marx and Engels, in different historical circumstances, called for in the *Communist Manifesto*, what opens up after the dissolution of what seemed solid and lasting: the very possibility of a cold look at predicaments and relations. Muñoz Molina offers, in the last pages of his book, a minimal political program whose specifics are less important than the fact that he explicitly proposes it (although he has taken his time, and it is only the last few pages of his book that in fact reveal it as a letter that means to reach a destination) as a gift or message for his children, or to the young Spaniards in whom he sees a reincarnation of his own person circa 1979, as he was looking to become administrative assistant in Granada. In the embrace and accord with reality and in the renunciation of fantasy— the "delirium" he dreads so much, which is also related to the distraction Abel permanently experiences until it is too late to redress it in *La noche de los tiempos*—he is simply calling for a restoration, or rather for an instauration, of democratic rule in Spanish politics, and contributing to making it possible precisely by not arrogating to himself a protagonic role. He is in effect talking to his children, as a father will.

I note there the reemergence of the old terms of our common generational experience—mourning and disenchantment, disenchantment and mourning, now reexperienced in the need for a legacy. Muñoz Molina speaks from that double instance, thirty-some years later, paying the price of having chosen to stay, of having given up on his original plan of leaving for good. To stay—we knew it then, vividly and unequivocally—was necessarily to postpone mourning, to disavow disenchantment, and perhaps to have to live on with eyes half shut, with dull ears, and with dormant thoughts. There would still be a lot of work to do, and no guarantee that an awakening could be sustained on the other side. But could Muñoz Molina have spared himself the pragmatic lucidity of the one who must dissemble and hide his panic in order to live a normal life? Could he have lived his Spanish life with totally open eyes, sharp ears, sleepless thoughts? Right around the middle of the book Muñoz Molina gives us a metacritical clue that we cannot not heed. He talks about the process of writing *La noche de los tiempos*, and he says:

> The disquiet, the feeling of danger and collapse that were at the same time the theme and the drive for the writing responded to a completely contemporary experience, but I was not able to account for them with materials from my own time. That produced a remorse that did not bring complete relief even when I was more thoroughly given over to the writing, more possessed by it. I wrote about the blindness of those who could not see what was happening in the middle of the turmoil of the present, out of distraction, out of irresponsibility, for just concerning themselves with their own business, for the ultimately fearful decision of refusing to accept the possibility of disaster, for the simple inertia of believing that things are much more solid than they really are. But I myself could not see anything, locked up in 2007 in my 1936 time capsule. (151)

The guilt and remorse Muñoz Molina mentions as what *Todo lo que era sólido* would assuage, are they not the trace of an anti-political or infrapolitical experience, of an experience more political than politics, in front of which politics, or whatever is meant by it, must pale? The restlessness of a time out of joint, spent in delirium, the history of a disaster that dwells in the disavowal of disaster—such is the infrapolitical legacy that prompts the need for the "great transformation" that Muñoz Molina now passes on to his children, as if politics could only find its truth in the crypt of time. What may seem terrible is that, in the absence of any other possible heritage, that is also the only unacceptable one. We inherited it from our parents, and it is such an inheritance that is finally and perhaps even exclusively explored in *La noche de los tiempos*, and its burden made us flee the country, or else to stay in it. It is the one who stays, as Muñoz Molina did, who must now insist that others, against all evidence, open their eyes and stop sleeping, because the one who has left has possibly forfeited his right to do so. It is no easy task for the 15-M generation, or it is an impossible task, such as it was for us. Whatever has gone up in smoke or melted into air will continue to recur as spirit or ghost. And the text knows, through the poison of its gift, that eliminating the ghost, whatever it is, and even if it were possible, is not quite for people like us.

That the times are out of joint, and that the experience of disaster is first of all the experience of the negation of disaster, is the very condition of politics, the need for politics, and the use of political engagement: in 1936, in 1977, or in 2012. It is so to such an extent that a down-to-earth, eyeball-to-eyeball look at one's circumstances and relationships is rarely possible, and when possible, it will still be weighed down by the burden of traditions that feel like a nightmare on the brains of the living. We cannot dispense with the conditions for politics. We can, however, attempt a political act every now and then, which is what I think Muñoz Molina has done on his own terms with his book sequence. There are, of course, no guarantees that it will have its intended effect.

Chapter 8

ETHOS DAIMON

The Improbable Imposture

> Who will boast of being a mere impostor? The drunken man who blurts
> out an absurd command, the sleeping man who suddenly awakes and turns
> and chokes to death the woman sleeping at his side—are they not, perhaps,
> implementing one of the Company's secret decisions?
>
> JORGE LUIS BORGES, "La lotería en Babilonia"

I

Heraclitus's Fragment 247, *ethos anthropoi daimon*, is one of the earliest,
perhaps even one of the most decisive statements of Western thought,
particularly in the absence of more extant fragments from Anaximander.
Hegel said of the Ephesian, in his lectures on the history of philosophy:
"Here we see land! There is no proposition of Heraclitus which I have not
adopted in my logic" (Barnes 57). At the same time, Heraclitus can also
be argued to furnish anti-Hegelian tools: it would be difficult to consider
him a thinker of the "cunning of reason" in history (see Hegel, *Lectures on
the Philosophy* 89). As to Fragment 247, "*ethos*" can refer, as the Liddell-
Scott Lexicon will tell us, to the haunts or abodes of animals, or to custom
or usage, also to manners and habits, so also to disposition and character. "*Daimon*" is an even more complicated word, as it is difficult for
us to imagine what it could have meant for a culture not inflected with
Christianity: yes, it means god or goddess, or what the Romans will call
"*numen*," but it also means chance or fortune, genius or fate, and the verb
"*daio*," which refers to the power of the *daimon*, talks about dividing or
distributing destinies.

 G. S. Kirk, J. E. Raven, and M. Schofield translate *ethos anthropoi
daimon* into English as "Man's character is his daimon." It is not much of a
translation. "*Ethos*" dubiously becomes merely "character," and "*daimon*"
is, well, daimon. For the human. Character is daimon, and not just any

daimon but "his" daimon, that is, daimon for man or for woman, a daimon for every specific human. What does that mean? In their gloss of the fragment, they say:

> 247 is a denial of the view, common in Homer, that the individual often cannot be held responsible for what he does. *Daimon* here means simply a man's personal destiny; it is determined by his own character, over which he has some control, and not by external and often capricious powers acting perhaps through a "genius" allotted to each individual by chance or Fate. Helen traditionally blamed Aphrodite for her own weakness, but for Heraclitus (as indeed for Solon, who had already reacted against the moral helplessness of the heroic mentality) there was a real point in intelligent and prudent behaviour. (Kirk, Raven, and Schofield 211–212)

In his "Letter on Humanism," Martin Heidegger translates the fragment very differently. He says: "The (familiar) abode is for man the open region for the presencing of god (the unfamiliar one)" (234). There is, of course, no reconciling the two versions, or perhaps there is, since "character," in Kirk, Raven, and Schofield, is far from explained, which means it is open to interpretation, and "*daimon*," vaguely translated as "simply a man's personal destiny" in the gloss, could be taken to be something dictated by the unfamiliar one, by the god making herself or himself present in the home of man, itself an open region or a place of hospitality, and turning it forever into a haunted place. Kirk, Raven, and Schofield's translation is a good example, I think, of the unthinking thought, the deadening or flattening that sometimes is presented not just as thought but as perfectly appropriate thought, by academic hegemony.

At least Heidegger complicates the issue, and does not give us translative mush. At least in Heidegger's rendering, the old word from Heraclitus becomes provocative and thought-worthy. Heidegger's own gloss is not so much indecisive as difficult. He refers in it to "a thinking more rigorous than the conceptual" (235), for which the old word "*ethos*" as abode of man, dwelling place, is enlisted. This other thinking, a kind of "original ethics" (235), is for Heidegger, as we may know, not only a thinking, "neither theoretical nor practical," he says (236), that would offer "directives that can be readily applied to our active lives" (236), but also a thinking that "conducts historical eksistence . . . into the realm of the upsurgence of the healing" (237). This "healing" (Heidegger is writing this in 1946–1947) will at the end of the essay be associated with "less philosophy, but more attentiveness in thinking; less literature, but more cultivation of the letter" (242). Of course it would be madness to undertake this in today's university. Or would it?

Javier Marías's 1994 novel *Mañana en la batalla piensa en mí* says: "but really all thought is sick, that is why nobody ever thinks too much or almost everybody prefers not to" (313; my translation now and throughout). Here Marías does not quite repeat what may have been a Nietzschean theme, namely, that the body reacts to disease, that thinking is one of the ways in which the body regulates, compensates for, tries to overcome disease. The thought is rather more radical: every thought is sick, every thought is sickness. How exactly are we to understand it? Is a remedy against sickness itself part of the disease? Is autoimmunity in itself, provided thought were an autoimmune reaction, a sick response of the body? And what is its purpose, if there is one? I suppose one could do worse than refer to the Heideggerian line just quoted: thinking leads into the "upsurgence of the healing."

But even this does not quite account for the particular use of "*estar*" rather than "*ser*" in the Marías quote: *todo pensamiento está enfermo*, all thought is sick, does not quite mean merely that all thought is sick thought. It means, rather, that all thought, any thought, finds itself with a temperature, dizzy, unstable, chilled, haunted. No wonder one would prefer not to think. But, if we must think, if we have no choice, for instance, in the university, do we do it with a regard to healing, do we do it with a regard to finding "directives that could be applied to our active lives," or is it just a matter of submitting to the disease, which of course could well lead us into the other side of the healing, which Heidegger identifies as "the malice of rage" (237), or even unto harassed death? But, again, perhaps these are mad thoughts, already sick thoughts, thoughts that are sick with a temperature, dizzy, unstable, and chilling, no doubt also haunted. Could we make of them the occasion for a little attentiveness to thinking, a little cultivation of the letter? For the sake of a certain healing: there would not be much to lose.

An even older or more conventional translation of Fragment 247 says directly: "Character is destiny." We know, of course, about Walter Benjamin's 1919 essay "Fate and Character," and we know that it incorporates, in very abstract ways, not just Greek tragedy and French seventeenth-century comedy but also Hegel and Nietzsche in its constellation of references. Well, Benjamin's essay is itself a gloss on Heraclitus's fragment, although the fragment is never mentioned, perhaps because the real idea in Benjamin is to break up the identification of character and destiny that the Heraclitus fragment seems to posit: to break it, not to the point of disassociating character and destiny, whatever they are, but rather to the point of complicating their relationship. To that effect, he begins by invoking what we could refer to as the two vulgar renderings of the equivalence (Benjamin himself does not use that term, "vulgar").

One of them would presume that "if . . . the character of a person . . . were known in all its details, and if . . . all the events in the areas entered by that character were known, both what would happen to him and what he would accomplish could be exactly predicted. That is, his fate would be known" (Benjamin, "Fate and Character" 201). In other words, once we get to know our own character, presumably by following the other Greek maxim, *gnothe seautón*, know thyself, or the character of some other person, your character, for instance, I would know your fate, your time, your life. Nothing happens to you that is not already inscribed in you: there is no pathos, nothing happens to you, nothing falls on you, or else pathos is always already singular, always already yours, and it has always already happened. Character is not identity; it is, rather, the *kharis*, the grace, as Rafael Sánchez Ferlosio would say or did say, that defines you as a singularity of time, a singularity in time.

(Toward the end of *Vendrán más años malos y nos harán más ciegos* [1993], Ferlosio incorporates a story that he names "Descubrimiento del 'carácter'" [Discovery of "character"]. The story tells how he was taken by his grandmother to a Capuchin Franciscan convent in Fuenterrabía. It was to be a first visit, and the grandmother instructed the child not to be indiscreet, as a hunchback would open the door: "Don't even think of saying anything to him or else!" But Rafaelito, irrepressible, tells us that when the door was opened, "what my eyes saw, suddenly taken by fascination, was the most wonderful creature they could ever have imagined," a gnome right out of his fairy-tale books, a little man with a long ashy beard, and he asked him: "Why are you so small, why have you grown so little?" The monk responded, with a sweet smile: "Because the Lord decided I should not grow any more." Ferlosio concludes: "I know today that singular divine grace is Character" [172–174]. Character is grace, not identity, from *kharis*, grace, favor, a gift.)

There is another vulgar conception that is the mirror opposite of the first. According to this second one, it is not that character absolutely determines fate, but rather that character and fate coincide, they are undecidably different, they are not distinguishable, since fate defines character and character refers to fate. Benjamin then rather ambiguously quotes Nietzsche: "Such is the case when Nietzsche says: 'If a man has character, he has an experience that constantly recurs.' This means: if a man has character, his fate is essentially constant. Admittedly, it also means: he has no fate—a conclusion drawn by the Stoics" (202). The point in Nietzsche is that eternal recurrence finds its utmost expressive site in *amor fati* as supreme character or, if you want, as a supreme characterization or internalization of character; character does not preexist fate, as it does in the first vulgar version; rather, character comes to be a thorough identification with fate as such.

But I will leave Benjamin for the moment, hence suspend his alternative rendering of the character/fate relationship. I will first attempt to analyze a particular feature in Javier Cercas's 2014 novel, *El impostor*. Although I should start by saying that the words "fate" or "character" are not to be found in *El impostor*, I also want to start by saying that *El impostor* is a rather fundamental and disquieting, even fundamentally disquieting meditation on the relationship between those two words. The words are certainly not alien to Cercas, as his readers might remember from *El vientre de la ballena* (1997, but rewritten in 2005) and even from the beginning of *Soldados de Salamina* (2001). In fact, *El vientre de la ballena* centers around a discussion of fate and character and, we could say, around a clear *parti pris* for character against fate. This novel in fact associates literature as such, or writing, with a defense of character against fate, or a strengthening of character against fate. Writing would be the healing of the diseases of fate, itself a sick writing, itself symptomatic or motivated, but whose primary function would be to assert the priority of character, and fate be damned. But I am now more interested in *El impostor*.

Let me begin, however, by quoting again some words by Rafael Sánchez Ferlosio, from a presentation he gave during the Premio Cervantes's awards ceremony, entitled, yes, "Carácter y destino," which Cercas abundantly mentions in *El vientre de la ballena*. Sánchez quotes Hegel's *Philosophy of History* in order to develop clearly anti-Hegelian thoughts. This is the quote, in H. B. Nisbet's translation:

> It is possible to consider history from the point of view of happiness, but history is not the soil in which happiness grows. The periods of happiness in it are the blank pages of history. There are certainly moments of satisfaction in the history of the world, but this satisfaction is not to be equated with happiness: for the aims which are satisfied transcend all particular interests. All

ends of importance in world-history must be secured by means of abstract volition and energy. The world-historical individuals who have pursued such ends may well have attained satisfaction, but happiness was certainly not their object. (Hegel 79; quoted in Sánchez Ferlosio, "Carácter" 641)

There is an active counterpoint between happiness and satisfaction in Hegel's words, and a certain clarity concerning the notion that the world-historical individual, that is, the hero, in the Hegelian sense, is not someone looking for happiness. Satisfaction is what the hero seeks or obtains in the accomplishment of his or her goals. Let us now transpose the notion of the world-historical hero into the notion of the man or woman of destiny, which is what Sánchez Ferlosio does. From that transcoding, a metonymic chain develops: the man or woman of character makes happiness, not satisfaction, her or his object; her temporality is not properly historical, unless we change the very meaning of the concept, and her expression or manifestation does not look for sense but rather for pleasure.

If one goes back to other Ferlosian texts such as *Mientras no cambien los dioses, nada ha cambiado* (1986), one will find the basic categories that regulate Ferlosio's anti-Hegelianism: one is not to be interested in the "acquisitive time" of history and progress, in teleological time, but in the exceptional temporality of the now, which regulates the use of the present, the consumption of the present, Ferlosio says, "consumptive time" against "acquisitive time": the use of the present, the use of the time of life, against the abuse of history, the abuse of deadly or nihilating accumulation, which must also be understood as the theft, even the auto-theft, of the time of life. Of course, pleasure must also deal with the disgust or the horror of empty consumptive time, in the same way that satisfaction must deal with defeat and catastrophe, with disaster and frustration. And one must eventually choose, unless others have already chosen for one.

(In the hilarious comic relief story Javier Marías introduces in *Mañana en la batalla piensa en mí*, we have the narrator visiting the king of Spain no less, certainly as close as we can come in Spain to the world-historical character, to the Hegelian hero in fallen times. The king needs someone to write his speeches for him, because, he complains, "I realize my personality is not known, how I am, and perhaps that must be so insofar as I am alive. But while I am alive I cannot stop thinking that, the way things are going, I am going to pass into history without attributes, or what is worse, without one attribute, which is the same as to say without character, without a neat and recognizable image" [169]. The king also complains that a host of speechwriters have managed to turn him into a character-less man, a nobody, and he wants to rectify that by getting himself a better speechwriter, that is, still within the "fantastic dissembling" in which we all live, but at least project a character, for God's sake, "there is a lot to choose from, but it would be good if we can have some authenticity in our farce, I mean a certain correspondence with the truth of my character and my deeds" [176–177]. We have a melancholy king who does not believe in the justice of the monarchic institution: "I doubt the very justice of the institution I represent, almost nobody would imagine it, that is certain" [177]. And this is because, he says, "I am not persuaded that a man or a woman must have their profession fixed for them from birth, and even from before, or his or her destiny, if you prefer to call it that . . . I do not believe that is just" [179]. Poor king, all he can do is "dissemble, of course dissemble all the time" [181]. All of this comes to a devastating attack on the Hegelian concept of the world-historical man, the historical hero, about which more later: a destiny is pre-fixed, and that annihilates character, or else: there is no character, and destiny is therefore bogus.)

II

What is the choice, then, in Enric Marco, the dissembling figure, the hero of dissembling, that organizes the narrative of El impostor? Of course Marco is an impostor, and Cercas conceives of the idea of investigating and interviewing him, letting him tell his story, as a "real fiction" or a "non-fiction novel." What does Cercas want? Whatever he may want or have wanted, what is beyond doubt is that Marco is an impostor. He modified, for instance, as the very last page of Cercas's book tells us, the name of Enric Moné, one of the Catalan prisoners in the Flüssenburg concentration camp, and turned it into Enric Marco, just a little calligraphic addition, in order to be able to hand over a xeroxed copy of the original document, clearly falsified, to the Amical de Mauthausen, that is, the Catalan organization that both commemorated and kept watch over the memory of those Catalans who were made prisoners and thrown into camps, concentration camps mostly, not so much death camps, although some were both, by the Nazi regime after the end of the Spanish Civil War. That xeroxed document, a false document, was essential for Marco to obtain his credentials as a camp survivor and become a member of the institution whose fate he would come to direct some time later.

Marco is an impostor also because he falsely represented himself in other endeavors, counterfeiting a past as an anarchist activist that helped make him Secretary General of the Confederación Nacional de Trabajadores in the 1970s in Barcelona, and lying and dissembling and bullshitting his way into, perhaps not the first, but the second or third line of memory activists in the Spanish transition, a hero of memory or a hero in memory. But Marco's memory heroics—heroics not only because successful, as they really made him into a hero for thousands upon thousands of high school kids and others, for instance, but heroics also because the memory itself, the memories themselves, referred to heroic behavior, not just to his status as a surviving victim, a victim whose survival was already a mode of heroism—were all lies. They were all lies, and Marco perpetrated a sham, little more than a sham, a pathetic sham. Of course the sham only became one when it was detected, and not before. What is the interest of such a figure? Why turn him into a literary hero as well, albeit a catastrophic one, an antihero?

One could say that Marco, a man of character, wanted to be happy, and his interest was not in satisfaction, or, equally plausibly, that he was looking for satisfaction and sacrificed his happiness to it—man of destiny, then. But this is a problem, the fact that we can say both, certainly so from the Hegelian or even the Ferlosian perspective, since for both of them one must choose character or happiness over destiny, or destiny and satisfaction over happiness (and those are the active and successful choices, because one can also opt for unhappiness and for catastrophe, even unawares). Can both options, then, be reconciled, and is that what Cercas's nonfiction novel tells us, the silent third perspective? The one who seeks satisfaction does it on the basis of some desire for happiness, and the one who looks for happiness expects to derive some satisfaction from it. There is no clear choice, against Hegel and Sánchez Ferlosio (although, to repeat, Sánchez Ferlosio is already against Hegel, an anti-Hegelian), between character and destiny. Are we then back to one of the vulgar interpretations in the Benjaminian reading? Whatever we decide, I think this issue is the basis of the infrapolitical, that is, existential reflection Cercas's novel deploys.

Let us put moralisms aside. It matters that he is, or be, an impostor, as that makes him interesting, even if in a pathetic sort of way. But perhaps it matters for reasons that are not evident. Cercas does not hide them, although it is perhaps fair to say that he does not quite reveal them either. Why is Cercas—Cercas the narrator; we can ignore Cercas the author, I

suppose—so obsessed with Marco, to the point of spending about nine
years agonizing over writing or not writing the book? Is it not the case
that we are all impostors, that we all falsify our history, we all falsify our
lives, we all falsify our work, even if we do not necessarily always cross
the material line into document falsification and even if we are not always
necessarily investigated by an impenitent historian whose mission it is
to reveal our falseness (although, as you know, increasingly, university
administrators take up that role quite willingly and gleefully, never mind
that they are generally the first and more monumental impostors). So, perhaps what really matters is something else, and perhaps we can attempt to
name it. The real question in the novel is not whether Marco is to be saved
or damned, condemned or celebrated, consigned to infamy or rescued for
a dubious pantheon of sympathetic rascals.[1] Cercas is not seeking to determine whether Marco has repented or is, as the cinema director Santi Fillol,
author of a documentary on Marco and also a character in Cercas's novel,
thinks, a reckless and unremorseful liar who "will never unmask himself.
He is always acting, he is always playing the role that interests him at a
given moment" (El impostor 409). Marco is like the Lacanian fellow who
manages to lie with the truth, whenever he tells the truth. Is it possible to
lie with the truth? Kant would be the first to say, as a mere consequence of
his moral law or concept of freedom, that such a thing, lying with the truth
at all times, which is hypothetically possible as the other side of always
telling the truth and being truthful even with our lies, would also be almost miraculous, improbable, a rare thing, although at the same time it is
all we ever do for the most part. But let us erase guilt from this equation.
Cercas is interested neither in finding guilt nor in cleansing guilt. What he
seeks is an equally miraculous, rare, impossible thing: to produce a book
about the truth residue of a monumental set of lies, to find what still might
stand up when all the lies are eliminated. Such is the technical exercise
in his nonfiction novel or "real fiction": how does one go about writing a
book where there are no lies, and what remains?

(I want to say something about Cercas's novel, and I hope to say something about Marías as well, I want to say something about Benjamin and
something about Hegel, and about Sánchez Ferlosio, but I also want to
finish my own book and reflect in it, as I finish it, on whether the search
for a kind of thought that, while accepting its own malady, its own
structural disease, could still aim at or for the upsurgence of healing is
only deluded. I want to do it through the thematization of the difference between character and destiny, or *ethos* and *daimon*, provided we

are still authorized to use the Greek terms. I have impossibly invoked the notions of attentiveness to thinking and cultivation of the letter as my own tools, thus setting the ground of my own critical demise, opting for the unhappiness and the catastrophe of failure, since it will be so easy for any reader to dismiss my attempt. A bit perhaps like what happens to the king of Spain in Marías's novel—comic relief. I will have become an impostor, like Enric Marco. So I can only go through him, in order to save myself, even if that is not what I want, least of all in the eyes of the readers.)

El impostor is an important text, perhaps even a masterpiece, in my opinion, because it deals with, it takes it upon itself to deal with, two very infrequent things—one hesitates to call them literary tasks, although they are undoubtedly only possible through writing, through the cultivation of the letter as attentive to thought—namely, what I would call a denarrativizing narrative on the one hand, and a will for testimonial deconstruction on the other—not for a deconstructed *testimonio*, rather for the deconstruction of *testimonio*. I am interested in both things— denarrativizing narrative, in opposition to mythographic or mythomaniac narrative, and the deconstruction of *testimonio* as a correction to the pretension of identitarian truth that has plagued political discourse over the last thirty years and continues to plague it. It is true that both procedures, which are the essential technical procedures of *El impostor*, are necessarily hard, even scandalous, and expose their author to ruthless recriminations. How does one go about denarrativizing narrative? Is that not a contradiction *in terminis*, an impossible endeavor? And how does one pursue a deconstruction of *testimonio* without leaving us all in the uncanniest form of exposure, having been denied the last shelter, to trust that others may trust our personal truth, which is ultimately only uttered as a request for respect and love? If you take away from us the double possibility of myth and testimony—both of them, myth and testimony, are negatively enframed by mythomania—then we are left with nothing, we no longer know what to grasp for. We would have to give up not just literature and philosophy, but also politics, in the necessary acceptance of a horizonless nihilism.

But perhaps it is not so bad. We know the primary intertext in *El impostor* is Don Quijote, and Don Quijote is after all both a denarrativizing narrative and a testimony in deconstruction, particularly at the end, at the terrible and necessary conclusion of the work, the death of Alonso Quijano once he gives up, thanks to that unpardonable idiot Sansón Carrasco, one of us, a critic and a humanist, on being Don Quijote. Reality does not save Alonso Quijano, it precisely consigns him to death—perhaps the ultimate form of lying with the truth—and ultimately, therefore, and here the novel ends, fiction does not save him either. Nothing saves him, nothing saves. That is what it is, in Don Quijote and in *El impostor*.

Marco's imposture, does it falsify a character or does it falsify a destiny? Is that imposture not in itself the means toward a sought-for destiny? Or is it rather the mechanism for consolidation, the necessary anchor of a character that remains absent, perhaps nonexistent, demanding presence through its very void? Marco—it won't do at this level to argue that one is only talking about Marco the character in the novel, not Marco in real life, as Cercas's narrative is built on erasing that difference—might well be incapable of responding to those questions even for himself, having become lost in his own imposture, and having done it from the initial realization that, from the start, Marco lacked, like the king of Spain, both a destiny and a character; both were missing, there was no option, and one could only, desperately, go for both, attempt to retrieve both, like the Yogi Berra–inspired character, who, when facing a crossroads, could only think of taking it. Blindly. Perhaps through a speechwriter smart enough to fake authenticity, which may be the precise role Javier Cercas takes upon himself as author of the novel on Enric Marco.

When, in one of the crucial passages of the book, Cercas attempts a description of Marco as the average man, another Spaniard or Catalan from the historical time he had to endure, so just another Spaniard or Catalan, a man without attributes, a fellow among others, what Cercas hints at but never says is that Marco has neither character nor destiny. This is, only partially, Cercas's page, in my translation:

> So that Marco's final enigma is his absolute normality; also his absolute exceptionality: Marco is what every man is, except in an exaggerated form, larger, more intense and more visible, or perhaps he is all men, or perhaps he is a nobody, a great container, an empty set, an onion that has been deprived of all layers of skin and is no longer anything, a site where all meanings converge, a blind spot through which everything can be seen, a darkness that illuminates everything, a great eloquent silence, a glass that mirrors the universe, a hollow that owns our shape, an enigma whose ultimate solution is that it has no solution, a transparent mystery that it is nevertheless impossible to decypher, and that it is better not to decypher. (412)

When a man or a woman is deprived of both character and destiny—and is that not the tendential accomplishment of our societies, the tendential accomplishment of our regime of labor, also at the university, the condition of existence today or the condition against which existence must be measured?—when neither one nor the other is accessible or practicable, it is only logical that the attempt to retrieve them be both desperate and reckless, as there is nothing to lose, nothing to be lost. The residual, tragic drama is not realizing that even in the absence of both one must choose between them, you must opt in the nonoption. To denarrativization, to the curious detestimonialization that Cercas investigates, there would correspond another counterclassic image: not Hercules at the crossroads, but somebody who is not a hero having to make a decision for which there is no decision, no deciding choices. Marco opts indifferently—either to give himself a destiny in order to gain character, or to project himself as a character in order to trap a destiny—and his option undoes him. But, at this point, at this particular crossroads, here and now, does it not undo every one of us, even if most of us have not yet found the rigorous investigator who will make our drama public? Or the speechwriter who will give it some desperate authenticity? Or the administrator who will dispose of us for good?

All of this proves Sánchez Ferlosio right: that the only intelligent thing, if we were only capable of it (the king, for instance, is not), would be to opt for happiness and never put our cards on any conceivable destiny. (That is, of course, also the secret, unconfessable and always already misunderstood, of Benjamin's second take on the idea of character, his 1931 essay "On the Destructive Character.")

III

What was the nonvulgar interpretation of the relationship between fate and character to which Benjamin opposed the other two, and then yet a third I have not yet clarified? Undoubtedly it is Hegel's rendering, as he discusses it in the vibrant pages of the *Lectures on the Philosophy of World History* I have already referred to. Hegel presents his notion of "the cunning of reason" (89) at the service of the Idea: "The right of the world spirit transcends all particular rights; it shares in the latter itself, but only to a limited extent, for although these lesser rights may partake of its substance, they are at the same time fraught with particularity" (92). The conflict between the universal and the particular is mediated by the cunning of reason through the figure of the world-historical hero—heroes are those who "in fulfilling the end of reason, ... not only simultaneously fulfill their own particular ends (whose content is quite different from that of the universal end), but also participate in the end of reason itself, and are therefore ends in their own right" (90). Others can be trampled: "A mighty figure must trample many an innocent flower underfoot, and destroy much that lies in its path" (89).

It is passion, reckless passion, as an attribute of character, that marks the hero and secures the coincidence between particular and universal ends that justifies the Hegelian system: "Passion is the absolute unity of individual character and the universal," says Hegel (86), "the way in which the spirit in its subjective individuality here coincides exactly with the Idea has an almost animal quality about it" (86). And then he will say, in words that cannot stop moving me, as much as I hate them:

> And the new world order and the deeds they accomplish appear to be their own achievement, their personal interest and creation. But right is on their side, for they are the far-sighted ones: they have discerned what is true in their world and in their age, and have recognized the concept, the next universal to emerge. And the others ... flock to their standard, for it is they who express what the age requires. They are the most far-sighted among their contemporaries; they know best what issues are involved, and whatever they do is right. The others feel that this is so, and therefore have to obey them. Their words and deeds are the best that could be said and done in their time. (83-84)

Passion sutures the separation of character and fate, which is also the separation between private or particular ends and the Idea of world history. Passion brings them together and makes them coincide, thus granting the truth of the *ethos daimon* saying in its modern translation: character is fate. Through passion, the hero can break an ethical whole and move toward a "higher universal," that is, a new moment in the deployment of the world spirit. The hero can or always must be a revolutionary, as heroes are the ones "who do not find their aims and vocation in the calm and regular system of the present, in the hallowed order of things as they are. Indeed, their justification does not lie in the prevailing situation, for they draw their inspiration from another source, from that hidden spirit whose hour is near but which still lies beneath the surface and seeks to break out without yet having attained an existence in the present. For this spirit, the present world is but a shell which contains the wrong kind of kernel" (83).

The Heraclitean daimon is here the world spirit, who reveals the new kernel every time, and ethos is the very opposite of ethics or morality, since it is ethos, as passion, that receives the command of the daimon toward revolutionary goals and leaves itself behind as a mere shell, like a snake does every fall. Needless to say, all of this reads very well if we could still believe in the march of humanity toward an end of times to be described as the triumph of the absolute spirit or, what amounts to the same, the Idea of and as world history. Without it, or provided it has already happened, the hero is nothing but the worst sort of villain, nothing but a bureaucrat of hegemony, an administrator of the ceaseless mobilization of life toward senseless change at the service of interests that can no longer be understood as the interests of the universal but are not yet the interests of the singular. The Hegelian edifice has collapsed. The righteous passion of the Hegelian hero is now either the insatiable greed of the corrupt or the stupid destiny of the deluded. We must choose, indeed. And yet we seem not to know how, or even that we must.

Benjamin goes at it through a clear demarcation: "Where there is character there will, with certainty, not be fate, and in the area of fate character will not be found" ("Fate" 202). Fate and character are separate realities, as they can no longer be identified through the passion of world history, much less through their vulgar equations. How to distinguish them? Benjamin considers fate, the daimon, consigned to the order of the law, itself "a residue of the demonic stage of human existence" (203). Tragedy, however, succeeded over law, "for in tragedy demonic fate is breached" (203). Tragic man "becomes aware that he is better than his god" (203), and the result is the consignment of fate to what Benjamin calls "the natural condition of the living" (204). But man is in excess of it, and he or she is in excess of it precisely through character. Character is no longer a tragic conceit—rather it belongs to comedy, the place, Benjamin says, "of an utmost development of individuality" that leads to freedom (205–206). Benjamin is finally saying that character is both an index and the site of the proper region of human temporality, as opposed to the inauthentic dwelling in misfortune and guilt that tragic understanding dismantles. Character is the site of freedom.

Can we still think of freedom, the grace of singularity, as the open region for the presencing of the god as the unfamiliar one, the uncanny guest? If so, can we facilitate its advent through an attentiveness to thinking, a cultivation of the letter? Is sick thought the very possibility for helping us leave behind the residual guilt and misfortune characterized by the onset of fate, by the intervention of fate, into our lives? Thought would be the haunted realm of events, and its function could not be coming to the end of itself, since that is death and termination. Haunted thought does not seek the termination of thought, the end of the haunting. What does it seek, then? What could healing mean in this context?

If writing and thinking can do something other than serve the fallen fate of universal history, if we can save or rescue ourselves from narratives of destiny that have in fact already lost their destination, it is to healing we turn, not as the reestablishment of health, but as the possibility of retrieval of the open region where freedom can still make an advent. Heidegger calls it "letting be," but there is nothing passive about it. In his Caracas speech, given at the Rómulo Gallegos International Novel Prize ceremony in 1995, and talking about *Mañana en la batalla piensa en mí*, Marías addresses himself to what I can only understand by now as a critique of fate. He says: "We all at bottom have the same tendency, that is, to see ourselves at the different stages of our life as the result and the sum of what has happened to us and what we have accomplished and what we have realized, as if that were the only thing that conforms our existence" (453). There is something we forget, and we forget that we forget it when we do theory or literature in mindless ways. But what if literature, as cultivation of the letter, or theory as attentiveness to thinking, could be understood to be sustained meditations on what fate keeps away from us, on what could have visited us but did not, on the sum total of possibilities unrealized in our lives not as destiny but as unused grace, unreceived grace, which now becomes receivable by virtue of a gaze that no longer looks at the exhaustion of those possibilities, but rather to their inexhaustibility? This is letting be, and it is perhaps this that Marías has in mind when he says: "People perhaps consist equally of . . . what we are and what we are not and what we have not been, equally of the provable, quantifiable, and memorable and of the most uncertain, undecisive, diffuse, perhaps we are made in equal measure of what was and what could have been" (453).

The bad Hegelian hero or counterhero, Richard III, who is, through the Shakespeare play, one of the fundamental intertexts in *Mañana en la batalla piensa en mí*, had a passion that could not be accorded to universal history. This is why those who haunt him, his victims, the flowers he trampled, come back to him before the battle and tell him to despair and die. Those very same ghosts also talk to Richmond, the future king, and tell him: "Good angels guard thy battle. Live and flourish"; "Awake, and win the day"; "Wake in joy" (Shakespeare, *Richard III* 5.3, 147, 152, 160).

Haunted thought could do worse than welcoming those visitations, particularly if they were addressed, not to Richmond, who thinks of himself in Shakespeare's play as the hero of providence, the hero of justice, God's man, but rather to someone, anyone, for whom there is only a life to be lived in the happiest possible way, and no destiny to speak of; as if we were mortal, and only mortal, instead of contemplating, as Hegel wanted, the foam of the infinite (Hegel, *Fenomenología* 91).

Chapter 9

A CONVERSATION REGARDING THE NOTION OF INFRAPOLITICS, AND A FEW OTHER THINGS

With Alejandra Castillo, Jorge Álvarez Yágüez, Maddalena Cerrato, Sam Steinberg, and Ángel Octavio Álvarez Solís, July 2014–January 2015; translation by Jaime Rodríguez Matos

The conversation was proposed and initiated by Alejandra Castillo. The first questions and answers were discussed indirectly in a Facebook group, which led to further questions and comments from the other signing interlocutors.

ALEJANDRA CASTILLO: In your book *Tercer espacio: Literatura y duelo en América Latina*, you indicate that autographic writing is index and ruin of the figurative project of writing. Described in those terms, autography seems to be framed between reflexivity, mourning, and survival. Following this thread, you indicated that figurality is both the condition of reflexivity and its very limit. In your forthcoming book, *Piel de lobo*, you take up once again the problem of writing and life. In the tie that binds those words together, you describe autography as a "writing in subjective destitution." I would like to begin this dialogue by asking about this description: what are you referring to when you say "writing in subjective destitution"?

ALBERTO MOREIRAS: The problem with figurative language is that it posits or invents the necessary existence of a nonliteral or catachrestic plane, and this plane is always and necessarily phantasmatic. If I say that the horsemen approach beating the drum of the plains, the noise of the drum is my phantasm: music. If I realize this, the music stops. And that has destituting effects. There is a destituting drive in what you call reflexive writing (I no longer remember what I said in *Tercer espacio*) that is always already tragic, and with which we can only relate in mourning if we are to survive, which can never be taken for granted. I suppose that there is constituting writing and destituting writing, though such a division is far from exhaustive as a phenomenology of writing. In any case, I speak of tendencies in writing, not of achievements: everything is always ambiguous and complicated in this terrain because nobody owns their writing, one can only struggle with it. For some, writing could be constitutive in a symbolic sense—for instance, if we accept Alain Badiou's schema, in which writing is fidelity to some event of truth in love, science, art, or politics. But I cannot believe that writing exhausts itself in that constitution of subjective truth, and I tend to think the opposite is the case: the writing that interests me does not seek to constitute a truth, rather it seeks truth and produces destitution. It seeks truth in the sense that it attempts to traverse the phantasm in every case, and it produces destitution in the sense that traversing the phantasm brings us closer to the abyss of the real. This is a Lacanian vocabulary, but we could rewrite it in deconstructive terms. Where Lacan would say *sinthome*, Derrida could speak of the secret. For me, in fact, there is no other writing than the writing of the secret. Or, there is another, but it does not work (for me). The question that arises, then, is that of the use of the writing of the secret, but that is a question that I don't think I am prepared to answer.

ALEJANDRA CASTILLO: While it is true that autographic writing leads us toward a certain politics of the proper name, it is no less true that such a name is but the inscription of death in the ownership of the name. In this sense, every auto-*bio*(thanato)-graphic gesture would imply the failed gesture of seeking to be faithful to writing one's self, while always writing, nevertheless, an other. In spite of this auto-hetero-graphic logic that is inscribed in writing, you seem to insist in some of the materials for your new book, *Piel de lobo*, on the necessity of giving testimony of the truth: "Books have to be true," you state. What is the limit between truth and fiction in an autographic project?

AM: I think that every act of writing fails; the only act without recoil would be total silence, which is also death. But, precisely to the extent that we write in spite of everything, death is inscribed apotropaically: we inscribe it in order to resist it. It does not seem to me to be so much the work of fidelity. It is more of an enterprise without fidelity, always ready to betray everything to achieve its ends, if one were shrewd enough to know when to betray, when betrayal is the best way to avoid the lethal inscription. That is why writing acts have to be true, because without that truth nothing works—as we know, in each case, only truth orients betrayal. Every reflexive act of writing is therefore never more than a theoretical fiction. But I would also resist the notion of testimony in this context. Testimony is only one modality of theoretical fiction among others; it does not define them all, although we could entertain the idea that testimony is always already nothing more than the theoretical dimension of fiction. We could say that there is always testimony in reflexive writing, there is always a testimonial dimension, but that testimony remains suspended in every case by what escapes it, by what the testimony produces as its own excess. That is what I call autographic writing.

ALEJANDRA CASTILLO: Is the definition of writing you are proposing related to the concept of "infrapolitics," which you have been developing more recently?

AM: Yes, and both are related to what, on a different occasion, I called the instance of the nonsubject. I suppose that the same intuition makes its way throughout this quasi-conceptual framework. Autography and infrapolitics refer to a practico-speculative space that is not regulated by even the slightest certainties, which are always ideological and which determine our relation with the everyday and thus remain outside of the horizon of capture defined by the legal apparatus, by the political and administrative institution, by the national instantiation, by gender, by sexuality, by ethnic origin—in sum, by any identitarian artifact. It is not only an attempt to think writing but also the course of experience itself, in what exceeds and from what exceeds that subjective capture.

ALEJANDRA CASTILLO: Could you elaborate on your idea of "infrapolitics"?

AM: I just spoke of it as a quasi-conceptual instance that resists every ideological apparatus of capture, which refers to an unregulated practico-speculative "third" space, which is to say, outside of rule and regulation. It is not that it is impossible to think it, for now (I think it is the easiest thing to think, what is closest to all of us, but someone said that the narrowest abyss is also the hardest to cross), but it is a contradiction to attempt to give it a theoretical formulation or a definition. It is important to invoke here the notion of "resistance to theory," not from the vantage point of the will that seeks to undo that resistance, but in order to fold into it, to understand it insofar as such a thing is possible for each of us. I imagine that what is important, then, is not to secure a stable definition, but to invoke a reflexive process that would allow for a liberation of the ear, the eye, the touch, and that leaves space, or makes it possible to conceive of an alternative site for thought. If I knew for certain how to do it, I would have already written four or five more books. But we can make an attempt: let us say that infrapolitics refers to deconstruction in politics, or that it is deconstruction of politics or politics in deconstruction. Jacques Derrida's 1964 seminar, at the École Normale Supérieure, on the question of being and history in Heidegger, was published last year. There Derrida comes very close to saying that deconstruction is the constant attempt to thematize the ontico-ontological difference, that is to say, the forgetting of Being that Heidegger diagnosed in *Being and Time* as infection or infiction of the metaphysical tradition as a whole, which is the hegemonic tradition of thought in the West. I would say, and it is clear that my genealogy of work has strong Heideggerian and Derridean ties, I would say, then, that infrapolitics is the name of deconstruction in politics, understanding deconstruction as the attempt (always unfulfilled) to thematize the forgetting of the ontico-ontological difference. To carry this thematic over to political reflection has proven a difficult task—it would be possible to think that Emmanuel Levinas, as much as Blanchot, Derrida, or Nancy, among others, were always attempting to come to terms with this, but, as we know, always in a manner that was not too frontal.

We don't have to abandon the project, however, to the extent that the modes of oppression most characteristic of our time, and perhaps of all times, always transcend what we might call representational politics, the politics that is mere confrontation between doctrines and positions, mere alternation of measures that come to take on the form of law—they always enter into the region of infrapolitics. If the latter is the place where the auto-heterographic inscription is or is not produced in its real form, that is, if infrapolitics is the place of experience and the instance of the singular manifestation of every politics, then the change of perspective, with regard to what could be termed the great "heliopolitical" parameters that define ostensible political life in modernity, would be of critical importance. As we know, the problem of liberalism, for example, is not liberalism in itself but the falsity of its application, and the same applies to communism.

For instance, the problem of a society politically structured according to Ernesto Laclau's theory of hegemony is not the given hegemonic articulation but what that articulation is incapable of dealing with. Let us say that every heliopolitics imposes a metaphorization, a way of understanding the space of the community. The infrapolitics of any politics is permanent demetaphorization. And in that always ongoing process of demetaphorization, which is, among other things, time, and what exceeds any will to control, and, accident and catastrophe, but which can also be freedom and *jouissance*, or an opening for pleasure—it is here where, I would say, the possibility of invention, which is also the possibility of revolt, of subtraction, of restitution, and even, why not, of vengeance is kept, even if it is in and through the retreat, the permanent retreat, of that very possibility. I don't think it is banal to insist on the idea that the attempt to resist this demetaphorization is the real name of antidemocratic authoritarianism, that is, of the oppression of the human by the human—from the Right or from the Left.

ALEJANDRA CASTILLO: Then, do we always have to search for the demetaphorization of any system?

AM: Demetaphorization happens on its own, since political life is always, in every case, a struggle that begins with the entropy of the concept. What is important, certainly in the university but not only there, not at all, is to remain alert to the constant attempts to avert the entropic demetaphorization of any system. Any project of justice and freedom for all, that is, of demotic equality, of preventing anyone from being more than anyone else, passes through the facilitation of the work of entropic demetaphorization, which in many cases has as a consequence the production of new alternative metaphors that are in turn provisional and subject to new losses themselves. Democratic republicanism is perhaps nothing other than that sustained process of rejection of any reification or biopoliticization of the concept. That is why I insist that we should recognize in it the call of forgetfulness. Western metaphysics constitutes itself in that forgetting, according to Heidegger, in favor of the onto-theological constitution of the *polis*, or of what takes its place, perhaps the state. Parmenides's poem incorporates in its very form the link between aristocracy and ontological ground, which is thus defined for the next two thousand five hundred years. To search for the difficult outside of onto-theology or in infrapolitics, to search for the difficult outside of politics, is not to wager on an anarchic demetaphorization, but its point of departure is that there is no stable -archy, that any -archy is already a consequence of the forgetting that constitutes it as such. Heidegger gave the name of Being to that instance of forgetting, to that instance that is always in retreat, because that was the word used in the tradition, but already in the 1930s Heidegger begins to emphasize that it is not necessary to speak of the Being of the tradition, that Being as it is understood in that tradition is not the reference. That is why he writes "Seyn" with a *y*, or he crosses out the word. Or he renames it Ereignis. But we could also call that forgetting infrapolitical experience. We can only refer to it in a tangential manner, itself metaphorical or metaphorized in every instance, precisely because it is not vulnerable to theoretical appropriation, because our language does not allow for theoretical appropriation without destructive capture. The forgetting cannot be fetishized into a new name of Being or onto-theological foundation, even as infrapolitics cannot constitute itself as a formal practice. Both forgetting and infrapolitics are only susceptible to a poetic quasi-nomination that makes possible the intuition of a trail, a trace in which the future of our planet is at stake, in my estimation. We can call it the Lacanian Chose, or the Freudian navel of the dream, the Derridean *différance* or the face of the other, or the neuter, or even all that appertains to the thought of the animal or the earthly outside of the Anthropocene—these are impossible names, catachrestic names for thinking the forgetting, in the same way that infrapolitics is an impossible name for thinking politics.

JORGE ÁLVAREZ YÁGÜEZ: One of the striking features of your thought is that you tend to use authors who are not generally regarded as political philosophers, who don't belong to any history of political thought as it is usually understood, whose thought is not, at least not in a central way, political, such as Heidegger, Lacan, Levinas, Derrida . . . , but you do it precisely in order to think the political or an alternative to the political as such.

AM: I have never had or attempted to have a technical relation with politics, neither in terms of what certain academic traditions call political science nor of what still others call political theory. In fact, I always thought or felt, as many others do, that politics oscillates, at least in what interests me, between being essentially corrupt and despicable and being charged with the greatest possible dignity and importance, and that this variation within existing politics has little to do with its concept. So when I decided, without a doubt driven, as far as I can remember, by contextual ideological pressures within the university, when I decided that I was to thematize politics or the political in my writing, it was always a matter of speaking from the place where I was, without any imperative for self-reformation whatsoever. Then I began, for example, to get interested in what there is of politics in processes of philosophical, critical, or literary writing and thought, perhaps paying undue attention to my own notion regarding the essential variation between its two abysses, its loftiness and its baseness. The truth is that one discovers, without setting out to do so, that real politics, at least in texts, is not where it says it is, or rarely. It is more common to find that the most radical democrat, as soon as one makes an effort to read his texts, ends up revealing, more or less naïvely, his intrinsic despotism, that the fiercest subalternist reveals himself as the perfect policeman, or that the noblest feminist could be understood as an extraordinary case of corrupt opportunism. Or that the internal contradictions of political thought end up producing the destruction of the concept of politics itself, as perhaps is the case in the work of Louis Althusser. It is also common, and this is obviously more interesting and productive, that people who usually prefer to remain on the verge of a direct confrontation with political matters, out of respect or disdain, as I mention, end up offering insights of great intensity regarding political life. Perhaps that is the case with the authors that you mention in your question: Heidegger, Lacan, Levinas, Derrida—all of them are people whose work cannot be directly classified as political but who have nevertheless provided insights, more or less indirect, which in many cases go further than their apparent intentions. I would say that Heidegger's work, for example, is not fascist in an organic manner, despite the catastrophic personal fascistization of the author that lasted many years, and that Lacan is not as conservative a gentleman as some suggest, and the writings of Derrida and Levinas, in different ways, have yet to be politically exhausted in relation to any possible understanding of the contemporary notion of democracy. In comparison with them, most political scientists or political theorists, certainly during the twentieth century, appear lamentably poor and narrow in spirit. Exceptions do exist, of course, but they tend to be exceptions that fall within that rule, thinkers like Hannah Arendt, Luce Irigaray, Wendy Brown, Miguel Abensour, or Claude Lefort—all figures with one leg or ear outside of the circumscribed social-scientific disciplinary field. Another way of saying the same thing, perhaps, would be to emphasize that what seems interesting today in the field of thought, at least for me, in relation to politics, is not so much political thought as thought that seeks to question the hyperbolic conditions of politics. This is not by chance—of course it has to do with the general conditions for thought during the twentieth century, which we now inherit. They are definable for me if I take as a point of departure what people like Althusser himself, and his more astute followers, in the wake of Marx, or people like Roberto Esposito or Carlo Galli, in the wake of Carl Schmitt, have termed implicitly or explicitly the conceptual end, that is, the productive exhaustion of the political architectonics of modernity.

JORGE ÁLVAREZ YÁGÜEZ: For some time now, your work has dealt with two key ideas, which we could say constitute two separate "research agendas," to use a concept from the theory of science, namely, posthegemony and infrapolitics. Could you comment on their relation?

AM: Speaking of hyperbolic conditions, one of my earliest memories is how I gutted my favorite toy, which was a model plane, I guess it must have been a Douglas or a Boeing, which the Three Magi had brought me. That spring my parents took me to a pigeon shooting contest at Vigo's Aeroclub, but I soon lost interest in the killing because I was much more fascinated by the two or three planes that came into or left the airport, which I could see directly beyond the firing range. When I returned home, I paid a visit to my friend Fidelín, with the purpose of finding out why my plane didn't fly like the ones at the airport. I couldn't think of anything other than borrowing the pliers that belonged to Fidelín's dad and setting to work. After much effort and great sadness, since after all it was my favorite toy, I saw that the plane had a wooden ball inside (which was by that time all that remained usable of the toy). I didn't know how to think about the connection between the ball and flying or not flying, and I think that experience of perplexity and disenchantment, and of loss, ended up causing a fixation of the Fort-Da type in me. I mean, it occurs to me that it could be like that, and that therefore we could relate your question regarding infrapolitics and posthegemony to this situation, for in the end both notions or figures are perhaps intuitively accessible as conditions for flying and conditions for freedom. That is to say, neither infrapolitics nor posthegemony is a goal to be achieved, but rather they are conditions of life, or of practice, and of thought, and one must reach them, perhaps, or if at all possible, through a certain labor of destruction. They require, to enter into themselves, a certain destruction whose end result is never assured. In my previous answer, I said that real politics is not usually found where it seems to be but in a different place. Wherever it is, whoever finds it, neither infrapolitics nor posthegemony claims to occupy that place; instead they occupy the place that allows for making the place of politics a question in each case. It is of course more complicated than it seems, above all because once the necessity of that step back appears, that step back opens another perspective, and then not even politics is a goal, and certainly not the privileged one. But, since you ask about the relation between the two notions, we could begin by saying that posthegemony is the intrapolitical transposition of what we have been calling infrapolitics. In other words, infrapolitics is not politics, it is not a modality of politics, but an other dimension of existence; yet if there is or if there were political infrapolitics, it would be posthegemonic politics in the precise sense of an opposition to any understanding of politics as a system of submission to hegemonic power qua hegemonic. It is therefore a radicalization of the so-called demotic principle of democracy. Infrapolitics understands that there is a region of existence, of existence in common, for which the political relation, although it far from exhausts it, is determining in every case, but it also tries to understand that that political relation, as a region, is not exhaustive, does not consume or map out the space of human existence. Which already tells us, for now, that politics is no goal at all, in any of its modalities, but is itself condition. To insist on posthegemony, in this context, is to insist on the fact that there is a region of common facticity, a sort of generalized state of things crossed by relations of exploitation and domination that any hegemony also sanctions factically. Posthegemony asks to live that state of things from a certain distance, which is to refuse the naturalization of every system of exploitation and domination. However, that refusal does not have a political naturalization either, that distance does not belong to politics and is not founded upon it, for nothing in politics, despite what Machiavelli claims, can be understood as mere abstention from participation in the exploitation or domination of others. Therefore, infrapolitics is, to that extent, a necessary conceptual correlate to the posthegemonic relation, or nonrelation. We could say that, even if there were infrapolitics without posthegemony, there is no posthegemony without infrapolitics, but posthegemony is a political practice, that is, it is a mode of inhabiting politics, whereas infrapolitics is rather the trace of a factico-temporal dimension of existence that precedes (or sub-cedes) and at the same time exceeds every political determination.

MADDALENA CERRATO: Infrapolitics points to a dimension of existence that exceeds both the political and the ethical dimensions, one that does not allow itself to be exhausted either by the two areas that have been understood since Aristotle as practical knowledge or by their mere sum; this is so because infrapolitics points to the excess, the nonsubjective remainder of experience, to the fact that not all experience falls within the subjectivist purview, not all action can be redirected toward a structure of decision. In doing this, infrapolitics reveals the aporetic condition of the political (which would be revealed also in the contradiction in Althusser between the theory of hegemony and aleatory materialism) and the exhaustion of the modern categories with which to think it, thus inaugurating the possibility of "inhabiting politics" in an an-archic and nonsubjective form, that is, making posthegemony possible as a political practice. What happens with the ethical? Does infrapolitics also inaugurate the possibility of thinking and inhabiting the ethical in an an-archic and nonsubjective manner? Would this be an ethics beyond the decision? And where would that lead? Who do you see as your interlocutors in that path? Would Lacanian psychoanalysis have a privileged place in it?

A M: I guess that we can say that the division of practical reason between ethics and politics belongs still, or belongs essentially, to what Heidegger in his "Letter on Humanism" called "the 'technological' interpretation of thought." That technological interpretation has a lot to do with the Platonic-Aristotelian division between essence and existence, perhaps really Helenistic in origin. The ethico-political relation would fall on the side of existence, but already from this fallen form of the division, and absolutely tied to the old metaphysical humanism that saw the world as a mere projection of the subjectivity of the subject. For metaphysical humanism, which is the master ideology that lives through us, the subjectivity of the subject is the only horizon for thought and action. Thus, ethics has to be understood necessarily as a rule of subjectivity or a field of subjective expression. From that understanding, the ethico-political relation is subjected to the narrow predicament of conceiving itself as predominantly ethical (in the person of the Kantian "moral politician") or predominantly political (in the person of the "political moralist"). The first attempts to follow the law rather than his own convenience, whereas the second, the subject of radical evil, does the opposite. But this determines our practical existence in a way that is too reductive—we are above all good or evil, or we are indeterminately bad-and-good, and politics is nothing but the field of action that justifies those appellations. Ethics, understood as technics, can only correct modalities of political conduct. But already in that text Heidegger is searching for an "other" thought "that abandons subjectivity." The step back from all of this, which the notion of infrapolitics announces and tries to think, is consequently also a thought that takes a step back with regard to ethics, understood technically. I wrote all I could about the mysterious and famous fragment by Heraclitus, *ethos anthropoi daimon*, in my first book, *Interpretación y diferencia*. I imagine that what was at stake for me at that time was to begin thinking that step back. For Heraclitus, the ethos is neither law nor a set of rules of conduct; rather it is essentially dwelling and inhabiting, a way of being, if we can venture that translation. In the concluding pages of his "Letter," Heidegger talks about an "originary ethics," although in the same paragraph he discards the term, because for him it was no longer a matter of rescuing old metaphysical terms, with their equivocal chronology and temporalization. If that "originary" ethics, assuming that we erase the first of those two words, promises a step back, promises the restitution of a thought that is no longer techno-conceptual, no longer crossed by the techno-ontological differentiation between essence and existence, we should understand that such a promise is nothing but the possibility of a difficult and destitute exercise that has no end. The word "exercise" can be useful if we understand it etymologically, from *ex-arcare*, unearthing what is hidden, unsecreting. Let us say, then, as provisional as it might be, that infrapolitics is an exercise in this sense—it seeks an exodus with regard to the technological ethico-political relation, it seeks its un-secreting destruction in order to liberate an other existential practice. I would not have any problem using in this context an expression I have used elsewhere, that of "savage moralism." Infrapolitics, in its reflexive condition, is an exercise in savage moralism, anti-political and anti-ethical, since it requires an exodus with regard to the subjective prison that constitutes an ethico-political relation ideologically imposed on us as a consequence of metaphysical humanism. Yes, that savage step back with regard to the ethico-political relation is an-archic, because it does not submit to any principle. And I harbor little doubt that it is possible that some kind of Lacanian or post-Lacanian analysis can serve to think it in its radical poverty.

ÁNGEL OCTAVIO ÁLVAREZ SOLÍS: In some of your work, particularly in *Línea de sombra*, you point to the possibility of a politics without a subject. A politics without a subject avoids the excess of subjectivity that comes with the arrival of the other and, by extension, makes possible a non-onto-theological politics. Nevertheless, recently your work has taken an infrapolitical turn in which experience and existence appear as a space for a "savage moralism," a space for avoiding the subjective and subjectivizing dimension of ethics. Is an ethic without subject possible? Is infrapolitics the anticommunitarian correlate of infraethics?

AM: Allow me to clarify that I don't believe I have ever proposed a politics without a subject and, in any case, certainly not to settle the problem of the "other" by eradicating it from the start. What I was after in *Línea de sombra* was a dismantling of the odd equation that identifies the political field with the field of subjectivity, as if the subject were the final horizon of politics. To say that there is politics also and immediately beyond the subject, that there is politics beyond any figure of subjectivity, even if there is of course a role for the political subject at the same time, this seems so scandalous that even today it is cause for all sorts of misunderstandings and confusions. Yet what exceeds the activity of politics with regard to the subject is everywhere and is in fact much more overwhelmingly self-evident than the naïve notion according to which politics is always what the subject wants and seeks. For my part, I confess that I don't understand why there are so many misunderstandings regarding this point. Or in any case, I should think that the constant misunderstanding is already proof of the ideological consecration of opting for the subject in politics. That our late modernity insists on making subjectivity and action coincide is of course consistent with the reluctant Cartesianism that still inspires our world, even when no one believes in it by now. But what one believes doesn't matter; what matters is that one kneel before the altar. And that is a busy altar—it looks like a bar. I think that what you call a "turn" with regard to *Línea de sombra* is in fact not the case. *Línea de sombra* is a book written against political philosophy, and from a certain deconstructive subalternism to which I sought to give some rigor. What has come after it, very slowly in terms of written production, for biographical reasons that are not irrelevant in this evolution, is an abandonment of politics as a primary thematic in my work, but it is a special kind of abandonment: it establishes itself as a critique of politics. It abandons politics insofar as it is a critique of politics and thus rather than depoliticize it hyperpoliticizes, though it hyperpoliticizes not according to a new political will, but precisely in accord with an existential exodus that I understand as infrapolitical exercise. This existential exodus has consequences at every level, and each one will have to decide if these consequences are to their liking or not. The classic figures are those of retreat, refusal, and abandonment, not by virtue of a quietist or contemplative path, but in relation with a possible radicalization of existential intensities, which in our world only find vulgar substitutions or ridiculous placebos. It is clear that the infrapolitical exercise is countercommunitarian, and that it does not seek any unifying subjectivizing process of the multitude à la Badiou or Rancière, Negri or Laclau (whose theories of politics seem to me ultimately consistent with the Cartesianism I was just alluding to). Clearly it is not a question of proposing an opposition between a politics of more or less dirty hands and an ethics of more or less clean hands, but of not giving a damn about either of the two options. Politics is a massive factum in our lives, which are traversed by it in ways that far surpass our control; but ethics, in our time, and without entering into what it might have been in other epochs, is either farce, pretense, and deceit (insofar as it is based by now on untenable faiths) or it is just pragmatic opportunism (a series of rules that it is convenient to follow to get along with friends, at work, or in the street). So there is no infraethics; ethics is always already fallen below itself. It is interesting but pathetic how ethics (as farce, pretense, and deceit) is offered in a generalized and unquestioned manner as, for the most part, the obvious justification for the politics of the Left in the academic world. Saying that can cost you your head if you still care about having one or are still carrying it (not me). In short, no, there is no infraethics because there is no ethics, and in turn, there is infrapolitics because there is politics. It is important to be precise regarding savage moralism; it is not a "new ethics," nothing of that sort. It is what befalls in a situation in which neither politics nor ethics are instances for an interesting praxis. Savage moralism is not a goal but a procedure, not a theology but a phenomenology, and the formation of style, without which there is no existential intensity, depends on its specific forms in each case. This is why it is still possible to say that savage moralism is a hyperbolic condition of democracy, hence of the only possible politics we should care for.

ÁNGEL OCTAVIO ÁLVAREZ SOLÍS: Literature in greater measure and cinema to a lesser extent are a constant presence in your writing. Yet this interest has been traversed by a preeminent concern with theory: literary theory as a modality of critical theory. Based on your way of writing, specifically in your latest texts and conferences, is there a critical nexus between autography and infrapolitical literature? If there is an infrapolitical cinema, what kind of images or what kind of thought about the image does infrapolitics produce?

AM: In fact, I have written what I have been able to on literature, but very little on film, even though I watch movies every day and incessantly. I imagine that I have the right to pose the question differently to be able to answer it. I don't think that there is in all rigor infrapolitical literature or infrapolitical cinema or anything of the sort—there are ways of approaching experience that can allow us to say, for example, that Gogol is closer to infrapolitics than Gorki, or Proust closer than Brecht, or Beckett closer than Faulkner. Without a doubt, one could extend that exercise to the whole of the Western canon. We could say that *Don Quijote* is an infrapolitical book, and *La Celestina* also, but not particularly *War and Peace* or *Demons*. The Cézanne of the Mont Sainte-Victoire series is an example of infrapolitical practice on the visible, or the Velázquez of *La mulata* at the Art Institute of Chicago. As far as film goes, certainly the work of Raúl Ruiz is infrapolitical reflection, but with moments of intensity that vary quite a bit. His *Poética del cine* could be understood as a manual for infrapolitical cinema, couldn't it? Albert Serra is infrapolitical also, but not so much Bernardo Bertolucci. Laura Poitras's documentaries are in a sense infrapolitical. However, what matters is not that we create a new canon, but that for these kinds of judgments to make sense, we change the way that we read. And the way that we read is always autographic. And autography changes, it moves. I have spent most of my life believing erroneously that the university is a friend to thought, and it is only recently that I have come to understand that this is not the case, that today the university is rather the enemy of thought, that it is necessary to think against the university, without negating the benefits we can garner from working in it. I always thought that in any given field, the absolute priority was to take that field to its limit, only to realize very late that the professional field is nothing but a roost whose denizens seek constantly to reproduce in the same form. I always believed that deep personal and institutional loyalty was a respectable moral value, until I found out that if it is, it is so only for a few unhappy ones. The philosophical figure that interests me is that of the stranger in Plato's *Parmenides*, whom I imagine as the archetypal infrapolitical being, for whom there is no thought that is not autographic, precisely to the extent that his personal experience does not count and does not prevail. The stranger comes from other places above all because he is always on his way elsewhere, and this movement defines his freedom: unshareable, dangerous, and so much more valuable insofar as it is the only conceivable dimension of real experience. To read others always as the stranger, to live narrated existence vicariously as the stranger—that is the best lesson of theoretical critique. And in comparison, banalities related to things like the eternal and interminable gloss of the novel from a particular country, or the poetry of such and such a generation, not to mention culture here or there, have little traction. I am not saying that these things are not necessary, or that there isn't a market or a desire for them. But it is not my desire. And it is less so every day. The other day in a discussion someone was telling me that in the United States I am not white, but also that I could not usurp the "person of color" denomination. Then, if I am not white nor a person of color, I don't exist, or I only exist as abjection, I am a stranger at the border line. Instead of lamenting it too much, I have to opt for making a virtue of such a paradoxical necessity—which was somehow chosen for me beyond any voluntary choice, and which also belongs to those nonsubjectivizable conditions of my life. Sometimes we prefer to act as if our lives were perfectly homologizable to those of others, but I believe one must have the courage to realize that this is not the case. Perhaps that is the first commandment of the infrapolitical catechism, because all others follow from it, whatever they might be.

SAM STEINBERG: In your writing, I have found a certain resistance to canonization or, to take up the term you used above, a certain intransigent task of demetaphorization—and I say this in a way that is necessarily equivocal and even foolish and naïve—which is governed, to say it somewhat ironically, by the development of different names that serve as a conceptual reserve against the instrumental capture of thought: third space, subalternity (at least in the sense you give it), posthegemony, infrapolitics, up to deconstructive practice (different from that practiced in Comparative Literature departments in the United States). Do you identify with this pseudo-genealogy?

AM: Yes, those terms, and others that you do not mention, but among which are many that once were my favorites, I don't know, such as dirty atopism, or critical regionalism, or second order; I guess they are at once something like milestones in my itinerary and concentrations of desire, indifferently. Bergson used to say that no one gets to really think more than one idea, and that it is possible to spend an entire life thinking, only to find out in the end, if you are lucky, that everything that was done goes to configure it. Maybe it is not true, maybe there are two- or even three-idea people around, perhaps even the occasional Don Juan of ideas who can have them all or buy them by the dozen—I have known some of those.

In my case, I think that it is true that I never stopped thinking the same thing, without ever realizing what it could be. In other words, everything I write or say in my classes or meetings or papers is stubborn approaches to the same thing—I can glimpse enough of it now to understand it is this way. Certainly the terms condensed in those constellations that you mention are so many fleeting fetishes, which are nevertheless indispensable for my own mental economy, and which after a time become useless and have to be renewed. Meanwhile, the truth is that nothing produces more solitary excitement than hitting upon one of those terms shining from the bottom of some drawer or some nook of the soul, as a Zahir that only the one who possesses it can feel as such, and which remains opaque or even irritating for others. It all depends on the kind of intellectual one has wanted to be. I don't think that I am or have wanted to be an organic intellectual or to militate in the name of any cause, that I am a specific intellectual or an intellectual of the state, that I can consider myself an academic intellectual except in an unbelieving and uncomfortable way, that I am an identitarian or that I enjoy unconditionally adhering to this or that. I am not even a specialist in anything. I have to entertain myself by allowing some stranger to arrive, perhaps a word that is usually announced by other words, and I honor it with a good meal and a glass of wine. That is why I like conversation. That has always been my problem—I like to talk to people who may not like to listen to me, I like to offer little naïve gifts that are sometimes received as shots. I get people's ears mixed up often—but then maybe not. But I haven't learned to domesticate my own tongue and to silence myself in the way that so many others keep quiet, which is by repeating what others say. In all modesty. The devil knows what it takes. But *la procesión va por dentro*, and in the end the important thing is to enjoy what one does.

SAM STEINBERG: As is always the case, one never finishes all the books that one should write or has to write or wants to write. What are Moreiras's unpublished books? And I am not only referring to future books (though I am also referring to those), but to those books that were left behind. I am thinking, for example, about a book on the narco. Where do you locate those books, from the past as well as the future, in the intellectual map?

AM: Thanks for the question, though I am going to blame you for the forced narcissism of the answer. Hell is cobbled with books that were left behind, and the truth is that it is a good place for them. The regime of intellectual production in which we live hypocritically wants our publications to proliferate on the basis of some vague appeal to competitive excellence—in which, moreover, no one, or no one in the administration, believes. For every Zizek or Derrida, capable of writing several books a year, and of making all the rest of us bite the dust, there are dozens of colleagues, excellent as they may be, from whom it is perhaps not advisable to ask that they write more than one book every fifteen or twenty years. I am not either Zizek or Derrida, and so everything that has been left behind deserves to have been left behind. The sorry fact, but there it is, is that I began my professional life mistakenly, I chose wrongly, got off on the wrong foot, for reasons that are hard to explain, and I had to take on the responsibility of training students, from the very beginning, for a career in an academic field that has inspired little personal interest in me, no particular passion (I don't think this is a mystery). For the last thirty years I have carried that like a bird hanging from my neck, after the novelty wore off, the mere curiosity. But it was too late. Now, on the one hand, it could well be that the world is thankful for my relatively low or, at best, medium rate of production. On the other, it is true that only recently (I can date it precisely: since July 2012) have I begun to think that there are books that I would like to write, and that are starting to knock at the door—strictly because now I no longer feel tied to any institutionally recognized professional field, and so I will never again write under a relative obligation to do so. Until now, truth be told, this has been a difficult issue. So, in addition to *Piel de lobo*, which will be published in Madrid in 2020, I have about five more or so in preparation—each one is semisecret—and I hope to finish them all in two years (which, of course, won't happen). Then I would like to write a book, I don't know, on the Marquis de Sade, and another on Antonio Gramsci, and another one on my favorite contemporary Spanish writers, Juan Benet and Javier Marías. And I have promised to write one on the infrapolitical cinema of Raúl Ruiz. But I am sure that, among all of these that I just mentioned, perhaps I'll only write one or two, and that, in turn, other themes will emerge. What I do believe that I will be able to do, now that I have decided not to move anymore and to decline any invitation that would distract me, will be to write one book every year or year and a half, until my time comes to watch movies and read detective novels *per omnia saecula saeculorum*. Or perhaps not. Perhaps I am rushing too much, when slowing down is what is needed.

Appendix

MARRANO RELIGION

Javier Marías's *Los enamoramientos,* and the Literary Secret

> He was always aware that we are here because of a conjunction of chances.
>
> MARÍAS, *Los enamoramientos*

1

I confess my fascination with *Los enamoramientos* (2011), and I cannot tell you why it fascinates me—its secret affects me also in that way, insofar as I can only establish a partial relationship with it that I cannot betray. I can only say it is connected to several aspects of the story this book has tried to tell—perhaps not the most evident ones, which is the reason why this is given as an appendix, a supplement, take it or leave it, for daring readers, if there are any, unless, of course, the author is the lunatic one and seeks links where there aren't any. I would like to explore that possibly deluded (or not) partiality through the notion of the marrano religion, if there could be one. My hypothesis, that is, the modality of my partial relationship, which makes the interpretation interminable, is that the novel becomes a sort of mise-en-scène of Isaac's sacrifice, which is at the same time its immediate erasure. If the history of Abraham refers to a law, marrano religion, necessarily betraying the monotheistic relation, would be a relationship to the secret beyond any law—a religion without religion. No other discourse but the literary can thematize and explore it—philosophy and theology will not do, anthropology will not do. In "Literature in Secret," Jacques Derrida says:

> Literature surely inherits from a holy history within which the Abrahamic moment remains the essential secret (and who would deny that literature remains a religious remainder, a link to and relay for what is sacrosanct in a society without God?), while at the same time denying that history, appurtenance,

and heritage. It denies that filiation. It betrays it in the double sense of the word: it is unfaithful to it, breaking with it at the very moment when it reveals its "truth" and uncovers its secret. Namely that of its own filiation: impossible possibility. This "truth" exists on the condition of a denial of power whose possibility was already implied by the binding of Isaac. (Derrida, *Gift* 157)

Binding Isaac is obedience to a command that binds unconditionally. Literature at the same time guards that command and voids it in betraying negation: marrano religion and impossible possibility.

Los enamoramientos makes patent that particular latency in all literature. The novel thematizes the secularization of Isaac's sacrifice and simultaneously erases it in the name of a secret that is not reducible to politics—a nonsecularizable secret, unshareable, incomprehensible for the community, which can only develop from it a sort of infinite rumor. Javier Díaz-Varela is the Abrahamic figure in the novel; María Dolz, the narrator, can only express a damaged incomprehension regarding him. María also feels dead, killed by Javier, she is the living dead, the displaced ghost who would want not to be who she is and not to know what she knows. In her utter abandonment, at the end of the text, she beautifully renders her religion without religion: "At the end nobody will judge me, and there are no witnesses to my thoughts. It is true that when we are caught in the spider web—between the first chance event and the second one [that is, between birth and death]—we fantasize limitlessly and at the same time conform ourselves with any crumbs, with hearing him—like hearing that time between chances, it is the same—, with smelling him, with glimpsing him, with having a presentiment of him, with still having him on our horizon instead of vanished from it, with not yet seeing in the distance the dust of his fleeing feet" (*Los enamoramientos* 216; my translation throughout).

As the novel begins, María's gaze is focused on the couple sitting at a nearby table in the neighborhood coffee shop. María is watching Miguel and Luisa, "What was most pleasing about them was to see how much they enjoyed being together" (15). Miguel and Luisa are in love. But Miguel dies, stabbed by a madman in the street. And certain circumstances allow María to meet Javier, Miguel's best friend, at Luisa's house. It happened during a visit in which Luisa tells María about the death of her husband, how terrible the murder was, and how devastating her mourning, her pain. María notices Javier's solicitude for Luisa. A short while later María and Javier develop an affair, and María falls in love with Javier. One afternoon, María is napping in Javier's bedroom after making love, and she is awakened by the doorbell ringing of somebody arriving at the apartment. María cannot avoid overhearing a conversation in which the worst is revealed: Javier had Miguel killed. After that, she knows her relationship with Javier must come to an end. Javier also understands it that way, but he explains to María what happened: it was not murder, just homicide, which Miguel had requested of him as an act of friendship. Sometime later, in the Chinese restaurant at the Palace Hotel, María finds Javier and Luisa dining together, happy, in love. "They were mutually absorbed, they chatted with vivacity, they looked in each other's eyes every now and then without saying anything, they touched across the table" (391). Between the first and the last scenes of the novel a terrible sentimental education is imparted.

2

Honoré de Balzac's novella *El coronel Chabert* has an important role in the intertext of *Los enamoramientos*.[1] Javier speaks of that text to María with a certain obsessive insistence. María finds and reads the novella, curious about why Javier, with whom she is already in love, would "use it as a demonstration that the dead are fine the way they are and should never come back, even if their death was untimely, unjust, stupid, gratuitous, or chancy, like [Miguel] Desvern's, and even if that risk, the risk of reappearance, does not exist. It was as if he feared that in the case of his friend, a resurrection were possible, and he wanted to persuade himself or persuade me of the error, the bad timing, even the evil that such a return would bring about for the living and also for the deceased" (179). We are already in the middle of the theory of the phantasm that Marías has used on other occasions. Javier seems to be preoccupied, perhaps even slightly deranged, by the prospect of a dead man's return, his intimate friend Miguel, murdered by a beggar, "stabbed to death for no reason and on his way to oblivion" (150). But the oblivion part is unclear. Miguel's return is implicit in the ostensible worry about Balzac's novella, the side-taking Javier does in favor of the colonel's wife or ex-wife, the now Countess Ferraud, who must confront the return of a husband she had thought dead in battle ten years before. The dead, even if they never return, have countless ways of returning.

When María reaches the end of Balzac's text and finds the words that Derville, the lawyer, tells his associate Godeschal on human wickedness and the usual impunity, she notices what she calls an "error of translation" (180) in the detailed narration of the novella Javier had given her. In an impromptu translation from the French, Javier had quoted: "I have seen women feeding the child of a marriage drops that should bring it death, so that the child of an illicit love could be favored" (172, 181). But the novella does not say "*des gouttes*," it says "*des goûts*," which means that the correct translation would have been: "I have seen women fostering in the child of a marriage tastes (or 'inclinations') that would lead it to its death" (181). María attempts to interpret the hidden sense of that translation slip, very rare for someone with such a great accent and mastery in the language. She imagines that "it is very different to cause death, whoever is not handling the weapon tells himself (and we inadvertently follow their reasoning), from preparing for it and waiting for it to occur by itself, to happen on its own; it is also different from desiring it, from ordering it, and desire and command mix at times, they become indistinguishable for those who are used to seeing their desires satisfied as soon as expressed or even hinted at, or used to having them fulfilled as soon as conceived of" (183). The novel introduces the infrapolitical dimension of a possible *actio in distans* in its structure: the action that is not directly political (or is it?) but will result in political effects, in this case identified with the capacity of "the most powerful and the most cunning" of never getting their "hands or almost even their tongues" dirty (183), of provoking crimes that would remain unrecognized and unpunished, above all unrecognized, of ruining the stomach of the likes of Monsieur Derville, the lawyer. Would it be possible for Javier to have had Miguel killed, Miguel, his best friend, not because the latter asked him to, but rather so that he could get his wife, Luisa; to clear the field for Luisa and be able to bring his desire to eventual fruition? How was María not to think that thought, from which possible perspective?

3

María imagines as she tries to deal with a difficult and entangled truth that turns her also into a peculiar kind of narrator: not just an untrustworthy narrator but rather a narrator who, as absolutely trustworthy, is precisely incapable of believing that her truth is the whole truth, or truth as such. Perhaps, to start with, María thinks that there are things one should not say, or should say only with great reluctance and care. What incalculable sequence of events could come into being if one told a friend—say, Miguel to Javier—something like "If something happened to me one day . . . if something definitive were to occur," please take care of my wife and my kids; "She must have you as a replacement" (*Los enamoramientos* 117). It is dangerous to play with fire, to ask your friend to collaborate in your final obliteration, because if you do, your friend might be tempted to do it. He would tell your ghost, "You asked for it, remember? Don't come now with reproach or accusations, when you are no more than a cold-handed ghost, when people barely remember you." What was a gesture of friendship, what implied trust and abandon, can end up provoking murder, clean or dirty, even if it is only the murder of a ghost. "It is better for your wife and kids that I remove you from presence totally, particularly now that you are dead; they will feel better, they will be happier. You yourself understood it that way when you asked me to do what you asked me to do, perhaps not fully knowing what you were doing, thinking it was a problem for the future, but the future lasts a long time, and the time came for you to be taken away terminally, my friend. Don't fuck with me; it was your idea, you asked for it."

Yes, one can think it was just a slight transgression, that is what friendship is for, to absorb them, not to dwell on them; one should be able to expose oneself to a friend without exposing oneself to unwelcome effects, without the incalculable coming into the picture, without the unexpected happening. I did not tell my friend to erase me, not now, while I am alive (or am I dead already?), and not when I am dead. On the contrary, I asked my friend to try to take up my role, in a sense for him to become me, to keep me alive among mine. Alive, not dead, giving my people what I myself have always tried to give them. I did not want erasure but survival, even knowing I would not be there, even knowing and accepting the vicariousness. That is what friends are for, I think. Otherwise, what are they for? Besides, you did not really tell your friend literally to substitute for you. You told him: "I am not asking you to marry her or anything of the kind. . . . You have your bachelor's life and your many women that you would never give up . . . But, please, keep close to her if I at some point become absent. . . . Be a kind of husband without being the husband, be my extension" (117). You asked him not to be you, but to be your surrogate, your secretary, your representative. It is not such a big deal, that alleged transgression. It is what is normal in these cases, what one expects, that is why one has friends.

Of course he did not like it, or he did not seem to like it, and he said: "Are you asking me to substitute for you if you die? . . . to become a false husband? ... and a father at a certain distance?" (118). "Do you realize how difficult it is to be a false husband without becoming a real one in the long term? ... If you were to die one day and I went to your home daily, it would be really difficult for what should never happen while you were alive not to happen. Would you like to die knowing that?" (119-120). He almost accused me of asking him to become a pimp, and that bothered me a little, to tell you the truth, for him to jump to the conclusion that he could occupy my place, which of course I would never have asked, which was well beyond what I was asking. I did not realize then that something had already opened up, perhaps at that precise moment, or it was already open, I do not know. What was incalculable, unforeseeable, was rearing its ugly head through my friend's very protest, and I tried to calm him down and I said no, how can you even think that, I said that my wife was not going to be interested in him in that way, she knew him all too well, for many years, for her he was a brother or a cousin, and to get the fuck out. I was not asking him to sweep me into nothingness, to remove all traces, to bury me, only for him to take some care once my own story had come to an end, if it did; that would calm me down and make me feel better, given my difficulties; it was just a promise, for me it would be just a promise, his promise that if something bad happens to me, he would take care of things, that is all. And I told him: "So I still ask you that, if something bad happens, will you give me your word that you will take care of them?" (124). And he, still a bit upset, I could see it, he said then: "You have my word of honor, whatever you want, count on it. . . . But do me a favor and don't ever fuck me over again with things like that, you've given me a bad feeling. Let's go have a drink and talk about less macabre things" (126).

4

Yes, I suspected something, of course, how could I not, Javier could say, but Miguel refused to confirm it then, or perhaps he himself did not yet quite know, he only suspected it. It was later, he said, that we had the other conversation, the truly terrifying one. He asked me to kill him, or to have him killed, but that day we only spoke of him, not about his wife or kids, it was more than enough. He told me the doctors had diagnosed him with a severe kind of cancer, an intraocular melanoma, really "a very evolved metastasized melanoma" that would give him no more than a couple of months of a livable life and would carry him to his death with atrocious pain, with or without supposedly palliative treatment (332-333; 334-335).

He asked me to plot his death within one and a half to two months. I lack the strength for suicide, he said, it is not to die but to die poorly that terrifies me, I am not ready for that, I do not want Luisa and the kids to have to go through it. My time will have passed, he said, and there is no extending the unextendable. Kill me, get me out of here. But do not tell me how or when, "do whatever you want, hire someone to shoot me, have someone run me over when I am crossing the street, let a wall fall on top of me or my brakes stop functioning, or the lights, I do not know" (345). At first I said absolutely not, "I told him that could not be, it was too much to ask, he could not charge someone with a task that only he could take on" (346). But "from the beginning I knew I had no alternative. That, difficult as it could be for me, I had to fulfill his request. What I said to him was one thing. What it was on me to do was something else. I had to get him out of the way, as he put it, because he would never dare do it himself, actively or passively, and what awaited him was indeed cruel" (347).

So I sought help, I asked for favors, and we plotted a plan that would allow his death, if everything worked out, without trapping me in the legal consequences. The bum who slept around the neighborhood and made some money reserving parking slots for people and who knew Miguel from that was the chosen one. We gave him a cell phone and we started to call him, sickening him on Miguel, telling him that Miguel was responsible for the prostitution of his daughters, and we gave him one of those butterfly knives, we left it where he slept, he could choose to use it or not. And he ended up doing it. And he stabbed Miguel to death, multiple times, the morning of his birthday, as Luisa waited for him at a restaurant for lunch. It was an act of piety on our side, not a murder, it was homicide, perhaps, a crime, also against the bum, although he is better off now at the psychiatric hospital than he used to be, living in his dirty abandoned car, but his death was what Miguel wanted, how he wanted it, and giving it to him was an act of friendship. And yet "I have always known I had to think and act like a murderer" to get it done (349). And now I am very tired. "Whatever you think, María, in spite of everything, is not too important. As perhaps you may imagine" (349).

5

Before knowing all of that, María suspected something fishy, or she did not suspect but felt there could be, since she herself, in her unrequited love for Javier, had started to realize that the disappearance or death of Luisa could be advantageous for her, could bring her Javier's love. If María herself can desire Luisa's death, there is no apparent reason why Javier would not have desired or would not have been capable of desiring Miguel's death. It is obvious to María that Javier is in love with Luisa, and that he is waiting for forgetfulness, the passage of time, the reparations of time, to end up occupying in Luisa's life the position of his old dead friend, assassinated. María knows that she herself is only a temporary substitute in Javier's passion, that Javier seeks Luisa, Javier is in love with Luisa. And she is terrified, given Miguel's death, that things may have been too serendipitous for Javier. Perhaps Javier long desired, desired for too long, Miguel's death. "One does not dare desire anybody's death, still less when somebody is close, but it is intuited that if a determinate someone would suffer an accident, or had a terminal disease, the universe would improve somewhat, or, better for every one of us, our own personal situation" (191–192).

María listens to Javier's version of what happened. Javier plotted Miguel's death. Javier is deeply in love with Luisa. The first possible version of what really happened is a sordid one, but who can avoid it? It is the logical one, the realist one, the obvious one. Javier's story, his tale, María says, is only "to deceive with the truth" (293). Javier is in love with Luisa, Javier had Miguel, Luisa's husband, killed. Those are facts. Will it even be true that Miguel had a very evolved metastasized melanoma? Will it be true that Miguel asked Javier to get him out of the way, a curious expression (was it Miguel's expression, or was it Javier's expression?) in order to spare himself a considerably more atrocious death, or suicide? All of those are or could be Javier's inventions. The newspapers mentioned nothing about any of it, the necessary autopsy for victims of violent deaths does not seem to have revealed the cancer, but newspapers aren't trustworthy, and "in Spain almost everybody does just enough for the record, never more, there is very little desire to go deep, to spend hours on what nobody requires" (359). After all, any coroner could see that Miguel had died from the nine or sixteen stab wounds. As far as what really happened, "nothing was conclusive" (393) for María, except that Javier had Miguel's blood on his hands, and now had Luisa in his bed. So it is perfectly possible that Javier is yet another one of the characters who makes Monsieur Derville, the lawyer, retire from his lawyer's office: "Our offices are sewers that cannot be cleansed. . . . I cannot tell you how much I have seen, because I have seen crimes against which justice is powerless. Anyway, all the horrors that the novelists think they are making up are always well below the truth" (Balzac, *El coronel* loc. 1162, Kindle Archive).

But there is another possible version, against María, although María cannot quite bring herself to dismiss it. María says: "Worse than the serious suspicions and the perhaps rushed and unfair conjectures was to know two versions and not know which one to accept, or rather knowing I had to accept both and that both would persist in my memory until the latter removed them, tired of the repetition" (354). Perhaps Javier did what Miguel asked him to do, and sacrificed himself for Miguel, in complete uncertainty regarding how that was to affect his relationship with Luisa, or even putting it radically in danger. Perhaps Javier did what Miguel asked him to do out of friendship and the loyal need to fulfill his friend's request, and there is nothing else. Or perhaps there was some other reason—not even friendship, not even loyalty, not any need to pay any kind of debt, something else, who knows? How is one to know? When Javier says that "from the very beginning" he knew he would have to fulfill his friend's request—Abrahamic mandate, turn yourself into a murderer, immediate suspension of everything that is normal in everyday life, an entry into an ecstatic relationship with the secret—Javier understands that his solitude, the solitude of an existence called into the secret, betrays not just Luisa and María, but ultimately also Miguel himself, and that his life has been mortgaged to the absolute, to an absolute. What is incalculable has come into his life beyond every justice and beyond every justification. Why should he expose himself to it? Javier's love for Luisa needs no assassination, needs no voluntary *actio in distans* from Javier if it is true that Miguel is suffering from a terminal cancer that will take him to his grave in a matter of months. No calculation justifies Javier's actions, but María cannot know whether it is calculation itself that establishes a consistently lying narrative: to deceive every time, to deceive with the truth. María, remembering that Javier had told him that what happens in novels does not matter, says: "Perhaps he thought that was not the case for the real facts, the facts of our lives. Things are probably true for the one that lives through them, but not for the rest. Everything becomes a story and ends up floating within the same sphere, and what happened is hardly different from what is invented. Everything ends up being a narrative, therefore sounding the same, fictitious even if true" (331).[2] Javier, to María's ear, can only deceive with the truth because Javier's truth is beyond any narrative and hooks up with radical denarrativization. Javier will have always told María: "You have understood that for me my longings are above every consideration, every brake, every scruple. And every loyalty, imagine. It has been very clear to me, for some time already, that I want to spend the rest of my life with Luisa" (307). But this savage, because unconditional, decision cannot explain his decision to abide by Miguel's desire—the latter remains outside every narrative, in the secret, in an obligation deemed unconditional that loyalty cannot explain, or brakes, or any scruples.

There are two versions, and only one of them has to do with calculations and narrative economy. The other version is alien to them, even if it can only narrate or be narrated. A narration without narration, the narration that starts itself by saying "from the very beginning I knew I had no alternative." And perhaps literature is nothing but the secular attempt to touch that edge of narration beyond narration. This is the infrapolitical dimension of literature, its *actio in distans*, without which literature can only be communitarian allegorization, fallen as such, unfree. In the last instance, perhaps Javier's words to María, when he is laboriously attempting to explain to her the story of Colonel Chabert, are apposite: "what happened matters the least" (166).

6

Derrida talks about Abraham's sacrifice not as an absolutely unique event in the life of Abraham, but rather as what he calls "the most common thing" (*Gift* 68). Derrida says: "As soon as I enter into a relation with the other, with the gaze, look, request, love, command, or call of the other, I know that I can respond only by sacrificing ethics, that is to say by sacrificing whatever obliges me to also respond, in the same way, in the same instant, to all the others" (69). Javier came into that relation when Miguel asked him to get him out of the way (if indeed he did). For Derrida, nothing can provide justification for such a responsibility or such an imperative, which he calls an "absolute sacrifice" (68). The sacrifice Abraham was asked to make is not the sacrifice of irresponsibility before responsibility, but rather "the sacrifice of the most imperative duty (that which binds me to the other as a singularity in general) in favor of another absolutely imperative duty binding me to the wholly other" (71-72). Isaac's sacrifice is the one that takes place every day for each one of us, insofar as we constantly sacrifice what we love the most to what we must do. Javier must suspend his own desire, even endanger it, in order to fulfill his secret obligation. If Abraham is ready to kill his son, or Javier, Miguel, beyond ethics, besides ethics (Javier's passion for Luisa precisely puts him in radical evil at the time of consummating his sacrifice, outside ethics, in the abyss of ethics), appearing thus, in the eyes of his neighbor, as a murderer, then we are all murderers, since we do in each case what we do and we sacrifice everything else to it. Something presses, constantly and overwhelmingly, and it organizes every decision as a passive decision, but what presses remains inscrutable. We are all murderers and we live in a perpetual suspension of ethics, given over to a savage moralism. But the temptation of ethical behavior through some notion of absolute responsibility is also, necessarily, the temptation of an infinite betrayal of ethics, maximally irresponsible. María learns it at the end of the novel, when she finally admits that "I could not care less about justice and injustice" (393). It was always something else—and it is the something else that binds.

NOTES

INTRODUCTION

1. Comments by Alejandra Castillo, Federico Galende, and Sergio Villalobos, respectively in "Nombres," "Umbral," and "Amigo," are in *Revista de Crítica Cultural* 34 (December 2006). My response, "Pantanillos," is also there (78–87).

CHAPTER 1. Marranism and Inscription

1. I am referring to chapter 4 in Deleuze and Guattari's *What Is Philosophy?*

2. This is probably a good place to say that there is no "appropriation" of the tragic history of a specific group of people, provided we can talk about marranos as a "group" in any meaningful sense, in the way I want to use the notions of *marranismo* or marrano register in this book and elsewhere. The very use of those notions should be understood as a personal homage to the victims of that history that refers to persecution, harassment, oppression, murder: a history of the Spanish and Portuguese "new Christians," or conversos, later accused of not being converso enough by hegemonic social or political power. The fact remains that the marranos were not only Jews by tradition or descent—they were also Spaniards, so they also belong in the national and cultural history of Spain. The metonymic use of some aspects of their historical experience (the double exclusion, the isolation, the potential disorientation, but also their commitment to freedom, their understanding of community without community, their potentiality for unfettered thought) to refer to an intellectual-institutional position today that, to me, has obvious links with the tradition, with my national tradition, means no disrespect. To the contrary . . . it is only radical solidarity.

3. Infrapolitics and its corollary, posthegemony, receive ample treatment in forthcoming books on those concepts—one of them to be published by La Oficina and the other by Biblioteca Nueva. Let me, meanwhile, direct the reader to the second interview in this volume, chapter 9, where the notion receives a treatment that will supplement the too-shallow indications offered here.

CHAPTER 2. My Life at Z

1. It is eight years at the time of this translation—and the reason why the translation took three more years is given in what happened.

2. Three years later, I have no specific recollection of my fearfulness, which was probably trembling shame rather than fear, and it had to do with the obligation I had imposed on myself of writing this piece and publishing it. I was told the piece, once published in a Spanish magazine, was the object of sick curiosity at Z, and that any number of people experienced the delights of Google Translate for the first time ever trying to decipher my poor Spanish. I hope they learned something. If not, they can do it now. Not that I care. But I never received any response. I will say here once again that writing this piece made me physically sick, and I still hate having had to do it—but I thought it was necessary, not just as a symbolic personal protest but because it can help other people when they are subjected to mob rule with the complicity of those who should have helped them against it.

CHAPTER 3. The Fatality of (My) Subalternism

1. As John has a special interest in *testimonio*, he will not object to the following: In the fall of 2005, within a few days of my having given the university administration notice that I would be leaving for an overseas position, given their lack of interest in my retention, which the deans had been advised against by my departmental chairs, when I could not quite believe what was happening and was confronting, in the name of dignity, the loss of everything that was important to me (my home, my dogs, my garden, my habits, twenty years of Latin Americanist work in the United States), and was still desperately expecting someone, a friend, to wake me up from a bad dream, some of my colleagues of fifteen years started conspiring with the clueless deans to bring John Beverley in as my replacement. They established a pact of silence, and they kept to it: whatever happened, I was not supposed to hear a single word. When, many months later, everything came out into the open, they tried either to dissemble their own involvement or to justify it: "Hey, you are leaving, I have to continue to live here" or "Well, we did not have a choice, it was us making the decision for John or someone else for somebody else" or "I am not your enemy, don't think of me as your enemy," respectively. I suppose they were trying to do what was good for them, or for their university. Who can blame them? No one (*nemo?*) can blame them. And John told me: "You could cut the mess with a knife. I was not going to accept." And he didn't.

2. Or not so secret. At the end of chapter 6, Beverley writes: "Our disillusion has not been *thorough* enough. It has not worked through the melancholia of defeat. As a result, it leaves (or seeks to impose) a residual guilt that shades into an acceptance of, or identification with, the powers that be. . . . In that way, the paradigm of disillusion has not prepared us to accept that the possibility of radical change has opened up once again in the Americas, North and South" (109). This is a strange logic. Because his generation, Beverley claims, was defeated in its revolutionary aspirations, they are now unable, generally speaking, to understand that the possibility of revolutionary change must be endorsed once again. Understanding such

a thing goes through a radicalization of disillusionment that would enable them to work through melancholic fixations, so that their desire finds open channels yet again. I confess I am unable to follow John here, perhaps because I have nothing to do with his generation, not really, and I have always been opposed to armed struggle as a substitute for politics. But let me offer a counterreading of the situation: Beverley is not trying to get rid of melancholia by working through it. He is simply trying to find a partial object that can act as a substitute formation, as he has done in the past with the Central American revolutionary movements, with ETA and the Basques, with the Colombian guerrillas (but see note 4), and with subaltern studies. In other words, his Latin Americanist desire has always been a substitute formation at the level of narcissistic identification. This is what I call ego Latin Americanism, of which Beverley is an exemplary character.

3. Most readers will have no reason to know with any precision that the breakdown and de facto dissolution of the Latin American Subaltern Studies Group took place through and at the end of a conference, "Cross-Genealogies and Subaltern Knowledges," organized by Walter Mignolo and myself at Duke University in the fall of 1998. I have already talked about this in chapter 1, but it bears repetition in the context of this chapter. Mignolo initiated early on in the conference discussions a move or a series of moves (later confirmed by the introductory essay to several conference papers he published in the first issue of *Nepantla* [see Mignolo, "Introduction."]) oriented toward breaking, analytically and politically, the group of Latin American subalternists into three different groups, roughly, the "founding members," among whom John Beverley and Ileana Rodríguez seemed to stand in a group of their own; the so-called properly postcolonial thinkers that would include Mignolo himself and his allies, among whom Enrique Dussel and Aníbal Quijano were certainly there (as far as I can tell, that very conference marked the beginning of the constitution of the decolonial tendency as such in the field); and a relatively undefined and motley but large bunch of so-called postmodernists who were at the time starting to use a new notion, "posthegemony" (whether appreciatively or critically, that depended), and who were more or less gently accused wholesale of being naïve Eurocentric sellouts. Things were not helped by the presence at the conference of an extraordinary group of Duke Latin Americanist graduate students, who seemed to hang out with the posthegemony crowd a lot more than with the other groups. At the final roundtable, John Beverley and Ileana Rodríguez made the political blunder of collapsing all differences between the two apparent or alleged groups that seemed not to include them and accusing both of them of together attempting to hijack Latin American subaltern studies in the service of a Duke institutional project. The Latin Americanist subalternist enterprise met its institutional death right then, as the three mentioned senior members, whom we thought of as the natural leaders of the endeavor, had managed to create a hostile and labyrinthine nightmare that not only spooked the rest of us but indeed alerted us to impending catastrophes of various kinds (which, of course, soon started to happen). When, a couple of years later, at the Subaltern Studies at Large Conference, organized by Gayatri Spivak at Columbia University, and to which both John Kraniauskas and myself had been invited as speakers, after it had become abundantly obvious for the most innocent among us that the Latin American Subaltern Studies Group

had collapsed and that Mignolo and his allies had decided and had been deciding to go their own separate way, Beverley and Rodríguez asked me, in the presence of John Kraniauskas, who, being Britain based, was possibly presumed to be unable to do it efficiently, to take over the leadership of a renewed Latin American Subaltern Studies Group. I had to decline, as I knew the idea was unviable because the damage done had been too profound. Sometime later, Rodríguez made the same proposal to Gareth Williams, who also declined. In retrospect, for me and for my "posthegemony" friends and students—and we were all too young then, or indeed naïve—the experience was finally an experience of bitter intellectual censorship. Our commitment to the group, which had already created all kinds of difficulties for us in the larger professional field (one of us failed to get tenure at his institution on the basis of his membership in the group, and that is simply the most egregious example of the difficulties), left us high and dry. I myself left Duke a few years later in the wake of a chain of events whose proximate cause was my difference with Mignolo. We are still living through the consequences of the conflict: those are the "Latin Americanist doldrums" people have talked about, which hurt not only us but many students and young professionals who came behind us and found a wasteland. "*Solitudinem faciunt*" indeed, but we did not call it peace. Perhaps somebody did. Obviously I am not talking about everyone in the larger field, only about people with certain theoretical and political commitments or interests in the subfield of Latin American cultural and postcolonial studies. See Williams, "Deconstruction," for further reflections on the implications of that episode.

4. Inconsequentially to my mind, but not to his, Beverley devotes a footnote to wonder why I may have never come to terms with my Galician origins and why I have never talked about Galicia in terms of "critical regionalism." He says: "As far as I am aware[,] Moreiras has not written about the 'critical regionalism' that is pertinent to his Galician identity" (134n13). Well, he missed, for instance, the full chapter in my book *Tercer espacio* where I talk about revolutionary projections in Galicia through the literature of my very own cousin Xosé Luis Méndez Ferrín, a radical Marxist-Leninist nationalist, by the way. And it does not take a lot of reading to find in that chapter the beginning of the thread for the whole book, if one continues, say, with the first Exergue. But never mind: the point is that John wants me to confront my own identity and thinks I haven't or am somehow unable to. Not like him: "In the extensive menu of postmodern 'identities,' I have discovered one of my own: as a child born and raised for the first twelve years of my life in Latin America by WASP parents from the United States, I am a 'third (or trans-)culture kid' or TCK" (136n9). He goes on to say that such a fact makes him similar to Roberto Bolaño or Barack Obama, which in my opinion is a more becoming set of identifications than the one he claimed a few years ago, shortly after the Lewinsky episode, when he said that he felt like a mixture of Bill Clinton and Mao Zedong. But we all have our fantasies. Mine is somewhere between Wile E. Coyote and the character played by Do-yeon Jeon in Sang-soo Im's *The Housemaid* (2010).

5. One of the questions nobody seems to want to ask is whether your religious or ontological or historical or cultural beliefs provide you with an identity, or whether identity, used in the ideological and militant sense, is already the name of your failure to believe in anything and your attempt to compensate for it: a common problem in postmodern, nihilistic

times far from being confined to the so-called Western world. Real believers, I have found, rarely appeal to identity: they do not need to. I find belief systems endlessly fascinating myself, and have a total and absolute respect for them—for any of them, including some I have run across that have baffled me. The point of my critique is not to contest the right of anybody to believe whatever it is they believe. On the contrary, I think. Fake believers destroy belief and the deep historical, imaginative wealth that comes with it. Fake believers represent a fallen state of ethical life, which is the reason why I do not think it is the task of academic scholars to promote the identity business: by definition, identities can only be respected not promoted (to that extent I value political programs oriented to respecting belief systems and the people who have them). The promotion of public identities by the state or state agents or political agents wanting to be part of the state is drastically suspect to me in every case, and it does not seem to me it has anything to do with democracy except as a means of controlling it, hence limiting it. I am aware of important trends in contemporary anthropology that are doing their best to suggest that indigenous belief systems, for instance in the Andes, can "force the ontological pluralization of politics and the reconfiguration of the political" (De la Cadena 360), but I do not believe that it is a necessary consequence of such theorizations that politics should be ruled over by new ontologies or even by a principled acceptance of multiple ontologies or worlds, whatever that might mean. While I understand the political power of ontology, I still refuse to ontologize the political even in the name of the subaltern. If those very anthropologists aim to critique the Western imperialist Nature-Culture divide, as an ontological mode that has been historically used to subalternize non-Western belief systems, it seems hardly persuasive that newly rediscovered ontologies should now be given leeway for a reconfiguration of the political, as opposed to seeking a reconfiguration of political power on democratic terms, whether in Latin America or elsewhere. To sum up: in my opinion, it is not ontology but democratic practice that should be privileged for any reconfiguration of the political as it is or could be. If the difference matters between a conception of "politics as power disputes within a singular world" and a conception "that includes the possibility of adversarial relations among worlds, a pluriversal politics" (De la Cadena 360), it only matters because, presumably, the latter might foster the cause of tendentially universal equality.

6. I have a distinct recollection, perhaps flawed, of Beverley's expression of support for the FARC (Revolutionary Armed Forces of Colombia) several years ago, as it made quite an impression on me. But he tells me in a private communication that he does not recall ever supporting them, and he certainly does not now.

7. If I recall correctly, the first version of this paper was presented at the conference "Marx and Marxisms in Latin America," organized by Bruno Bosteels at Cornell University in the fall of 2006.

8. Cf. Arturo Escobar's otherwise brilliant essay "Latin America at the Crossroads," where the main idea is actually to orient *marea rosada* governments to proper doctrine—the doctrine is, of course, highly arguable, but it constitutes perhaps the best and most cogent formulation of a radical decolonial state project to date.

9. José Luis Villacañas and I have coedited the Latin American sections of the

Wiley-Blackwell *Encyclopedia of Postcolonial Studies* (2015), with about seventy contributors, where we hope to have set some things straight. The subtitle for our work was "A Metahistory of Material Practices of Power."

10. On the at best preparatory character of intellectual work vis-à-vis politics, Beverley's question is: "How should we judge that claim today?" (51). My answer is: same as yesterday. I have no pretensions, as a writer, that I am a political actor, and tend to think that any leaking of disciplinary work into the political sphere is for the most part based on a misunderstanding. I suppose sometimes the misunderstanding can be productive, but that probably happens rarely.

11. Mark Driscoll's accusation of "looting" against Hardt and Negri, apparently after extensive consultation with "decolonials," because it was claimed that Hardt and Negri used the mantra "coloniality of power" without immediate and unmediated attribution, gave rise to a considerable amount of possibly unintentional academic ridiculousness. See Driscoll's "Looting."

12. On this, see the curious dance of complimentary quotations of one another that crosses many of the contributions in Moraña, Dussel, and Jáuregui's *Coloniality at Large*. There is a circular structuration of the argument that hides an otherwise blatant hole: everybody talks about a great discovery made by someone else within the group, who in turn refers the attribution to another someone else within the group, but the discovery is simply, at the end of the day, that there has been a claim of a discovery shared by all and consecrated by the common consensus. This is the mechanism of charismatic reception: a gospel is announced, and the announcement is the gospel.

13. In a general sense, of course, Spanish imperial reason is Roman, adjusted to territorial idiosyncrasies through the church and many centuries of everyday life, hence already a critique of Roman imperial reason. In another sense, the Spaniards developed their own premodern forms of imperial reason, still in nascent ways, in the everyday contact with non-Christian life and through settlement operations, in Andalusia in particular. Be that as it may, the precise categorical determination of Spanish imperial reason needs to be undertaken with as much specificity and complexity as possible. It is a preliminary step toward the practical possibility of its democratic critique. A lot of work needs to be undertaken, conceptual and historical, and it is a generational task, the way I see it.

14. For me, as was stated earlier, the critique of the total apparatus of Latin American development is the ground zero of Latin Americanist postcolonial subaltern studies and the very possibility of a radically anti-imperial, a-principial, and democratic configuration of Latin Americanist thought. See Kraniauskas, "Gobernar," for his definition, and see also Kraniauskas's critique of development in "Difference."

15. I hope it is clear that I am simply glossing, parodically, on what Beverley himself says. I have not been to Venezuela and cannot pass judgment on the Chávez regime, on whether or not it constitutes an improvement on its predecessor, or whether or not it is in fact better than any of the proposed alternatives within Venezuelan political life. I suspect the situation is far more complicated than it seems from a distance, and it does not allow for facile position taking.

16. See Esposito, *Categorie*. See also Bruno Bosteels's *Actuality* 75–128.

17. I am very grateful to Teresa Vilarós, Sam Steinberg, Gareth Williams, John Kraniauskas, Benjamin Mayer, Bram Acosta, Federico Galende, Patrick Dove, José Luis Villacañas, Laurence Shine, David Johnson, Vincent Gugino, Justin Read, Alejandro Sánchez Lopera, and Juan Pablo Dabove for their reading and feedback on preliminary drafts of this chapter.

CHAPTER 4. May I Kill a Narco?

1. Yes, Latin American Subaltern Studies Group again!! It returns, like that fellow in the *Friday the 13th* movies, and will keep returning in this book, obsessively, uncannily, unfortunately. But I have chosen to leave all those references in the various chapters (prepare yourself for more) more or less unchanged, because the repetition will produce its own readerly effects, one hopes.

CHAPTER 5. The Turn of Deconstruction

1. What would be called for here is what Ernesto Laclau and Chantal Mouffe refer to as the long tradition of popular and democratic struggles, struggles of position or systemic struggles, struggles of maneuver, identitarian or class politics, solidarity politics, and politics of representation. I am referring to both popular and democratic struggles as famously theorized in *Hegemony and Socialist Strategy* in particular, but it is clear that Laclau and Mouffe have a lifelong interest in the phenomenology of political struggles within this first register of interpretation.

2. It is worth quoting Zibechi: "I wouldn't call this type of organization democratic. I think it is something more complex. Félix Patzi says that the Andean community is not a democratic [sic] but rather a form of 'consensual authoritarianism.' To be honest, I do not advocate democratic forms as if they were superior. The family cannot function democratically, because not all members have the same responsibilities and duties or the same abilities to contribute to the collective. I think that we call democracy a mode of domination created by the West, but that is an altogether different question" (309). Is it, really?

3. Yes, sorry, here we are again with the Latin American Subaltern Studies Group. I recognize that my insistence on it is a symptom of something or other, but I am helpless to avoid it, or else insisting is the cure.

CHAPTER 6. We Have Good Reasons for This (and They Keep Coming)

1. See Moreiras, "Democracy in Latin America: Álvaro García Linera," and the rest of the contributions in that issue of *Culture, Theory and Critique*.

2. Regarding a-principial or an-archic thought, an obligatory reference is to Reiner

Schürmann's *Heidegger on Being and Acting*: a successful attempt to use Heideggerian thought for a leftist understanding of political practice, incidentally in spite of Bosteels's dismissal of such a possibility in *Actuality* 123–124n25.

3. Álvarez Yáguez ("Cinismo") understands cynicism as a radical ideological consequence of financial capitalism, already foreseen in Marx's *Capital*. This might well be behind Jameson's position on the very possibility of a democratic and Marxian politics.

4. It is difficult to resist making the point that, as far as I know, no sane European today, if questioned, would agree that the ideology attributed to her by the decolonialists is in fact hers. The eye-of-God thing, in matters not religious, is probably a residue of some hardcore nineteenth-century natural scientific ideology at best. In religious matters, there is nothing specifically European about monotheistic dogmatism.

5. I have been and remain profoundly grateful to Bruno Bosteels for the attention he has paid to my work in his book. It was an act of generosity that he did not have to do, as he could have chosen any number of other attempts at thought for his purposes, and I appreciated it greatly, and will always do so. This is not, however, the time or place to engage with his discussion of my conception of "infrapolitics," which I leave for another essay perhaps.

6. See Sam Steinberg, "Cowardice," on the question of a "communism of communisms."

7. I am grateful to Jaime Rodríguez Matos for bringing this passage to my attention.

CHAPTER 7. Time Out of Joint in Antonio Muñoz Molina's *La noche de los tiempos* and *Todo lo que era sólido*

1. Santos Sanz Villanueva says that *La noche de los tiempos* deals with "the origins of contemporary Spain," hence making a connection that I think must be at the same time strengthened and displaced. Cf. *Todo lo que era sólido* 151. Muñoz Molina writes about 1936 "hauntologizing" his present, and at the same time 1936, 2009, and 2013 are dates in or about which Muñoz Molina writes that mark his own conditions for writing, which are not the conditions of Spain.

2. I have already mentioned "hauntology" in the previous note, for which see Derrida, 51 and passim. I will also be referring to Heidegger's essay "The Anaximander Fragment," which is a powerful intertext in Derrida's book. In his essay, Heidegger translates Anaximander's fragment as "along the lines of usage; for they let order and thereby also reck belong to one another (in the surmounting) of disorder" (57).

3. But see Loureiro 32 for comments on how Muñoz Molina rejects the notion of the "two Spains," hence also the notion of a "third Spain" whose presence is overdetermined in Azaña's text by the abysmal conditions of the Republican government in the early spring of 1936.

4. Of course, those indefatigably lucid and oh so committed antifascist intellectuals, namely, José Bergamín and Rafael Alberti, are presented as rather sinister characters in *Noche*: grotesque would be an even better word.

5. Many years later (1998), my wife, Teresa M. Vilarós, would publish her book *El mono del desencanto: Una crítica cultural de la transición española (1973–1993)*. On the impact of

Chávarri's film, see 47–53, and for commentary on the Born *Don Juan* and related happenings during the period, see 187–194. See also, for graphic materials, Castillo, ed., *Barcelona, fragments de la contracultura*.

6. Faber's essay is a thoughtful critical reading of Muñoz Molina's book in which Muñoz Molina is brought to task on the basis of his assumption of the role of the intellectual as a "moral guide" for the political life of the nation. It is perhaps on that basis that Faber ends his commentary by accusing *Todo lo que era sólido* of engaging in a "defensa del *status quo*. No en términos de modales, quizás, pero sí en términos de sistema económico y relaciones de poder" (n.p.). I will simply indicate my disagreement in this latter regard—a defense of democracy and of a democratic regeneration of public life should not be equated with a conservative defense of the political and economic state of affairs. On the 15-M movement, which starts on May 15, 2011, see http://es.wikipedia.org/wiki/Movimiento_15-M for a general description. A number of books on the movement have appeared, of which I will mention Roitman, *Los indignados*, Taibo et al., *La rebelión*, and Álvarez et al., *Nosotros*.

CHAPTER 8. Ethos Daimon

1. Has it become clear yet that investigating imposture at this level is hardly distinguishable from imposture as such? The two join in an improbable psychic mirror—if I am right, Cercas harbors the same fearful sympathy for Marco that I do; we could have been there ourselves, we were and we are there, because we have been told, both of us, at some significant point in our lives (or has it always happened and been happening?), that we are impostors, that we live under the mark of the marrano, that we work in the marrano register. One survives those accusations, mob accusations, preposterous, pathetic, but the damage is undeniable. Until, of course, one adjusts. Cercas's novel is a courageous marrano confrontation with his own fear of *marranismo*. Perhaps the same thing can be said about my own project in this book. Yes, fear, but we love it, as there is nothing else.

Appendix. Marrano Religion

1. Javier refers to it first, identifying not with Colonel Chabert but rather with the latter's former wife, for whom the sudden reappearance of the colonel is potentially catastrophic. But María reads the novel, and she comes to identify with Chabert as an unfortunate character in demand of an improbable justice or even thoroughly exhausted by the futility of his situation. Toward the end of the novel, María says she tried to "conjure away the danger" of memory by confronting it, and she decides to publish in her publishing house an edition of *El coronel Chabert* and some other Balzac novellas (it is, incidentally, a real book, published in a collection where Marías has interests). Other intertexts in *Los enamoramientos* are certain lines about dying in a timely or untimely manner from Shakespeare's *Macbeth*, the passages of Alexander Dumas's *The Three Musketeers* where Anne de Breuil's story is narrated (she was supposedly executed by her husband, the Count of la Fère, the future

Athos, when he found the infamous fleur de lis tattooed on her shoulder), and the definition of "envy" in Sebastián de Covarrubias's *Tesoro de la lengua castellana o española*. Every one of those references could generate several pages of analysis in the context of my own book's ending. But I will let it go.

2. Nobody reads footnotes; nobody will read the last footnote in this book. This radical impression of unreality—or rather, the fight that gathers one's existence into fighting the shadow of unreality, the shadow of fictitious truth, which is the uncanny counterpart of true fiction—is that not finally the mark of the marrano? This book attempts to be a reflection on that mark—therefore, also a modest contribution to a theorization of the role of an intellectual *infra rebus publicis*. There is an autographic interest here, but please don't tell anyone. After all, this is only a book, "and what happens in them is forgotten, once one comes to the end. What is interesting is the possibilities and ideas they inoculate and bring up through their imaginary cases" (Marías, *Los enamoramientos* 166).

WORKS CITED

Acosta, Abraham. *Thresholds of Illiteracy: Theory, Latin America, and the Crisis of Resistance*. New York: Fordham UP, 2014.

Agamben, Giorgio. *Il mistero del male: Benedetto XVI e la fine dei tempi*. Rome: Laterza, 2013.

Álvarez, Klaudia, Pablo Gallego, Fabio Gándara, and Óscar Rivas. *Nosotros los indignados: Las voces comprometidas del #15-M*. Barcelona: Destino, 2011.

Álvarez Yágüez, Jorge. "Cinismo, nihilismo, capitalismo." *FronteraD*, May 12, 2013. http://www.fronterad.com/?q=cinismo-nihilismo-capitalismo.

Avelar, Idelber. *The Untimely Present: Postdictatorial Latin American Fiction and the Task of Mourning*. Durham: Duke UP, 1999.

Azaña, Manuel. *La velada en Benicarló*. In *Obras completas*, edited by Santos Juliá, 6:33–92. Madrid: Ministerio de la Presidencia, Secretaría General Técnica, Centro de Estudios Políticos y Constitucionales, 2007. Originally published in 1939.

Balibar, Étienne. "Ambiguous Universality." *Differences* 7, no. 1 (1995): 48–74.

Balzac, Honoré de. *El coronel Chabert, seguido de El verdugo, El elixir de larga vida y La obra maestra desconocida*. Translated by Mercedes López-Ballesteros. Madrid: Random House Mondadori, Kindle Archive, no date.

Barnes, Jonathan. *The Presocratic Philosophers*. New York: Routledge, 1982.

Beasley-Murray, Jonathan. *Posthegemony: Political Theory and Latin America*. Minneapolis: U of Minnesota P, 2010.

Benjamin, Walter. "The Destructive Character." In *Selected Writings*. Vol. 2, *1927–1934*: 541–542. Cambridge, MA: Belknap Press, 1999.

———. "Fate and Character." In *Selected Writings*. Vol. 1, *1913–1926*: 201–206. Cambridge, MA: Belknap Press, 1996.

Beverley, John. *Latinamericanism after 9/11*. Durham: Duke UP, 2011.

Borges, Jorge Luis. "El milagro secreto." In *Ficciones: Prosa completa*, 1:507–513. Barcelona: Bruguera, 1980.

———. "La lotería en Babilonia." In *Ficciones: Prosa completa*, 1:441–447. Barcelona: Bruguera, 1980.

Bosteels, Bruno. *The Actuality of Communism*. New York: Verso, 2011.

——. "Translator's Introduction." In Alain Badiou, *The Adventure of French Philosophy*, vii–lxiii. London: Verso, 2012.

Brown, Wendy. "Resisting Left Melancholy." *boundary 2* 26, no. 3 (Fall 1999): 19–27.

Buckley, Ramón. *Miguel Delibes, una conciencia para el nuevo siglo*. Barcelona: Destino, 2012.

Cabezas, Óscar. *Postsoberanía: Literatura, política y trabajo*. Buenos Aires: La Cebra, 2013.

Castillo, Alejandra. "Los nombres del 'no-sujeto.'" *Revista de Crítica Cultural* 34 (December 2006): 78–80.

Castillo, David, ed. *Barcelona, fragments de la contracultura*. Barcelona: Ajuntament, 2010.

Castro Orellana, Rodrigo, ed. *Poshegemonía: El final de un paradigma de la filosofía política en América Latina*. Madrid: Biblioteca Nueva, 2015.

Cercas, Javier. *El impostor*. Barcelona: Random House Mondadori, 2014.

Coates, Ta-Nehisi. *Between the World and Me*. New York: Spiegel and Grau, 2015.

Collingwood-Selby, Elizabeth. *El filo fotográfico de la historia: Walter Benjamin y el olvido de lo inolvidable*. Santiago: Metales Pesados, 2009.

Dean, Jodi. *The Communist Horizon*. London: Verso, 2012.

De la Cadena, Marisol. "Indigenous Cosmopolitics in the Andes: Conceptual Reflections Beyond 'Politics.'" *Cultural Anthropology* 25, no. 2 (2010): 334–370.

Deleuze, Gilles, and Félix Guattari. *What Is Philosophy?* Translated by Graham Burchell and Hugh Tomlinson. New York: Columbia UP, 1991.

Derrida, Jacques. *The Gift of Death and Literature in Secret*. Translated by David Wills. Chicago: U of Chicago P, 2008.

——. *Heidegger: La question de l'Être et l'Histoire: Cours de l'ENS-Ulm 1964–1965*. Paris: Galilée, 2013.

——. "Penser ce qui vient." In *Derrida, pour les temps à venir*, edited by René Major, 17–62. Paris: Stock, 1997.

——. *Specters of Marx: The State of the Debt, the Work of Mourning, and the New International*. Translated by Peggy Kamuf. New York: Routledge, 1994.

d'Ors, Pablo. *El amigo del desierto: Relato de una vocación*. Barcelona: Anagrama, 2009.

Dove, Patrick. *The Catastrophe of Modernity: Tragedy and the Nation in Latin American Literature*. Lewisburg, PA: Bucknell UP, 2004.

Driscoll, Mark. "Looting the Theory Commons: Hardt and Negri's *Commonwealth*." *Postmodern Culture* 21, no. 1 (2010).

Escobar, Arturo. "Latin America at the Crossroads." *Cultural Studies* 24, no. 1 (2010): 1–65.

Esposito, Roberto. *Categorie dell'impolitico*. Bologna: Il Mulino, 1999.

Faber, Sebastiaan. "Review Essay: Antonio Muñoz Molina, *Todo lo que era sólido*

(Barcelona: Seix Barral, 2012)." *Revista de ALCESXXI* 1 (2013): 733–747. http://alcesxxi.org/revista1/revista1/pdfs/Faber2.pdf.

Ford, John, dir. *The Man Who Shot Liberty Valance*. Feature film. Paramount, 1962.

Fornazzari, Alessandro. *Speculative Fictions: Chilean Culture, Economics, and the Neoliberal Transition*. Pittsburgh, PA: U of Pittsburgh P, 2013.

Galende, Federico. *Filtraciones: Conversaciones sobre arte en Chile*. 3 vols. Santiago: Cuarto Propio, 2007–2011.

——. *La oreja de los nombres*. Buenos Aires: Gorla, 2005.

——. "Umbral." *Revista de Crítica Cultural* 34 (December 2006): 81–83.

——. *Walter Benjamin y la destrucción*. Santiago: Metales Pesados, 2009.

García Canclini, Néstor. *Culturas híbridas: Estrategias para entrar y salir de la modernidad*. Mexico City: Grijalbo, 1990.

Graff Zivin, Erin. *Figurative Inquisitions: Conversion, Torture, and Truth in the Luso-Hispanic Atlantic*. Pittsburgh, PA: U of Pittsburgh P, 2014.

Greene, Graham. *The Confidential Agent: An Entertainment*. New York: Viking, 1967.

Grosfoguel, Ramón. "La descolonización de la economía política y los estudios postcoloniales: Transmodernidad, pensamiento fronterizo y colonialidad global." *Tabula Rasa* 4 (2006): 17–46.

Hegel, George Wilhelm Friedrich. *Fenomenología del espíritu*. Translated by Manuel Jiménez Redondo. Valencia: Pre-Textos, 2006.

——. *Lectures on the Philosophy of World History*. Translated by H. B. Nisbet. Cambridge: Cambridge UP, 1975.

Heidegger, Martin. "The Anaximander Fragment." In *Early Greek Thinking: The Dawn of Western Philosophy*, translated by David Farrell Krell and Frank A. Capuzzi, 13–58. San Francisco: Harper and Row, 1984.

——. "Letter on Humanism." In *Basic Writings*, edited by David Farrell Krell, 193–242. New York: Harper and Row, 1977.

——. *Parmenides*. Translated by André Schuwer and Richard Rojcewicz. Bloomington: Indiana UP, 1992.

James, Daniel. *Doña María's Story: Life History, Memory, and Political Identity*. Durham: Duke UP, 2001.

——. *Resistance and Integration: Peronism and the Argentine Working Class, 1946–1976*. New York: Cambridge UP, 1988.

Jameson, Fredric. *Representing Capital: A Reading of Volume One*. London: Verso, 2011.

Jenckes, Kate. *Reading Borges after Benjamin: Allegory, Afterlife, and the Writing of History*. Albany: SUNY UP, 2007.

Johnson, Adriana. *Sentencing Canudos: Subalternity in the Backlands of Brazil*. Pittsburgh, PA: U of Pittsburgh P, 2010.

Johnson, David. *Kant's Dog: On Borges, Philosophy, and the Time of Translation*. Albany: SUNY UP, 2013.

Johnson, David, and Scott Michaelsen. *Anthropology's Wake: Attending to the End of Culture*. New York: Fordham UP, 2008.

Kant, Immanuel. *Religion within the Limits of Reason Alone*. Translated by Theodore M. Greene and Hoyt H. Hudson. New York: HarperOne, 2008.

———. *Toward Perpetual Peace*. In *Practical Philosophy*, edited and translated by Mary J. Gregor, 301–351. Cambridge Edition of the Works of Immanuel Kant. New York: Cambridge UP, 1996.

Kirk, G. S., J. E. Raven, and M. Schofield. *The Presocratic Philosophers*. New York: Cambridge UP, 1983.

Kraniauskas, John. "Difference against Development: Spiritual Accumulation and the Politics of Freedom." *boundary 2* 32, no. 2 (2005): 53–80.

———. "Gobernar es repoblar: Sobre la acumulación originaria neoliberal." *Revista Iberoamericana* 69, no. 203 (2003): 361–366.

Lacan, Jacques. *The Seminar of Jacques Lacan, Book II: The Ego in Freud's Theory and the Technique of Psychoanalysis, 1954–1955*. Edited by Jacques-Alain Miller. Translated by Sylvana Tomaselli. With notes by John Forrester. New York: Norton, 1991.

Laclau, Ernesto, and Chantal Mouffe. *Hegemony and Socialist Strategy: Towards a Radical Democratic Politics*. London: Verso, 1985.

Legrás, Horacio. *Literature and Subjection: The Economy of Writing and Marginality in Latin America*. Pittsburgh, PA: U of Pittsburgh P, 2008.

Levinson, Brett. *The Ends of Literature: The Latin American "Boom" in the Neoliberal Marketplace*. Stanford: Stanford UP, 2002.

———. *Market and Thought: Meditations on the Political and the Biopolitical*. New York: Fordham UP, 2004.

———. *Secondary Moderns: Mimesis, History, and Revolution in José Lezama Lima's "American Expression."* Lewisburg, PA: Bucknell UP, 1996.

Leyte, Arturo. *Heidegger: El fracaso del ser*. Madrid: Batiscafo, 2015.

Long, Ryan. *Fictions of Totality: The Mexican Novel and the National Popular State*. West Lafayette, IN: Purdue UP, 2008.

Loureiro, Angel G. "En el presente incierto: *La noche de los tiempos* de Muñoz Molina." *Insula* 766 (October 2010): 30–33.

Marías, Javier. *Los enamoramientos*. Madrid: Alfaguara, 2011.

———. *Mañana en la batalla piensa en mí*. Madrid: Alfaguara, 1994.

Marx, Karl. *The Communist Manifesto*. http://www.marxists.org/archive/marx/works/1848/communist-manifesto/ch01.htm.

———. *The Communist Manifesto*. In *Later Political Writings*, edited and translated by Terrell Carver, 1–30. Cambridge: Cambridge UP, 2007.

———. *The Eighteenth Brumaire of Louis Bonaparte*. In *Later Political Writings*, edited and translated by Terrell Carver, 31–127.

Mignolo, Walter D. "Introduction: From Cross-Genealogies and Subaltern Knowledges to *Nepantla*." *Nepantla: Views from South* 1, no. 1 (2000): 1–8.

——. "Introduction: Immigrant Consciousness." In Rodolfo Kusch, *Indigenous and Popular Thinking in América*, xiii–liv. Durham: Duke UP, 2010.

——. "Preamble: The Historical Foundation of Modernity/Coloniality and the Emergence of Decolonial Thinking." Edited by Sara Castro-Klarén, 12–32. A Companion to Latin American Literature and Culture. Oxford: Blackwell, 2008.

Moraña, Mabel, Enrique Dussel, and Carlos A. Jáuregui, eds. *Coloniality at Large: Latin America and the Postcolonial Debate*. Durham: Duke UP, 2008.

Moreiras, Alberto. "Democracy in Latin America: Álvaro García Linera, an Introduction." *Culture, Theory and Critique* 56, no. 3 (2015): 266–282.

——. *The Exhaustion of Difference: The Politics of Latin American Cultural Studies*. Durham: Duke UP, 2001.

——. *Interpretación y diferencia*. Madrid: Visor, 1991.

——. *Línea de sombra: El no sujeto de lo político*. Santiago: Palinodia, 2007.

——. "Pantanillos ponzoñosos: Respuesta a Alejandra Castillo, Federico Galende, Sergio Villalobos." *Revista de Crítica Cultural* 34 (December 2006): 78–87.

——. *Piel de lobo*. Madrid: forthcoming in 2020.

——. *Tercer espacio: Literatura y duelo en América Latina*. Santiago: LOM, 1999.

Muñoz, Gerardo. "The Exhaustion of the Progressive Political Cycle in Latin America and the Return to the Commons." Unpublished typescript in author's possession.

Muñoz Molina, Antonio. *La noche de los tiempos*. Barcelona: Seix Barral, 2009.

——. *Todo lo que era sólido*. Barcelona: Seix Barral, 2013.

Negri, Antonio, et al. *Imperio, multitud y sociedad abigarrada*. Buenos Aires: Waldhutter-CLACSO, 2010.

Ortega y Gasset, José. *El tema de nuestro tiempo*. In *Obras completas*. Vol. 3, *1917–1925*, 557–662. Madrid: Taurus, 2005.

Postone, Moishe. "Rethinking Marx (in a Post-Marxist World) (1)." Paper read at the theory workshop "Reclaiming the Arguments of the Founders," 90th Annual Meeting, American Sociological Association, August 19, 1995. http://obeco.no.sapo.pt/mpt.htm.

Richard, Nelly. *The Insubordination of Signs: Political Change, Cultural Transformation, and Poetics of the Crisis*. Durham: Duke UP, 2004.

——. *Masculine/Feminine: Practices of Difference(s)*. Durham: Duke UP, 2004.

Roitman Rosenmann, Marcos. *Los indignados: El rescate de la política*. Madrid: Akal, 2012.

Sánchez Ferlosio, Rafael. "Carácter y destino." In *Babel contra Babel: Asuntos internacionales. Sobre la guerra. Apuntes de polemología*, 631–651. Ensayos III. Madrid: Debates, 2016.

——. *Mientras no cambien los dioses, nada ha cambiado*. Madrid: Alianza, 1986.

——. *Vendrán más años malos y nos harán más ciegos*. Barcelona: Destino, 1993.

Sanz Villanueva, Santos. "*La noche de los tiempos*: Antonio Muñoz Molina." http://www.elcultural.es/version_papel/LETRAS/26180/La_noche_de_los_tiempos.

Schürmann, Reiner. *Heidegger on Being and Acting: From Principles to Anarchy.* Translated by Christina-Marie Gros. Bloomington: Indiana UP, 1990.

Shakespeare, William. *Richard III.* Folger Shakespeare Library. New York: Washington Square P, 1996.

Sófocles. *Oedipus at Colonus.* In *The Complete Sophocles.* Vol. 1, *The Theban Plays,* edited by Peter Burian and Alan Shapiro, 301–404. Oxford: Oxford UP, 2010.

Steinberg, Samuel. "Cowardice—An Alibi: On Prudence and *Senselessness.*" *New Centennial Review* 14, no. 1 (2014): 175–194.

Taibo, Carlos, et al. *La rebelión de los indignados: Movimiento 15 M: Democracia real ¡ya!.* Madrid: Popular, 2011.

Thayer, Willy. *El fragmento repetido: Escritos en estado de excepción.* Santiago: Metales Pesados, 2006.

——. *Tecnologías de la crítica.* Santiago: Metales Pesados, 2010.

Vilarós Soler, Teresa María. *El mono del desencanto: Una crítica cultural de la transición española (1973-1993).* Madrid: Siglo XXI, 1998.

Villacañas, José Luis. *¿Qué imperio?* Sevilla: Almuzara, 2008.

Villalobos, Sergio. "El amigo del pensamiento." *Revista de Crítica Cultural* 34 (December 2006): 84–87.

——. *Soberanías en suspenso: Imaginación y violencia en América Latina.* Buenos Aires: La Cebra, 2013.

Williams, Gareth. "Deconstruction and Subaltern Studies, or, a Wrench in the Latin Americanist Assembly Line." In *Treinta años de estudios literarios/culturales latinoamericanistas en Estados Unidos,* edited by Hernán Vidal, 221–256. Pittsburgh, PA: Instituto Internacional de Literatura Iberoamericana, 2008.

——. *The Mexican Exception: Sovereignty, Police, and Democracy.* Basingstoke, UK: Palgrave Macmillan, 2011.

——. *The Other Side of the Popular: Neoliberalism and Subalternity in Latin America.* Durham: Duke UP, 2002.

Zibechi, Raúl. *Territories in Resistance: A Cartography of Latin American Social Movements.* Translated by Ramor Ryan. Oakland, CA: AK Press, 2012.

INDEX

Schmitt, Carl, 49, 60, 136, 190
Schofield, M. 167–168
Scotland, 8, 21–22, 45, 52, 54, 56, 70
Scott, James C., 49
Serra, Albert, 196
sinthome, 184
socialism, 90, 131, 158, 217n1
Solanas, Fernando Ezequiel, 97
Sophists, 78, 80
Spinoza, Baruch, 40, 44
Spivak, Gayatri, 23, 133, 213n3
Stavrakakis, Yannis, 43
Steinberg, Sam, 183, 197–198, 217n17, 218n6
structuralism, 6
subaltern studies, 88–89, 134, 212–213n2, 213n3, 216n14; and Latin Americanist subalternism, 24–25; and the Latin American Subaltern Studies Group, 16–17, 23, 27, 89, 97, 115–116, 213n3, 217n1, 217n3; South Asian, 16, 22; and the subalternism of difference, 32, 33; and subalternist deconstruction, 76
subjectivist voluntarism, 163

testimonio, 15, 38, 95–96, 176, 212n1
Texas, 1, 4, 38, 40, 55, 56
Thayer, Willy, 1, 8, 115, 117
Theory Colloquium, 113

ultraleftism, 45, 91, 101, 119
unconscious, 72–74, 81, 154
University of Barcelona, 12–13, 30, 161
University of Georgia, 4, 12, 30, 112–113
University of Wisconsin-Madison, 4, 13, 113–114

Valderrama, Miguel, 8
Velázquez, Diego, 196
Vilarós, Teresa, 11, 59, 68–70, 114, 217n17, 218n5
Villacañas, José Luis, 1, 10–12, 17, 19–21, 39, 42, 51–52, 54, 104, 215n9, 217n17
Villalobos, Sergio, 8, 45, 105, 115, 117, 211n1

Whitmore, Katherine, 154
Williams, Gareth, 11, 23, 44, 89, 106, 114–117, 213–214n3, 217n17
Williams, Raymond, 15

Yampara, Simón, 139–140
Yúdice, George, 46, 96

Zapatism, 100, 110
Zibechi, Raúl, 110, 217n2
Zinnemann, Fred, 72
Zizek, Slavoj, 126, 146–147, 199
Zorrilla, José, 161–162